The Art of Daily Activism

Judith L. Boice is a writer and photographer. Her writings have appeared in *One Earth* and *Cultural Survival;* she is the author of *At One With All Life* and *Mother Earth: Through the Eyes of Women Photographers and Writers.* She graduated from Oberlin College, lived at the Findhorn Community in Scotland, and has worked as a teacher, gardener, and violinist. Ms. Boice currently lives in Portland, Oregon.

The Art
of
Daily Activism

Judith L. Boice

Wingbow Press
Oakland, California

Printed in the United States of America

Design by Andrea DuFlon
Cover illustration by Julie Cohn
Typography by Rick Heide
Printing by Walsworth Publishing

Wingbow Press books are published and distributed by
Bookpeople, 7900 Edgewater Drive, Oakland, California
94621.

First edition: April 1992

ISBN 0-914728-74-1

Contents

My gratitude to Stanton Nelson and the staff at Wingbow Press for their skillful, good-natured support in the creation of this book. Thanks to the Standing People, the trees, who have given away for the production of this paper. Thanks to Gaia and the Muses for their ongoing inspiration and beauty. Finally, my gratitude to all those who have touched me by the example of their lives, whose ideas and actions have moved me to alter my own. You are, and will continue to be, my teachers.

To those visionary activists
who have made the flesh and bones of their lives
an expression of the world
they wish to live in.

Part One
What You Are

I need to embody the qualities that I want to
see manifest in the world. Fighting for peace
does not produce peace. Fighting produces
fighting, just as I have learned that "righteous
anger" makes other people defensive and angry.
The method of accomplishing something is as
important as the outcome.

One

Inner Work

WHILE LEADING A WORKSHOP at the Findhorn Foundation, an educational and spiritual center in the north of Scotland, I learned the power of "small" acts of transformation. A German woman shared an experience from her childhood that had shaken her deeply. As a shy little six-year-old, she watched other children running through the bombed-out ruins of buildings on the edge of her village, their gaping doors and windows a reminder of the horrors of World War II. The children dared each other to run through the dark, rubble-strewn houses. One day she screwed up her courage and ran through one of the buildings like the other children.

"Halfway through," she recalled, sobbing, "a little boy hiding in the house reached out and grabbed me and wouldn't let me go." This dignified woman, a powerful executive in a German corporation, sat crumpled in her chair, shoulders collapsed like protective wings around her, eyes streaming with tears. After a few minutes she looked up. "And you know," she declared, eyes suddenly defiant, "if that happened again, I would kick him. I would hit back. I wouldn't ever let anyone take my power like that again. I never want to be a victim like that again."

The group of people around the table fell silent, still. Inwardly I applauded her step to move away from acting the part of a victim, but at the same time I believed that to strike out in retaliation was a twisted show of power as well.

"Edith," I said quietly, "would you be willing to do an exercise with me?"

She nodded, tears still bright in her eyes. I led her through an Aikido exercise, having her press on my arm three times. The first time, I resisted her pressure with all of my strength. We grimaced and strained as we struggled.

The second time, I collapsed on the ground and refused to look at her. I was the "victim." She reached out her hand to me, feeling terribly guilty for having pushed me.

I looked up at her and smiled. "Who has the power now?" I asked. She looked mystified. "I got you to bend down and feel sorry for me. I'm extraordinarily powerful right now."

The first glimmerings of comprehension passed through her eyes as she realized that I had a lot of power in my crumpled position on the floor. "That's what I've always done," she said. "I've always played the victim."

"And that's a very powerful position. You can manipulate a lot from down here."

The third time, I had to center myself. My aim was to take all of the energy that Edith used to push my arm and to pass it through myself and back to her. As she pushed, the force went through my belly and out my heart, connecting with her heart. My arm was stronger, but that was not my focus. She could still move my arm, which told me that I was not fully centered, but I wasn't straining at all.

We reversed positions. I pushed on Edith's arm three times. The third time, after Edith centered herself, I tried to describe the feeling of passing the energy through my body and back to her. She looked doubtful. "Edith," I said finally, "I can't really describe it. You'll have to experience it for yourself."

When I pushed on her arm, she looked at me, face placid. Her arm felt like a thick, iron rod. My shoulders were trembling with the effort of pushing on her forearm. She looked puzzled. "You aren't pushing," she said.

I gasped and looked at the people around us. "Edith, look at how I'm shaking. I'm pushing with all my might."

Edith's eyes widened, and her mouth opened in a silent "oh." A look of wonder shot through her eyes. When I moved away, we looked at each other, smiling. "How did that feel?" I asked her.

She stood speechless for a moment. "Like you weren't pushing . . . and I felt very centered . . . I think I understand now what this thing 'love' is all about. I've never felt it in my body like that before, really moving through my heart and arm and . . . well, it was . . ."

Words failed her. But I could see from the transformation in her face, eyes, and posture that she understood something on a deep level. She had experienced, and now she knew. All the lectures and books and tapes in the world could have described and explained the use of love to transform energy, but only the experience could open her to knowing for herself. Tell me something, and I understand. Let me experience, and I *know.*

When I know something, it becomes part of the fabric of my daily life. As one thinks, so one becomes—something akin to "you are what you eat," but on a much deeper level. The thoughts in my mind constitute the mental diet that feeds the experiences of my everyday life. What I sow in my mind, I reap in my life. "What goes around, comes around." And if I don't like what's coming, I had better look for new seeds for the garden, because unless I sow new strains, I'll get the same crop of weeds next year, and the year after, and the year after that.

"There is no way to peace," said A.J. Muste. "Peace is the way." I need to embody the qualities that I want to see manifest in the world. Fighting for peace does not produce peace. Fighting produces fighting, just as I have learned that "righteous anger" makes other people defensive and angry. The method of accomplishing something is as important as the outcome.

Personal and Planetary Change

Personal change leads to planetary change. Any kind of meaningful change originates in self-change, an individual's shift in awareness. This holds true for any sort of transformation, on any scale—in one-to-one relationships, family dynamics, political, social, spiritual, or planetary change—all begin with individuals who shift their conceptual framework of the world. Choosing to speak from love instead of frustration and anger increases the pool of love on the planet. Moment by moment we make choices, and those choices have a profound effect upon the world in which we live.

When I was fourteen, I collected signatures for a statewide "bottle bill." The bill got on the ballot but was voted down; the bottling companies launched a multimillion dollar campaign to defeat it. They didn't want to be responsible for the disposable containers that they generated, and they glossed over the fact that the returnable bottle business would generate jobs. In the end, reusing the containers would reduce their own costs. But the changes would require a radical shift in awareness, a quantum leap which made their corporate legs quiver with dread.

I came to understand that most legislation is remedial. When enough individuals change their perspective to one of value and respect, then a true social/cultural shift occurs. In the meantime, legislation helps to protect the endangered sector, whether human (the Civil Rights Act) or otherwise (e.g., the Clean Air Act), until individual values shift on a large scale and the endangering behavior ceases. The bottle bill aimed to instill an awareness of recycling combined with the incentive of money, the deposit refunded when containers are returned.

I learned firsthand that similar legislation, which passed in other states, had an effect. While I was working as a counselor in a summer camp in Vermont, a friend and I spent our day off at a beautiful hiking shelter a few miles away from the camp. We decided to stay in a tent rather than in the shelter, and had just finished staking the tent when the whine of a motor straining up the dirt road interrupted the dusky stillness.

Two men and a woman came clanking down the path, carrying a cooler full of beer, a huge radio/tape player, and three lawn chairs. They asked if we were sleeping in the shelter. "No," we told them.

We passed the night regretting our answer. They built a fire by dousing some logs with kerosene, unfolded the lawn chairs in the shelter, and spent the night drinking beer and blaring the radio twenty feet from where we were trying to sleep.

Around one in the morning I heard one of the men head for the edge of the campsite where the flat fell away suddenly into a gorge with a river running far below.

"Hey, where ya goin'?" asked the woman.

"Gonna throw this shit over the side," he said. I could hear the clanking of cans in a bag.

"Hey, man, we can get money for those. Don't throw 'em over, you asshole."

They took the cans with them, not out of concern for the Earth but because they were interested in their wallets and having enough money to party next week. Although the legislation had an effect in this case, it was still remedial. These people had not fundamentally shifted their attitude toward the planet.

Catalysts for Change

Listening to impassioned speeches or reading inspirational books can help catalyze change, but ultimately direct experience actually leads to fundamental change. After I shared stories at a Quaker Meeting one Sunday about demonstrations at the Fernald Nuclear Reprocessing Plant, a man talked to me for nearly an hour about his feelings of envy toward people who participated in demonstrations and his own feelings of inadequacy and guilt for not joining them. "I'm just one person," he lamented. "What can I do?"

I encouraged him to look at ways he could enact his concern here and now. "Every act is important," I told him. "All individual shifts in awareness add up to a mountain of change."

He asked what experiences had shaped my view of the world. I told him about sitting on a mountain when I was sixteen and suddenly knowing that everything in the world was alive, full of spirit. "It didn't change my life all of a sudden," I told him. "But slowly, over the years, that experience began to change everything in my life."

He nodded. "You know, one time I had an experience after I was running—I used to run marathons and did a lot of training. And one day, after I'd finished running, I felt really high. I was standing at the base of a mountain in this beautiful place, and suddenly I had this feeling, like I was hearing something . . . and it was saying, 'You can have anything you want.' Anything. And I felt like I could choose whatever I wanted.

"So I started thinking about being wealthy. But that wasn't really it. And then I thought about fame. That wasn't really what I wanted. And then power. But that wasn't it, either. I thought about it for a long time, and finally I came up with this: I don't want to be responsible for hurting another living thing in any way."

The next day he went to the restaurant where he had been working in the kitchen. He looked at the live lobsters that he had been putting into boiling water to cook.

"I looked at the cook and told him, 'I can't do that anymore. I can't kill those lobsters. And I'm never going to eat meat again.' He looked at me really funny, but since that day I've never eaten meat. I just can't do it. I had no idea what to eat at first . . . but that was almost eighteen years ago. I've learned now."

To me, his experience and the choices that he made as a result are as powerful as marching through the streets of Washington, D.C. All of the personal changes on the planet, when added together, create an avalanche of fundamental change. When people live through an experience of fundamental change, they release a huge amount of energy. They recalibrate to a new level of living and experience. That energy is transformation, and it affects the planet as a whole. The number of people involved in the transformation is as important as the quality of the energy shift because the effects ripple out like a stone cast into a still pond. Ultimately an individual's fundamental change ripples out to affect all those who encounter her or him.

Fundamental Change

Tom Brown, in his book *The Vision,* shares the story of a vision in which he was shown the construction of a nuclear power plant in an area of the Pine Barrens that was very special to him. He watched the destruction of the trees, the bulldozing of the land, and the rerouting of a creek. He listened to the noise of machinery and shouting. He saw a crowd of people outside the gates protesting, carrying petitions, and preaching to others about the dangers of the plant. Inside the main construction trailer, a young man pleaded to stop the construction of the plant—the people obviously didn't want it, and it certainly wasn't safe. His boss ordered him to talk to the protesters and to lie if necessary to calm the crowd.

Tom turned to the spirit who had guided him to see this future vision. The spirit reminded him that petitions and protests would result at best in temporary victories. Wilderness would be preserved only when humanity changed consciousness, by restoring contact with the wilderness and the old ways, and learned to respect the earth again.[1]

"To change the world for the better," says Seth in Jane Roberts' *The Individual and the Nature of Mass Events,* "you must begin by changing your own life. There is no other way. You begin by accepting your own worth as a part of the universe, and by granting every other being that same recognition. You begin by honoring life in all of its forms. You begin by changing your thoughts toward your contemporaries, your country, your family, your working companions."[2]

David Spangler, at one time a co-director of the Findhorn Foundation who developed its educational work, and currently a teacher and writer whose latest book is *Reimagination of the World,* offers these words of insight from his communications with John, whom Spangler describes as "... a non-physical friend of mine, an inhabitant of the spiritual worlds." I offer this quote to encourage inner listening:

> ... To do small actions well and to fill them with the quality of the spirit, no matter how remote those actions may seem to be from the great and urgent challenges of your world, is to do more for earth than to attempt great actions through glamour and enthusiasm but without skill and completeness ... To save a planet may be the act of nourishing a flower or honoring a relationship, as much as averting a war or restructuring an economy, if these can be done with the care and attunement that allows the spirit of God entry into the world.[3]

During a weekend workshop at the Findhorn Community I came face-to-face with the painful reality of my own underlying reasons for pursuing environmental and peace issues. Facilitated by Willis Harman, one of the founders of the Noetic Institute in California, the workshop focused on the power of thought to create a peaceful world. "What I hold in mind produces in kind" was the basic premise.

After a topsy-turvy weekend of marginally facilitated, free-for-all discussions, Willis asked a key question. What was our greatest fear? We were asked to look inside and then, one by one, speak and release that fear.

I didn't need to look very deeply for my greatest fear. It came screaming to the surface. "I'm afraid that the world will blow up before I have any time to do anything about it." The words tumbled out, urgent, paralyzing me with their fearful intensity. I realized suddenly that my drive to do things quickly, as soon as possible, was fueled largely by my belief that the world would soon end. Ironically, enacting that belief, organizing my life based on the fear of the world's destruction, actually empowered that final doom. Outwardly I was doing lots of "politically correct" things, but the foundation of those actions was a hotbed of fear. All of the "politically correct" actions in the world could not cancel out the vision of destruction I was carrying in my mind.

The realization of my own motivations, carefully hidden from myself, shattered me. When the session ended, I ran into the snowy woods, crying to the trees and stars, crying for forgiveness, crying for myself. I had to learn another way, and I had no idea what that way was.

My life changed radically in the months following the workshop. I wanted to work on saving myself, to rebuild my inner landscape on a foundation of how I wanted life to be, rather than to continue frantically trying to save the world. I became a member of the Findhorn Community in Scotland.

Nearly four years later I returned to the United States. A few months after my return, I attended a training course for the "Technologies for Creating" workshop designed by Robert Fritz. Certainly after my years of inner work and support of other people's transformations, I would find myself prepared. During the five-day training, though, I came face-to-face, once again, with my "world savior" stance.

During one of the afternoon sessions, Robert talked about actions aimed to fix something, whether that "something" was oneself, an organization, or the planet. Trying to fix something is not creating something new. At best, if the action is successful, an element is eliminated. Nothing new is created.

His words jarred me. My inner foundation tilted—my world, I suddenly realized, was based on fixing people and things. Who would I be if I wasn't helping someone or something? During the dinner break I donned my coat, wrapped a scarf around my head, and paced the bitterly cold, windy streets of a January night. As I walked, my mind turned over my work of the past few years. I had traveled, lectured, taught, shared, gardened, written, read, and breathed the work of "planetary transformation." What would I do, I asked myself, if I didn't have to save the world?

The question terrified me. So much of my identity was related to my burning need to save the planet. But was I really working for the planet? Were all of my actions actually aimed at supporting a different sort of world? Or was working for fixing the problems of the world, merely a thin cover for a problem-solving orientation?

Inwardly, I clenched hard. I was trying to hold together the crumbling edifice of my life orientation. "Breathe, damn it," I muttered to myself. Sweat broke on my back. I opened my coat to the bitter wind.

For a moment, I let go. I imagined what I would do in a world that didn't need to be saved. I saw myself sitting around a campfire in the desert, the night stars brilliant overhead, singing and sharing stories with people whom I loved. I sensed that I was still "working," if such enjoyment could be called work, to help people experience the Earth in a direct, powerful way. My reasons for the work, though, were to share my love of the planet, not to try to change these people for some larger "good" that I held in my mind. In a sense, my work would not be so drastically different from what I was doing, but my reasons would change, as well as the terrible inner urgency I thought I had left behind in the woods of Scotland four years before.

I returned to the seminar in time for the evening lecture, having gained some foundation of peace amidst my inner crumbling. I had gained another insight, too—that lessons are not learned all at once. As I move around on the spiral of my life, the "same" lessons greet me, but I approach them from another level of the spiral.

Magic—Bringing Thought into Form

One August afternoon I stood outside the community church in the Massachusetts town of Wendell, taking pictures to use up a roll of film. As I adjusted my camera, a young woman walked from a neighboring house. "You're the third person this week photographing that church," she rumbled as she strode across the grass outside the meeting house. She was less than five feet tall and built like a Mack truck.

I stuttered some sort of reply. She grinned and stuck out her arm, firmly grasping my hand in her own. She introduced herself and asked my name. "You live here?" she asked.

"Well, I'm just about to move. I've been living down by Jennison Road."

She nodded and started into a story about rebuilding the tiny house behind us that she had bought for her father. She recounted how she could have made the money for the house by paying attention to her intuition about the price of gold skyrocketing in the mid-seventies.

"I wanted to invest a thousand dollars in gold, but my family said I was crazy, so I didn't do it. We could have made nearly a hundred thousand dollars on that money."

Story after story astounded me with her ease at moving through the physical world. She was steeped in practical work with her hands and blessed with an innate sense of financial wizardry. She thought nothing of saving $50,000 and then spending it on her family. "I always know I can make more," she said, nodding with satisfaction.

"I tell my sister," she said, muscled arms folded over her broad chest, "you gotta do things because you want to, not because of the money. Way I look at it, what goes around comes around. One time," she said, face breaking into a grin, "I was helping this friend whose daughter was having a hard time. They wanted to put her in an institution. I got hold of her one day and told her, 'Look, you keep this up and they're gonna put you in a correctional home. Just play it cool for a few more years, and you'll be out on your own.' She's been as good as gold since then, good as gold.

"Well, I went over one day to help them put a shower in their trailer. So I shopped around and we put it together one Saturday afternoon. They wanted to give me some money, but I told them, 'No, give it to somebody who needs it. I did this because I wanted to, 'cause you're friends.' I knew I would be helped by them or somebody else someday.

"When we finished, they asked me if I wanted to go play bingo, you know, my sister and her mother and the kids. I told 'em I didn't go to bingo, I don't gamble on money—it comes easy enough anyway—but I'd go to be with them. Well, wouldn't you know her mother won a round, I won the door prize, and then I won two hundred dollars.

" 'See,' I told them. 'I always get paid for my work. What goes around, comes around.' But even I didn't expect it to come so fast!"

Her words were a soothing balm during a time when I was petrified about my ability to find a new house, pay the rent, find a job. I had learned all of the "New Age Doo-dah" principles about creating my own reality and expecting the best and visualizing what I wanted. In this moment, though, I gravely doubted my ability to manifest much of anything. Here was a woman who had probably never heard of *Creative Visualization* or *The Path of Least Resistance* or any of the myriad other spiritual self-help titles, and yet she embodied all of the principles with the ease of a mistress of the creative arts. She was the Queen of Pentacles in the tarot, a creator at ease with the physical world and her ability to move in it. That calm, inner knowing of her own rooted wisdom ensured that the results would continue.

"To do small actions well and to fill them with the quality of the spirit . . ." John's words to Spangler rang in my ears as I listened to her stories.

"Here," she said as we finished our conversation. "I'll share some of my luck with you. This," she said, slapping her hands on my outstretched palms, "is for good luck. And this," she said, gently brushing her hands over mine, "is some *soft* luck. Take it easy!" She swung around and strode back to the house where she was rebuilding the interior and adding a back porch.

"There," I thought, "is a true magician." And I'm not even sure that she was fully aware of her wizardry. It wafted around and within her, as close as the air in her lungs, as pervasive as the pulse of blood in her veins. Through her life she has learned to envision her world and then to act, to offer her love in a practical way. Hers is not the self-satisfied love of the philanthropist, always concerned about the tax credit for items given. Instead she gives with the full-bodied love of a lover of life, unselfconscious about the rewards or effect of her work. In that moment of my own doubt, she awed me. I had never seen her before, nor have I seen her since. She gave me what I needed that day—I can still sense the place on my palms where the good luck entered—and then quietly went about her business, and I about mine. A magician never rechecks her magic; she knows her work is complete.

The Rate of Change

The fundamental shift that comes with personal realization often is accompanied by a newfound conviction. For some, as with my own realization that the Earth is alive, the new awareness may not manifest immediately in a radical shift in action and thought. For others, the transformation changes them in a moment, irrevocably. With that flash of realization, they set their feet onto a new path and continue to tread forward without a moment's hesitation.

Martin Luther King was 26 years old and just beginning his career as a preacher when Mrs. Rosa Parks, a 42-year-old black seamstress, chose not to give up her seat in the front of a public bus in Montgomery, Alabama. Her arrest sparked Montgomery's black population, and plunged King into a period of deep contemplation. King spent a sleepless night considering the plight of his people.

The next morning, King announced his belief that a concentrated

drive against this state of racial injustice could bring tangible results. He chose to rock the boat of the status quo, to risk his career
and eventually his life, to speak out against what was, and for what
could be. That single act began a lifelong pursuit of justice and
freedom for the oppressed blacks of the United States.

King's commitment and conviction quickly sent waves into the
surrounding population. On January 30, 1956, King's house was
bombed. His response called for love, not anger, to meet the injustice. Before a gathering of hundreds of angry people, he affirmed
that violence was not the answer; he called upon them to manifest
love, and to carry on their struggle for justice with dignity and
discipline.[4]

Although King had not yet labeled his efforts "nonviolent resistance," his inner compass steered him to speak and act from a core
of love. His adherence to the law of love shaped the following
twelve years of his life and the lives of millions of people who
were touched by his message and his work. Although King was
deeply rooted in the black Christian tradition, his work has been
compared with that of another man of color who also worked with
the principles of nonviolent resistance on two other continents,
in South Africa and India.

Mohandas K. Gandhi was a privileged young Indian lawyer, having just completed his legal education in London, when he arrived
in South Africa. In the course of arguing his first case, he had his
first personal experience of racial discrimination.

While Gandhi was traveling in the first class train compartment
from Durban to Pretoria where he was to represent a client, the
guard examined his ticket and demanded that he move to the third
class section. Gandhi protested, saying he would not voluntarily
leave the first class section. The constable came, took him by the
hand, and threw him from the train. His luggage sailed after him.

Gandhi sat at the railway station in Maritzburg, in the high region
of South Africa, shivering in the chilly night. His overcoat was in
his luggage, but rather than ask for it and be insulted again, he sat
and endured the cold.

In that incident, Gandhi experienced racial discrimination for
the first time and then faced himself, choosing the response he
would make to injustice. The decision made on that solitary, bitterly
cold South African night shaped the rest of Gandhi's life. Although
his work did not blossom fully in that night, the seed was planted,

and the first sign of growth was his continued struggle with the railway guards and constables until he finally reached his destination. His experiences and struggles in South Africa also laid the foundation for his later work in India.[5]

Both King and Gandhi are examples of people who were confronted with crises in their lives—personal crossroads that were crises of conscience as well. The Chinese character for "crisis" is a combination of the characters for "danger" and "opportunity." These two men faced dangerous, life-threatening consequences when they chose to act from dignity and love. The crises became opportunities to apply their inner convictions, to make their religious beliefs into a "living force." The conversion from "belief" to "living force" is the process of transformation, the butterfly that emerges from the chrysalis of untested faith.

The great movers of our planet do not all win Nobel Prizes or elicit a vast, devoted following. One woman, who identified herself only as Peace Pilgrim, spent the later years of her life, from 1953 to 1981, walking back and forth across the United States, sharing a message of peace with all whom she met. "I shall remain a wanderer," she declared, "until mankind (sic) has learned the way of peace, walking until I am given shelter and fasting until I am given food." She refused to carry money and did not affiliate herself with any organization. Her only possessions were her clothing—a pair of sneakers, a pair of long pants, a long-sleeved shirt, and a tunic that read "Peace Pilgrim" on the front. In the two pockets on the front of her tunic were a worn paper with some of her favorite peace quotations and a comb.

Her pilgrimage did not begin, however, until after many years of inner work. "We begin to prepare for the work that we have to do and customarily we have no idea what we are preparing for. So as a child I had no idea what I was preparing for. And yet, of course, I was in many respects preparing. . . ."

After a childhood remarkably free of religious instruction, Peace Pilgrim entered a successful business career. Material success, however, did not satisfy her.

> As I looked about the world, so much of it impoverished, I
> became increasingly uncomfortable about having so much
> while my brothers and sisters were starving. Finally I had to
> find another way. The turning point came when, in desperation
> and out of a very deep seeking for a meaningful way of life, I

walked all one night through the woods. I came to a moonlit glade and prayed.

I felt a complete willingness, without any reservations, to give my life—to dedicate my life—to service. "Please use me!" I prayed to God. And a great peace came over me.

I tell you it's a point of no return. After that, you can never go back to completely self-centered living . . . However, there's a great deal of difference between being *willing* to give your life and actually *giving* your life, and for me fifteen years of preparation and inner seeking lay between them.[6]

Willingness is the seed, and inner work the fertilizer. To believe is to hold an inner conviction. To bring beliefs alive, to turn them into a living force with power to transform, is to choose and then act upon those private convictions. Beliefs birth outward, and have the ability to effect others when they are acted upon. The inner transformation, though, is necessary before the outward birth can take place. Gandhi's chrysalis was the bitterly cold night of Maritzburg—quite literally his dark night of the soul. King's chrysalis was the hotbed of Montgomery, Alabama and his own sleepless night of struggle. Peace Pilgrim's chrysalis was the moonlit glade of a forest. They each had to come to grips with their own application of conscience, their own response to oppression and struggle, before the seed of their life work could be planted.

Embodying Change

The key to transforming the world is to embody the qualities that we want to see manifested in the world. "If we are not happy," writes Vietnamese monk Thich Nhat Hanh,

if we are not peaceful, we cannot share peace and happiness with others, even those we love, those who live under the same roof. If we are peaceful, if we are happy, we can smile and blossom like a flower, and everyone in our family, our entire society will benefit from our peace . . . Meditation is to be aware of what is going on—in our bodies, in our feelings, in our minds, and in the world. Each day 40,000 children die of hunger. The superpowers now have more than 50,000 nuclear warheads, enough to destroy our planet many times. Yet the sunrise is beautiful, and the rose that bloomed this morning along the wall is a miracle. Life is both dreadful and wonderful. To practice meditation is to be in touch with both aspects. . . .[7]

Thich Nhat Hanh and many other young Buddhist monks practiced this awareness of embracing both aspects during the war in
Vietnam. They moved into bombed-out villages to help rebuild.
They were shot down by both sides, greeted with suspicion because
they refused to choose sides.

> We were able to understand the suffering of both sides, the
> Communists and the anti-Communists. We tried to be open to
> both, to understand this side and to understand that side, to be
> one with them. That is why we did not take a side, even though
> the whole world took sides. We tried to tell people our percep-
> tion of the situation: that we wanted to stop the fighting, but
> the bombs were so loud . . . We wanted reconciliation, we did
> not want victory. Working to help people in a circumstance
> like that is very dangerous, and many of us got killed . . . Recon-
> ciliation is to understand both sides, to go to one side and
> describe the suffering being endured by the other side, and
> then to go to the other side and describe the suffering being
> endured by the first side. Doing only that will be a great help
> for peace.[8]

Being Peace begins with the assumption that inner attitude,
inner awareness, determines one's effect upon the world. If I want
to live in a peaceful world, I must discover peace within myself
and then enact that peace. Hanh inspires me because he does not
stop with embodying peace. He goes a step further to say that we
must enact our awareness of peace, even if that awareness requires
us to change our lifestyle, or even risk our lives. The call is not to
martyr oneself but to embody peace in the most immediate ways:
to smile, to love, to appreciate, to give of oneself without prejudice.
Being peace means enacting peace in the fabric of one's life.

The awareness extends to more than the human companions
who accompany us on this planet. Awareness extends to the plants,
minerals, and animals with whom we share this Earth.

After three years of living at the Findhorn Community in Scotland,
I had grown weary of people who were intent on "meditating
away" the world's problems, but were wary of direct action, labeling
any forthright statement about the world "political" and quickly
dismissing it. "We are a spiritual community," I was reminded many
times. "We do not make political statements."

During a visit to Australia in 1987, I met rainforest activists in
Tasmania and New South Wales who combined their spiritual work

with direct, nonviolent action for the Earth. Although these two groups were lobbying for different geographical areas of Australia's wilderness, both had a similar approach to their work. They combine their love for the Earth with their spiritual outlook on life, and transform that union into action.

Rob Blakers, a photographer living in Tasmania, combines his spiritual discipline of Ananda Yoga—which recognizes the sacredness of Earth, unlike many religious orders that seek to escape the "illusory" physical world—with his work.

Each morning Rob begins his day with an hour of meditation and chanting. When he is in his house, he adds some yoga postures. In the forest, he walks and photographs, taking pictures to alert people to the wonders of Tasmania's wilderness, to inspire them to care enough to take action for the temperate rainforests. After spending a few days with him in the wilderness, I know what he must endure to take those photographs. I know, too, why truly great wilderness photographers are so few—they are a special breed, like the gold miners of the last century, able to endure, even thrive, in the most difficult conditions. Their treasures, though, are not minerals wrested from the mountains; their prize is the image of the mountain itself, the first snowfall among the peaks, the blossom of autumn colors on the ridge. They take only a shred of the mountain's soul, not her innards, captured on film for posterity.

From Tasmania we traveled to Lismore in New South Wales. Here we met John Seed and the other members of the Rainforest Information Center (R.I.C.). Once again we were inspired by the depth of these people's commitment to their spirituality as well as their dedication to nonviolent direct action.

John had recently been in India speaking to the Satyagraha Foundation about R.I.C.'s nonviolent work protecting Australian forests. This organization, composed of followers of Gandhi's principles, felt that its members had grown lax in their commitment to nonviolent action, and invited the Australian activists to inspire its flagging membership.

John returned from the trip with a new understanding of the lack of basic amenities in India. After seeing village after village struggling without drinkable water, he could no longer justify having hot water in his house, headquarters for R.I.C. He stopped short of ripping out all the water pipes; instead, he tore out the water heater. If visitors want to bathe, they can take a cold shower or go for a swim in the river behind the house.

Ten years ago, John Seed never would have dreamt of being a rainforest activist. While traveling in India in the early seventies, he was introduced to Tibetan Buddhist and Vipassana meditation. He returned to Australia and helped establish a community outside Lismore dedicated to family, organic farming, and twice-daily meditations.

One day his life underwent a profound and irrevocable transformation. "There was a dispute over logging at the end of Terania Creek Road, only four or five miles from my home," John recalls.

> To show the level of my disinterest in such matters, I had never gone to the end of that road and had no idea there was a rainforest there.
>
> I can't remember what motivated me to go. I've tried to, because it was such an important turning point in my life. From that moment on, everything changed. Maybe it was the combination of experiencing the rainforest itself, which is totally different from the regrowth forest at Bodhi Farm, and the heightened circumstances of civil disobedience, danger, and arrest. No one else was affected the way I was.[9]

John's passion for the rainforest spread to a passion for the whole planet. He completely involved himself in the Terania Creek demonstrations, placing himself in front of bulldozers, joining others who were chained to logjams or perched on top of trees. After having exhausted every means of legislative action, the demonstrators were putting their bodies on the line to save the rainforests. After months of protest that gained national media attention, the loggers finally left Terania Creek. John continued to join other protests around Australia before he turned his attention to the international scene.

In our talks while visiting the R.I.C., John told me, "Nonviolent direct action is the most direct path for self-change. It brings up everything to look at."

To his statement I would add that any sort of action based on your deepest convictions for a better world will necessarily launch you onto a path of self-change. Inner changes are the foundation for outward action. And the vision of the world that you want to create is the inner compass that points the way and keeps you on the path.

Two

The Root of Vision

We are made of dreams and bones . . .
   —*David Mallet, folksinger*

The wild dream is the first step to reality by which we set our highest goals and discern our highest selves.
   —*Norman Cousins*

Some men (sic) see things as they are and ask why. I dream things that never were and ask why not. —*Robert F. Kennedy*

You have to know where you're going before you can buy the ticket. You can't walk into a bus station and buy a ticket until you know where you're going. And you can't get anywhere in your life until you have an idea of where you want to go.
   —*Phyllis Rodin*

THE ANSWER TO WHERE I WANT TO GO shapes my life vision. Because so many people associate visions with "being in the clouds," I carefully chose the title for this chapter. I associate vision with roots, the foundation of effective action. Vision begins as a seed that sprouts when one makes choices. Effective action fertilizes the seedling. People who claim to have visions but never act on them give visionaries a bad name. In truth, they are not visionaries, but rather dreamers, and a world of difference separates the two.

Vision is a prerequisite for any sort of effective living. Without a guiding vision, you drift aimlessly from job to job, or from cause to cause. "I can't do such-and-such because of so-and-so. . . ." You can blame your circumstances, but all the complaining in the world is a lie if you don't really know what you want to do.

In many Native American societies, no one is considered an adult until she has a vision for her life. Without a vision, how can someone know how to act? Note that the frame of reference here is internal. One's own guidelines come through personal experience: praying, questing, and seeking vision. The society respects the integrity of the individual's vision; no one is expected to fulfill anyone else's vision. However, she is expected to fulfill her own.

Guboo Ted Thomas, an Aboriginal elder from Australia, emphasizes two teachings for people who come to his "Dreaming Camps," which are organized to teach about the Dreamtime. The first is love, the underpinning of his approach to life. The second is the elimination of three words—should, if, and but. "You eliminate these from language, and you'll be 'lot happier," says Guboo, nodding quietly and then breaking into a grin. "Should, If, and his lesser brother But. Get rid of 'em."

Shoulds, ifs, and buts are dreary energy drains that can be replaced with wants, wills, and choices once you identify what you truly want to do.

Visionary Leadership, Individual Dreams

In Western culture, individual visioning is the exception rather than the rule. Instead of searching for personal visions, we have relied first on institutions and later on visionary individuals to supply our visions. Historically, the focus of visionary leadership in Western European culture evolved from the realm of the nobility—the Goddess/God or Queen/King—to the Church. Medieval visionaries such as Hildegard von Bingen (abbess, mystic, poet, composer, 1098–1179) and Martin Luther questioned and challenged the Church on the basis of their own revelations, but overall the Church continued to fulfill the role of "visionary leader" through the Middle Ages. Leadership then passed to the State during the "Age of Reason," a period dominated by the rise of "objective thought" among philosophers, scientists, and political reformers. This era spawned the "modern philosophers" (Descartes, Kant, and Hegel), "objective" scientists (from Descartes and Newton to Darwin), and a variety of new systems of government—democracy, socialism, and communism among them. In the twentieth century, the focus shifted to the visionary politician (whether it be Hitler or FDR) and finally to visionary activists, unaffiliated with particular institutions. A personal vision of a different kind of world, not an institutional policy, motivates their actions. Gandhi and Martin Luther King, Steven Biko and Maggie Kuhn are examples of the visionary activist, each acting upon his or her own vision of a different world.

A common aspect among these visionaries is their focus upon the world they want to create, not on what they want to eliminate. After all, if society is devoid of one undesirable element, it may be marginally better off, but it certainly is not changed. Creation means bringing forth something out of nothing. When human beings harness the power of creative vision, we claim our purest aspect—the seed of the Creator within each us, a seed latent in many individuals.

Enter yourself to discover the seed of creative genius that dreams, gestates, and finally births as your own life, lived within the context of a planetary vision. In truth I cannot act alone, for I am connected with all of life through the web of creation, but my actions can strengthen the web or tear it asunder. The quality of my impact depends largely upon the quality of my vision and the way in which I act upon it. My larger vision becomes the touchstone by which I measure all of the choices in my life, large or small, planetary or mundane.

This book is for those who have dreamed, awakened to disillusionment, and remained determined to realize the stuff of dreams in the daily waking world. Visionary power is shifting from institutions to the individual. The heroes and heras are you and I, and our time is now.

"No more Gandhis," proclaimed Danaan Parry in one of his talks. Parry, founder of the Earthstewards Network and a major proponent of conflict resolution on both local and international levels, was fully conscious of his "blasphemy." "'No more Gandhis,'" he explained, "means that we stop looking for epic heroes to solve our problems. Instead, we take on the task ourselves. You and me. Doing it the best way we know how, in our daily lives."

"No more Gandhis" also requires that you and I reclaim the visionary role filled by these epic figures. They excused the masses from exercising visionary responsibility. They supplied ready-made blueprints for those who had not undertaken the same inner questioning, the inner searching that leads to a personal direction, integrated with a vision for the whole.

Dream. Visualize. Sit quietly, allowing dream-seeds to root and grow. Knit some socks. Take long walks. Be conscious of the dreams growing in the belly of your soul. Talk little, think long, dream hard until one day the growth pains start. They take many forms— the dissolution of a marriage, the loss of a job, disillusionment with authority figures, the awful realization of impotency in the face of planetary destruction. The awakening begins, flecked with moments of realization and joy, breaths of fresh air gulped before resubmerging in a sea of pain. Awakening is not always pleasant, and reality is not always pretty, though the power of some moments can forever imprint you with their beauty.

Birth and Growth of a Vision

Through the pain I am laboring, straining, stretching that soul-belly, enduring until it softens to release its cargo, the beginnings of a fully fleshed life vision. It emerges breathing, squalling with good intentions, but still ever so tiny. "A mind that is stretched by a new idea," said Oliver Wendell Holmes, "can never go back to its original dimension."

The newly birthed vision thrives on the milk of action, at first the daily mundane sort. Now that I have a vision for my life and the world, how do I function? What do I eat, what do I wear, how do I speak, how do I dispose of the garbage, with whom do I live, how do I interact, how do I go about walking on this Earth in an appropriate way?

These are not trivial questions. They form the very foundation of the visionary's existence. Without addressing these basic considerations, the newly birthed vision has no chance of becoming a full-fledged reality.

The growth continues. Summertime. Apply your vision in the sphere of the home and then take the first tentative steps outside. Move into the neighborhood as the toddler learns to walk, then run, then dance.

Autumn. The second wave of disillusionment. Time to deepen the vision, readjust the direction and the details, grasp its significance on a deeper level. And who am I, with or without this vision? Do I even want it? (I'm beginning to suspect it may have been imposed by someone else, and I don't like it.)

Late autumn. Adulthood. Maturity of the vision. It rests comfortably upon my bones, as close as flesh, as pervasive as the flow of blood in my veins. I am becoming that vision, the dream incarnate, realizing its magnitude in fits and starts, in small and in far-reaching actions.

Winter. Old age. Ripened fruits hang heavy on the bough. From a seed I have grown a tree that has replicated the life force of that dream-seed many times over. The act of creation breeds more creation. The realization of vision brings greater vision. One cycle of creativity dies into another, the fruits of the old providing an abundance of seed for the new.

The cycle wheels through Creation, wielding an ancient truth—action breeds more action. Inactivity breeds lethargy. Who do you choose to be? The vision is yours to create. Remember, it does not come ready-made. You provide the seed. You fertilize and prepare the ground. The dream is yours to birth and finally to become.

And where does the dream come from? Out of nothing. And nothing is one of the most pregnant, fertile states imaginable. You can't dream it "wrong," for there are no external measurements for comparison. It is undeniably your own. And that is what gives it power.

◆　◆　◆

The following visioning exercise is designed to help guide you to your vision for your life and for the planet.

Set aside an hour of quiet, uninterrupted time. You might consider waking an hour early one morning to savor the dawn and the stillness. The pathways to the heart, to the depths of one's inner world, are least cluttered during the first and last hours of one's day.

Settle into a comfortable sitting position with the spine tall and straight. Take a few deep breaths, expanding the abdomen, the ribcage, the upper chest. If you notice any tight spots, send the breath into that area, releasing any tension. Imagine the body is made of butter, and you are sitting under the midday sun, melting in the heat. Feel the shoulders grow heavy. Allow the muscles around the eyes, ears, and jaw to grow heavy and relax. Allow the neck to soften.

Follow the breath moving in and out of your body. Become aware of the air and how it nourishes the body. Feel the flow of blood moving through your body. Notice where you can feel the pulse in your body.

Turn your attention to your inner ear. Notice the sounds—sometimes like a hum or buzz, other times like ocean waves.

In this relaxed state, allow yourself to imagine your life, exactly as you want it to be. For the moment, disregard the details of how you will reach this place. Simply enjoy visualizing your environment . . . living situation . . . relationships . . . work. (long pause) Allow yourself to be surprised by what you see.

When you are ready, bring your awareness to the place where you are sitting. Notice your breath, heartbeat, and the sounds of your inner ear. Stretch your body and open your eyes. Write in your journal, recording what you saw and experienced in your journey.

◆   ◆   ◆

You can supplement this exercise by answering the following questions. Record your answers in your journal. Read the explanations that follow only after you have answered the questions.

1. Ask yourself, "What five things do I value most in life? What am I willing to work for, to fight for, to live for?"
2. In 30 seconds or less, write down the three most important goals in your life.
3. If you won a million dollars in the lottery today, what choices would you make in your life? If you had all the time and money in the world, what would you do? What would you aspire to?
4. If you knew that you would live in perfect health for another six months and then die, how would you live? Whom would you see, where would you go, what would you do?
5. What have you always wanted to do but been afraid to attempt?
6. What kinds of activities give you the greatest sense of importance, self-esteem, and self-worth?
7. Imagine you had one wish from a genie, or a magic pill that you could swallow. What one goal would you wish for, what one great thing would you dare to dream, if you knew that you could not fail?

Question One helps you to identify the most important values in your life. These values provide clues that help focus your life vision. When answering Question Two, be sure to give yourself only 30 seconds and no more. This "quick list" method, developed by Joyce Brothers, bypasses the "shoulds" programmed in the subconscious mind. Question Three reveals what you would do if you had no mental or physical limitations. The fact that you can vision it means that you have the ability to accomplish it. You may need more time and have to work harder than if you had won the lottery, but with perseverance you can accomplish these goals. Your response to Question Four reveals what is most important to you, your true values. If the answer to this question is different from "What would you do if you won a million dollars" and "The three most important goals in life," look again at the goals that you are setting and make sure that you incorporate your responses to this question in your day-to-day activities. For Question Five, remember the fear that holds you back is usually the result of early conditioning. "I can't do such-and-such because my mother (father, teacher, minister, whoever) told me I couldn't/shouldn't/wouldn't." You may limit what you want to do according to what you think is possible. Question Six highlights your "area of excellence." Activities that utilize your greatest gifts usually generate feelings of satisfaction and self-worth. Identifying your area of excellence provides clues as to how to manifest your life vision. Not everyone was born to be a dancer or an engineer or a telephone operator. We each have different strengths—for good reasons! Find your innate abilities and expand upon them. Question Seven again asks you to look at what you really want to do, without imposing any restrictions or limitations.

After answering these questions and completing the above meditation, choose one major definite purpose for your life. Otherwise, you diffuse energy and disperse your efforts. Brian Tracy, in a tape series entitled *The Psychology of Achievement,* emphasizes the importance of this focusing: "Every great life only becomes great when the individual picks one thing which is more important than all of the other things put together, and the accomplishment of which will lead to the attainment of many of the other minor goals in life, and then commits all of their efforts and attention and energies to achieving that one thing."[1]

For a multi-talented person, this may be a difficult task. For someone who has a hard time making decisions, it may seem an insurmountable task. In my own life, I have come to realize that I expend a lot of energy trying to keep all of my options open. Instead of choosing whether to pursue music or writing or a medical career, I have tried to do all three, or at least keep the doors to all three possibilities open. In the process, however, I have split my attention and done justice to none of the three.

During the summer of 1989, after completing a book manuscript in April and recording an album of Celtic music in May, I spent three months in a one-room cabin searching inwardly, agonizing over how I could best focus my life. Despite all my efforts, though, no clear vision emerged. Occasionally I walked two miles to the nearest pay phone. I was desperate for contact after my lonely inward vigils.

"Look, Judith," said a medical clairvoyant whom I telephoned during this time, "you need to choose one area of your life to focus on."

"But I can't decide which one," I moaned. "I'm afraid I'll choose the wrong one ... why can't I do them all at once?"

"You need to focus on one. You can think of the areas of your life as majors and minors. Your other talents won't go away. In fact, you'll find that they also develop as you learn to focus on one area. The process of choosing is as important as what you choose. If you aim for prestige, you'll meet a lot of nasty, competitive people. They will mirror your own motivations. If you choose humbly, if you do what you really love—no matter how crazy it may look on the outside—you'll find your way."

During these months of contemplation, a vision was slowly emerging. Perhaps I was so afraid of acknowledging my greatest desire that it had to sneak up slowly, quietly, so as not to scare me off. One morning early in October, I awoke, began my usual meditation, and then opened my eyes. In that moment, I knew. After all those months of vacillation, I took a deep breath, sighed, and made a choice. In fact, I was bored with the struggles of the past months and wondered why I hadn't seen the obvious sooner. The birth was ridiculously simple after the months of difficult labor. I wanted to become a naturopath and, despite my fears about finances and academic demands, I was going for it. Period.

Making Peace with the Unexpected

As I look back at my own life and listen to other people's stories of transformation, I realize that vision cannot be forced—at least not the major, life-changing kind. I cannot choose to have a peak experience next Wednesday at 7:13 a.m. I cannot schedule a life-shattering revelation during a 10-day Vipassana retreat, nor can I orchestrate planetary transformation simply by publicizing it. Major transformations arrive with the flow of life, not through directing it. Although I can meditate, pray, and fast for vision, I am not guaranteed that "the big moment" will arrive as a result of my efforts.

Although I cannot force a vision, I can move toward the visionary life. As I orient myself away from societal "shoulds" toward my deepest inner promptings, the visionary stance requires listening to the wholeness of creation. Once I have learned to look inward, quieting the logical chattering of the mind, I can hear my own heart—the true "mind" that guides me in the ways of wisdom. Then I can also hear the wisdom of the outer world, the signs and portents woven into the fabric of daily life.

I first experienced vision questing on Vision Mountain outside Spokane, Washington. Local tribes have visited this mountain for thousands of years to pray for vision to guide their lives. After a hectic summer of living at the Bear Tribe, a community based on Native American ways located on the mountain, I was eager to join a group of people on a four-day vision quest. I also wanted the time to re-evaluate the decisions that I had made before graduating from college. After a year-long break from academic studies, I planned to study naturopathic medicine. I simultaneously desired and dreaded a vision; I was nervous that it might guide me away from my plans.

After a sweat lodge and blessing ceremony, we were guided to isolated places on the mountain. Once I had unpacked my sleeping bag and arranged the writing materials that I brought with me, I leaned back against a rock in the center of the circle where I was to spend the next four days.

Within an hour, my stomach growled viciously. My mind was bored with studying pine bark and watching passing clouds. By the end of the afternoon I had relived every relationship in my life, combed memories that bristled in my awareness, and made lists of what to keep and what to discard in my life. I revised the lists over and over—to keep myself sane; to keep my mind from forcing my body to run screaming back to the Long House and some form of entertainment; to feed myself with information and activities to make my mind feel useful and therefore safe.

For two days I struggled with my mind before it finally ground to a halt. Lack of food, sleep, and outer stimulation had finally quieted my racing thoughts. I was lying on my sleeping bag, spacy-exhausted after two days of fasting and a sleepless night watching the movements of the stars and the moon. I could finally look around the circle at the pine tree and rocks that had become my closest companions without any thought waves entering my awareness. Only then could I began to hear the voices of the beings around me—the rocks, the pine trees, the blue-tailed skinks living under the rocks, and the squirrel that chattered in the tree. I began to hear my own voice as well.

Listening to the self is not enough. The purpose of the quest is to align the voice of individual self with the voice of creation, the wholeness of life. I was "alone" on the mountain, questing for vision, and yet that aloneness introduced me to the voices of all the beings around me, the ones who speak through the heart, not the talkative world of humans.

Tom Brown, in his book *The Vision,* relates how his teacher Stalking Wolf introduced him at a young age to the Vision Quest. To Stalking Wolf, the quest led to self-realization, which served to prepare the soul for connection with the Creator and the unity of all things. The pure connection of self and Creator gives rise to Vision, the Creator's command and knowledge of one's life purpose.[2]

Vision Questing as a Way of Life

Grandfather taught Tom that questing is more than a one-time event. Questing rarely yields grand visions all at once; it is a continuing process, and those on a spiritual path need to repeat the Vision Quest, perhaps several times a year, throughout their lives.[3]

During my own quest, I "heard" that I was to continue to take time in wilderness areas, specifically one day a month to fast and sit alone. Presumably I fall into that category of "seeker" who receives vision through a long, slow process rather than a momentary bang. I admit that I have not faithfully kept the once-a-month directive, but I set aside time at least once a year to sit alone in a sacred area and listen for guidance.

My most recent quest was a four-day fast/vigil in a burial cairn in northern Scotland. Like the native people of North America, the indigenous peoples of Europe had rituals to mark rites of passage. The cairns are round, domed structures built of stone with a long, low tunnel leading into the round central cavity. Some of these burial cairns, besides being the final resting place of powerful people within the community, were places of initiation. Candidates would spend the four days preceding the winter solstice (the shortest day/longest night of the year) fasting inside the womb-shaped, earth-covered chamber. On the morning of the fourth day, the rising sun's light "pierced" the vaginal tunnel entrance to the chamber, illuminating the inner chamber where the candidate sat. Metaphorically, the shaft of sunlight, the male principle, entered and fertilized the earthen womb, the female principle. Presumably the candidate, too, was fertilized—with the gift of vision.

Unlike the first quest, in the burial cairn I was not concerned about the outer form of the ritual. Few true wilderness areas remain in Scotland—humans have shaped and scarred the land for thousands of years—so I did the best I could with what was available. Without a sweat lodge or a stream to cleanse myself before the ritual, I took a shower before driving to the site, and smudged myself and the cairn before entering. (Smudging is a cleansing performed by drawing smoke—usually from burning sage, cedar, juniper or sweetgrass—around the body.) Because the cairn is marked on the tourist maps, I shared the site from time to time with other people, mostly curiosity seekers. I had a long talk with a Danish man who crawled into the cairn and sat beside me. He described how he had struggled to understand his own visionary experiences according to his intellectual background. Failing to rationally explain them, he had dismissed them. He had visionary experiences, but refused to believe in them. I laughed with him, because my stance was just the opposite; I believed in visionary experiences, but refused to have them—perhaps not consciously, but I had a much easier time believing in "otherworldly" experiences when they happened to someone else.

Perhaps I was also dismissing the power of my own visions by comparing them with those of others. Because they did not resemble the experiences of Black Elk, Brooke Medicine Eagle or other members of the Bear Tribe, I was sure that the wisdom and insight that I gained was not "right," not the grand vision that I was "supposed" to have. The power of my own vision, though, is precisely that it is mine. I cannot look outside for confirmation of an inner event.

During my quest in the burial cairn, I was directed in how to balance my life. At that time I was preparing to return to the United States. I was questing for direction on how best to live my life as I moved away from life in a large community into a relatively secluded, "mundane" situation. The answers came to me during the quest through dreams and meditative moments. I was to divide my life between four activities—meditation/inner work, gardening and work with the Earth, writing, and music. Each activity would feed a different aspect of my being and provide inspiration for the other areas of concentration.

The information from this quest provided guidance for that section of my life's journey. I cannot assume that the directives will apply for the rest of my life, or even for a full year. Questing is an ongoing lesson in attuning to the needs of each moment, of each segment of the journey.

Being True to Your Vision

The process of questing and clearly visioning an ideal life often unblocks energy invested in the half-truths that we tell ourselves. One woman, when she first completed this exercise, spoke of her vision of being a powerful healer. "It was wonderful," she said, eyes glowing. "But then," she said, face falling, "I said to myself, 'I can't be *that* powerful,' and the vision begin to dim. I want to be a great healer, but I don't want all that power!"

In this case, she immediately began to compromise her vision. "But I couldn't have that" is a common response. We diminish our vision to make ourselves more comfortable in the moment; "more comfortable" means closer to our present circumstances. The vision causes us to stretch beyond what we know; otherwise, it merely reports our current situation. Visioning means stepping into areas that are unexplored, unknown, and uncharted.

"Your imagination is your preview to the future," Einstein once said. That preview brings excitement or trepidation, depending on how we respond to change. Nothing can be created before it is envisioned. Someone conceived of a computer before it was built. In fact, the leaders in computer technology were those who could envision the whole product or system and then work backwards from the vision, step by step, to work out the actual technological challenges.

The discrepancy between your vision and your current situation generates tension. Do not, however, confuse this kind of tension with debilitating stresses that cause "tension" headaches and other illnesses. The difference between what is and what you want forms a creative tension that propels you towards what you want.

A note on "what we want." From a young age, I was taught that polite people, especially children, were never supposed to ask for what they wanted. I learned to be wishy-washy as a way of avoiding making direct statements. The art of social interaction is to skirt around the obvious and avoid ruffling both friend and foe. Instead of connecting deeply and speaking truthfully, I was taught to be innocuous. I've decided, though, that I'd rather be a truthful heretic than a pleasant jellyfish. Actually stating what I want feels much "cleaner," both in my interactions with other people and with myself.

Robert Fritz relates a story about working with handicapped people to identify what they really wanted in life. One woman struggled with the exercise of identifying what she wanted in life—which, Robert reminded her, was different from identifying what she thought was possible.

The woman insisted that she could not have what she wanted.

"I can tell you what you want," said Robert. "You want good health."

The woman agreed, but insisted that she could not have it. When she finally allowed herself to acknowledge her desire for perfect health, she felt "physically lighter, as if a weight has been lifted off my shoulders. I feel clearer. It's almost as if there is an energy flowing through me now."

> Whether or not her illness persisted, she no longer had to bear
> the additional burden of feeling obligated to misrepresent to
> herself the truth about her desire for health.[4]

Having a vision does not immediately solve every problem in life. In fact, the path to realizing the vision may stretch and bend and reform the visionary in unforeseen ways. The only sure knowledge of the way ahead is that you have never been this way before. The moment you begin to veer, to make life more "comfortable," you move away from your vision. One step towards comfort may be followed by another and another until that series of more comfortable steps takes you to very familiar territory—right back where you started from.

A clear vision provides a map that clarifies decisions, from daily schedules to career plans. I know, for example, that if I want to write a book, I need to set aside time every day to write. I cannot work an eight-hour job, cook and eat meals, write the book, and practice the violin four hours a day. As much as I would like to pursue all of the loves in my life at once, I can never do justice to any one of them when I spread my energy and attention so thinly.

Planetary Vision

Having created a vision for your personal life, focus now on your planetary vision. The acts of your daily life fulfill the vision of your personal life. In turn, your personal life fulfills a planetary vision.

◆   ◆   ◆

Repeat the visualization exercise, but this time emphasize your planetary vision.

Set aside 30 minutes of uninterrupted, quiet time. Take a couple of deep breaths, letting go of any tension in the body.

Close your eyes. Imagine that your body is made of butter, and you are melting in the sun. Allow yourself to relax completely.

Feel your awareness expanding to fill the room where you are sitting. Expand farther, filling the house. Feel your awareness grow even larger, expanding until it fills the community and then the state in which you live. Expand to encompass the continent, then the northern hemisphere. Expand even more. Feel your awareness grow large enough to encompass the entire planet.

From this position, look down at the Earth. Take note of the condition of the entire planet—the oceans, land masses, the animals and plants, the minerals and humans— all of the ecosystems on the planet.

Now envision the planet as you would like it to be. If you desire a healthy ocean and water system on the planet, envision that. If you desire food for all creatures, envision that. If you desire justice and freedom for all living beings, imagine what justice and freedom would look like. If you desire a healthy environment, visualize that. If you want a peaceful world, imagine a world at peace. Envision any other aspect of what you would like to see created on the planet. At this point, don't worry about the how; you are simply creating a vision of what you want for the planet. Give yourself plenty of time.

Ask yourself, "If I could have this world, would I move in? Would I take it?" If the answer is "yes," then choose to live in this world.

When you feel ready, bring your attention back to where you are sitting, and open your eyes. Record anything you want to remember in your journal.

◆ ◆ ◆

You may want to follow this exercise by writing out your vision for the planet as if it already existed. If drawing or painting is your medium, portray the world you wish to live in. Write a song, compose a symphony to celebrate your vision. Place your creations where you can see them and return to them often for inspiration. Be aware, too, that your vision may change over time as you move along your path. You may choose to add more detail or focus on different aspects of planetary life. Transformative experiences may cause you to rework your vision entirely.

Be aware, too, of preparing yourself emotionally and mentally for the task of creating a vision. Edith Stauffer, writing about the "Power of the Will," emphasizes "... the incredible power of the will and the importance of using deeply emotional experiences to plant positive goals or ideas in the unconscious. We should frame no judgments and cease all action and goal formation while our attitudes are negative ... While attitudes are positive, sound goals (conscious and unconscious) may be achieved. ..."[5]

Focusing on what we want to create is powerful, something to be approached with awareness, but certainly not with fear. We move away from reacting to what we don't want in our world and toward creating what we do want. "For most people," writes Robert Fritz, "when they begin clearly to know what is important to them, they discover what might be called their 'natural goodness.' As Robert Frost put it, not some 'tenderer-than-thou collectivistic, regimenting love with which the modern world is being swept,' but an authentic and practical caring for higher values, both for the individual and for the planet."[6]

Create a vision that truly expresses your highest, deepest good. Don't compromise your vision for fear that you are not perfect or prepared or powerful enough. Envision a life worthy of your living. Make sure that it is yours. No one can create a vision for you; it must come from your own inward searching. Most importantly, no one can live a vision for you. You must clothe the bones of your vision with the flesh and blood of your own life.

Three

Choice and the Use of Will

"Would you tell me please, which way I ought to go from here?"
   "That depends a great deal on where you want to get to,"
said the Cat.
   "I don't much care where—" said Alice.
   "Then it doesn't matter which way you go," said the Cat.
   "—so long as I get somewhere," Alice added. . . .
   —*Lewis Carroll,* Alice in Wonderland

I learned at least this by my experiments. That if one advances
confidently in the direction of his dreams, and endeavors to live
the life which he has imagined, he will meet with a success
unexpected in common hours. He will put something behind
and will pass an invisible boundary. —*Henry David Thoreau*

THE POWER OF CONSCIOUS CHOICE is the activist's greatest
tool. The definition for "activism" gives two major clues in pursuing
a life committed to action—doing things with energy and decision;
in reality, the two are inextricably linked. Decision unleashes
energy, while indecision traps it in swamps of despair. To work
halfheartedly is to move forward with the brakes on, fearful of
every curve in the road. Eventually movement ceases altogether.
"The very best way to relate to our work," writes Marsha Sinetar,
author of *Do What You Love, the Money Will Follow,* "is to choose
it. Right Livelihood is predicated upon conscious choice. Unfortunately, since we learn early to act on what others say, value, and
expect, we often find ourselves a long way down the wrong road
before realizing we did not actually choose our work. Turning our

lives around is usually the beginning of maturity since it means correcting choices made unconsciously, without deliberation or thought."[1]

Conscious choices are primarily commitments to oneself. They are not generated in response to other people's approval or disapproval, but arise from the necessity of the soul, from uncovering our deepest wants and desires.

> Choosing rightly, and in direction with what we truly want, we learn about our strengths. We also notice our weaknesses. As we choose what is most helpful to us, we feel our power growing. Every time we consciously choose something, however insignificant it might seem, in line with what we feel is highest and best in ourselves, we support our true life goals. Also, we reinforce the idea that we are good, valuable and worthwhile. This reinforces our next proper, healthful choices. Thus, a more positive cycle takes hold of our habits, thinking and outcomes.[2]

Choices unleash unseen resources, attract hitherto unknown people, and generate further action. Mary Link, director of Peace Brigade International, completely reoriented her life after hearing an inner voice that led her to focus her life on peace work. Several years later, she was preparing to shift her focus within the peace movement. She spent a restless night considering her options. "That night," she said, "I made my decision. And then," she said, smiling, "the phone didn't stop ringing for three days. That's how my life works."

Choice is invocation, inviting the Universe to support our endeavors. The channel is clear, ready to receive inspiration, energy, and the substance to realize the choice.

Intending Versus Choosing

A word of caution about "intending" to do something: "Intending" differs vastly from "choosing." I have grown weary of people who "intend" to do things. This use of the word "intend" is, I believe, an outgrowth of "personal growth" seminars; the theory is that if I "intend" enough, eventually I will accomplish something: "I intend to do that next week," or, if I really mean to do something, "I have a strong intention around that project." Unfortunately, "intend" often becomes a substitute for "I'll try." How often do you or others say, "I'll try to get there next Wednesday," or "I'll try to finish this

CHOICE AND THE USE OF WILL 39

article by the end of the week"? How often is the project actually completed? I'm willing to bet that completion happens with alarming rarity, because the word "try" impacts as doubt on the subconscious mind, just enough to weaken the mind's assurance. In our lives, "trying" causes us to falter from our true direction, from our intended goal. I have worked to eliminate the word "try" from my own vocabulary, especially in giving instruction to others. The words "try" and "intend" are particularly damaging when referring to goals and life direction.

Forget about trying, or its lesser brother intending—just do it! If you choose to finish the article by next week, say so—and then be sure to do it. If you are going to Millie's house on Wednesday, say so. If you really don't want to go, tell Millie that you won't be there. Forget about "trying" or "intending." These words are usually polite coverups for "I don't want to" or "I can't."

Evaluating the Here and Now

Choice activates, but the impetus to move will be fruitless unless you take stock of your present position. In order to get to where you want to go in your life, you need to make a clear evaluation of your present position before embarking upon a journey. Make choices, and then evaluate where you are.

If you are honest about your current situation, you are most likely a long way from your vision. Don't despair; if you were close to your goal, it wouldn't be a vision, it would be a pleasant activity, a stroll on a lazy summer afternoon. The disparity between what is and what you envision creates tension. Like a magnet, the vision draws your current situation towards it—or conversely, you could say that reality propels itself toward the vision. In such a situation, the greater the tension, the better. Increased tension means more potential energy propelling you to your goal.

A taut rubber band has more tension, more potential energy, than a slack rubber band. The two points that anchor the rubber band are the current situation on one side and the vision on the other. Simply loosing the rubber band without direction produces haphazard results. The creative process involves aiming the taut rubber band and then releasing the potential energy into directed action.

The intensity of the "snap" of the rubber band varies from one life to another, and from one creative process to another. Usually the release happens over a considerable length of time, with the tension slackening as you move closer to fulfilling the vision. As the tension lessens, the need to re-evaluate the current situation increases. Recognize and guard against the tendency to discard visions once the initial "juice" of the germination and growth stage have passed. After the initial "rush" of conception wanes, visionaries rebuild energy and enthusiasm through completing day-to-day activities that fulfill the dream. These secondary choices, made to support the primary vision, generate momentum. Moment-by-moment choices either support or undermine the creative process. Momentum and endurance build as a result of the choices made in these situations.

The Use of Will

Choices also aid or undermine the development of will. "Willpower" applies to more than diets and athletic regimes—the correct use of will affects the whole of one's life by bonding the knowledge of the head with the experience of the heart. The energy of will is located in the throat chakra (energy center) of our physical bodies—note, ahem, that energy moving between the head and the heart must pass through the throat chakra. How I use my will—the choices that I make, the words that I speak, and my accountability for those words—either links or separates the heart and the head. The destination on this inner journey is to marry the head and the heart, to bring wisdom into feelings and actions. I may know in my head that I need to set aside time for writing, but until I use my will to make choices that support that understanding, the knowledge is not enacted in the heart of my daily experience. I use will when I apply the truths I know in my head to the daily actions in my life. To use will means to bring wisdom— the things that I know—into the experience of my life.

Caroline Myss, co-author of the book *The Creation of Health,* links the energy of the fifth chakra (the throat) with:

> the development of personal expression, and, especially, the use of individual willpower . . . Cause and effect is the study of the use of willpower and its relationship to what is created in our personal worlds. In the language of energy, the act of using personal willpower is equal to the act of commanding energy to take form according to the map of emotional desire and mental intention that one is holding in one's consciousness.

Thus, the expression, "that's not what I had in mind," is given genuine authority when you actually realize that "having something in mind" does, in fact, precede every action of personal creation in which you participate. . . .

The study of cause and effect also teaches a person about the significance of learning to "follow one's dreams" and that you can "do anything so long as you believe in yourself." In order to succeed in realizing your dreams, you have to hold on to your goals, keep your intention clearly focused and make choices that empower your ambitions. The study of cause and effect— actions and consequences—is, in fact, the study of the power inherent in each of us to create our own realities.[3]

Taking Yourself Seriously

Ultimately, the choices I make say something about how seriously I take myself and my vision. "Serious" doesn't mean arrogant or snobbish. The people whom I have met who take their visions seriously are some of the most good-natured, generous people imaginable. Because they know the power of vision and direct action in their own lives, they are not threatened by others' visions. In fact, they usually actively support and encourage other people to follow their own individual inspirations.

One day I asked myself what I would do differently if I took myself seriously. After a few moments' thought, I realized that the first thing I would change would be how I responded to what I perceived as other people's wants or needs. As long as I did not take myself seriously, others' needs would take precedence over my own. I would always choose giving my time to other people's projects. (My sense is that this modus operandi is a basic social response imprinted in women. We are taught to nurture others— not our own creations.) As long as I refused to take myself seriously, I would choose to spend the evening with a lonely, boring co-worker from the nursing home rather than writing or studying herbalism or going circle dancing. I would continue a friendship because I felt the other person needed the support, not because the relationship was mutually beneficial. My choices say a lot about how easily I can be swayed by outside expectations or needs, and how willing I am to use my own internal directives as guidelines for my decisions.

In essence, I am deciding how to "spend" my energy. By deciding in favor of my vision, I place value in my life. I vote with my time, attention, and energy for what is most important to me. I prioritize my actions according to fundamental decisions that I have made about what is most important in my life.

Fundamental Choices

For an activist, the fundamental choice is change. The type of change is dictated by one's vision—or lack thereof. Karen was a happily married mother of two boys when her back gave way, precipitating a year of intensive inner work. Six months into the crisis, she traveled to England with her family. She had already begun the process of discarding elements of herself that no longer served, and identifying areas that needed to grow. During that trip, filled with many magical, unplanned meetings, something fundamental came "unglued." The last vestiges of what she identified as "herself" gave way and disintegrated. "I was terrified that nothing would be left when I let go of what I call the 'ego,' or the 'little self.' When I let go into the nothingness, thank goodness there was a tiny, tiny being of me still there inside, very stunted, very tiny. I had the image of a blackened fetus, but it was still alive . . .

"At that point, I knew that I could choose to go crazy, or I could choose to take what had happened to me and put it into my life. At that moment, I knew that it would be easier to go insane. I've never been one to take the easy way. I chose to put it into my life, whatever that meant, whatever it took."

What came out of that blackened, shriveled self was "beauty. So much raw beauty. Poetry and dance and music and song . . . I had been afraid of this Self, and it was so beautiful."

Karen made a fundamental choice when faced with the disintegration of her "ego," or outer self. Her choice to integrate her experiences into her daily life established the foundation for the rest of her life. Her reference point became internal rather than external. She chose to transform and then to integrate the newness into her daily life. In essence, Karen chose to be true to herself rather than continue responding to outside influences.

Robert Fritz identifies four fundamental choices that underlie a creative orientation to life. These choices include 1) being the predominant creative force in one's life, 2) being true to oneself, 3) being healthy, and 4) being free.

When Karen chose to live life on her own terms, she made two of the four fundamental choices—to be true to herself and to be the predominant creative force in her life. Becoming the "predominant creative force" in your own life means relying on an internal sense of direction to guide your life. You identify what you want in life and make choices to fulfill your greatest desires. You take responsibility for the outcome of decisions and actions. You are no longer the victim of external forces, real or imagined, visible or invisible (such as "fate" or "luck"). You are the primary force behind your own creativity, and thus your own ability to bring about change.

For those walking the path of activism, I add a fifth fundamental choice—to be a catalyst for change. Every activist whom I have ever met desired to bring about change. The truly great activists have a vision for the change they want to see enacted on the planet, and they take action to bring about that vision through their own being as well as through their actions. Like Dr. Edward Bach's directive for the physician, "Healer, heal thyself," the activist who desires planetary change must also work to change him- or herself.

The Domino Effect

Be aware, too, that a single choice may precipitate a whole series of changes in your life. Caroline Myss tells of a woman in one of her workshops who struggled for a long time to identify a "choice point" in her life that affected many later decisions. Caroline reminded her that any change has the power to alter one's life. Finally, in exasperation, the woman said, "I decided to paint my house this summer. Big deal."

"Start there and see where you go," advised Caroline.

Forty-five minutes later the woman jumped from her seat and waved her paper.

> "Look at this," she said to me (Caroline). "Last year my life was a mess. I wanted to change everything about my life and myself, and it was so overwhelming I didn't know where to begin. Out of frustration I decided to paint my house because it was something I could do immediately. Then I decided my furniture looked pretty shabby next to the painted walls, so I refurnished three of the rooms in my house. Then I guess I was feeling better about myself because I decided I needed a new look. I took up an aerobics class and three months ago I invested in a new wardrobe because I was losing weight. When all that was finished, I still had my life to deal with, but I felt better about

myself. I decided to pursue my own development—my own personal development—and that decision led me to start reading spiritual literature. And that eventually led me to this workshop."

What this wonderful woman was describing was the process of transformation that she had set in motion through the initial choice to paint her house. Now, at the non-physical level what she chose was secondary to the fact that she put herself in motion, and therefore the Universe could assist her with guidance and with grace.[4]

During a time in my own life of great indecision, a good friend encouraged me to take action, any action, to begin the process of transformation. "Move!" he exclaimed. "Think how hard it is to steer a truck when it's parked. It's much easier to change direction when the wheels are in motion. Get moving and trust that God will do the steering!"

♦   ♦   ♦

The following is an exercise to help you identify how many changes are generated by a single choice in your own life.

In your journal, or on a large sheet of blank paper, write a choice that you have made in the center of a page and then circle it. As you recall changes or further decisions that resulted from this choice, note them as branches radiating from the center circle. Continue to note subsequent changes and decisions, connecting them with lines to their originating source. Branch outward as you identify more decisions and changes that followed as a result of preceding decisions.

♦   ♦   ♦

This exercise, though simple, dramatically illustrates the power of a single choice in your life. When you are finished, your notes will look like a tree with many branches radiating from a central point. You can see graphically how the effect of a single choice affects many areas of your life. Each choice ripples like a stone dropped into a still pond—the effects reverberate through many areas of your life. Each choice generates change which in turn brings about new decisions and more action in your life.

I cannot predict exactly how a choice will effect the rest of my life, how the energy of a stone dropped in the pond will affect the surface of the water. In my life, I cannot predict—or sometimes even imagine—the changes that a single choice may catalyze. When the choice is to enact a radically different world, both on personal and planetary levels, the aftershocks may cause innumerable changes.

"Your natural temptation at this point," writes Robert Fritz, "would probably be to ask for an example of how this shift (to be the predominant creative force in one's life) might look in a person's life. But in the creative orientation, we cannot predict what the shift will look like, for it will be unique in each case. In fact, it is probably more useful not to have a model or picture of how it might look, because then your temptation would be to try to match your reality to the picture in the example."[5]

Be aware, too, that you need not memorize, or even know, every twist and turn on the path to realizing your vision. Choices attract resources, people, and information that were unavailable or unknown to you before you made the decision. You cannot know the path because the essence of creativity is bringing something from the void. No one has trod this way before, so no maps of the journey exist. You may glean navigational skills from studying others' journeys, both contemporaries and ancients, but realize that the path itself is yours to forge. You enter a frontier of your own creation. The only assurance is that it will be unknown, and the only constant, change.

Working With Creation

Your navigational tools include your ability to evaluate your current situation and to adjust your actions and choices accordingly. Create and adjust, says Robert Fritz. No one reaches their desired goal without some alteration of their original plans. Conscious choice steers you toward what you truly want in life.

Another important factor is desire. The more reasons you have for attaining a goal, the stronger your motivation will be, and the more irresistible the goal becomes. You must truly, passionately desire the vision that you have created for your life. Remember that the vision acts like a magnet, drawing you forward in your life. Desire increases the pull of that magnet and galvanizes your resolve to align your life toward the realization of your vision.

Frequent reminders of your vision aid the steering process. One powerful method is to write your vision, and any secondary choices that you are pursuing to fulfill that vision, each morning. Writing your choices imprints them deeply in your awareness for the whole day. You may find that many "chance" meetings or bits of information come to you, or opportunities present themselves that you would otherwise overlook, with the potential to help fulfill your vision. If you cannot write all of your choices each day, at least post them in a prominent place where you can read them each morning.

Another effective morning exercise is to create a mental picture of your vision. With your eyes closed, use your inner sight to envision your life and the planet as you desire them to be. Clearly see the vision, and then clearly depict current reality. Ask yourself, "If I could have my vision, would I take it? Would I move into such a world now?" If the answer is yes, then choose your vision.

Asking yourself if you would accept your vision is of vital importance. Many people, when given what they claim is their greatest desire, either balk or walk away from it. If I am unwilling to accept the reality of my vision, it will never come into being. For years I may have fantasized about buying a new car, but if someone drove up my driveway with the car of my dreams right now, would I accept the keys and sign the registration? I may dream of a peaceful, environmentally sound planet, but if I awoke to such a world tomorrow, would I choose to stay? Your answer to "if I could have it, would I accept it?" provides clues to how either you or your vision needs to change.

If you would not take the vision, ask yourself if the picture is complete. Have you left out some aspect of the vision? Does your dream car have a blue interior instead of the red plaid in the car that you've been offered? Does your ideal world include bicycle pathways as well as mass transit systems? Check to be sure that you have the entire vision. Details may be added or subtracted at any time. And don't compromise your vision according to what you think is possible. Remember, the larger the disparity between what is and what you envision, the more tension and therefore potential energy is available to propel you toward your vision.

Four

Befriending Change

IN THE MIDST OF one of the most difficult periods during my stay at the Findhorn Foundation, I sat on the steps outside Cluny Hill with my head buried in my arms, crying. My anticipated nirvana working in the Cluny vegetable garden had soured into a nightmare—not with the plants, but rather the humans with whom I worked.

In the depths of my agony, David Earl, one of my closest friends and an unfailing support, sat down beside me and circled me with his arms. He allowed me to cry into the woolly shoulder of his sweater for several minutes before he asked what was wrong. Between tearful gasps, I briefly outlined my struggles with the other people working in the garden.

"I feel like such a failure," I confided. "I don't know if I'm going to make it as a member here. I seem to go from one emotional crisis to the next."

"But you're still riding the roller coaster," said David Earl.

I look up, puzzled. "What do you mean, roller coaster?"

"The roller coaster of change. You're still riding it. You haven't tried to jump off."

His words momentarily stopped the flow of tears. "But other people don't seem to go through these difficulties, this questioning. Like you—you've been here for almost ten years. You know this is where you belong, you don't have to question it."

David smiled patiently. "Every day I have to choose to be here. I go through periods of questioning all the time. I think everyone who's a member here does."

47

I was shocked. Somehow I had imagined that joining the community and becoming a member eliminated doubts and questioning.
My Goddess, everyone else was going through this, too?

"And," said David Earl, meeting my eyes, "you are more than
your emotions."

I sat for a moment, sniffing. Who was I, I wondered, if I wasn't
my emotions? In that moment, I was aware only of being swamped
with feelings. I had given up trying to keep my head above the
murky emotional depths. I was that sea of feelings—was there
anything of me left if I wasn't those emotions?

"But my emotions are part of me," I blurted out. "Are you trying
to say that I shouldn't feel them?"

"Of course not," said David Earl, squeezing my shoulder. "The
emotions are part of you, but they are not all of you. The 'you,'
the real you, is much more than your emotions—or your physical
body, or your mind. I have a body, but I am much more than my
body. I have a mind, but I am much more than my mind. Do you
see what I mean?"

I had a glimmering of his meaning. Yes, I could sense something
of myself that was beyond these emotions, that was looking on
with amused compassion. This larger "me" seemed to be on vacation, but still in touch via satellite. I wanted desperately to establish
closer contact. Perhaps I could even woo it to become a permanent
companion in my life.

David Earl gave me several important tools that afternoon. The
first was the image of a roller coaster to represent change. Yes, I
lived through ups and downs, periods of joy that alternated with
self-loathing, but until then I had never understood that they were
movements within the larger pattern of my "ride" through life.
Somehow I had convinced myself that if I was "on track" in my
life, I would never experience difficulties. "Going with the flow,"
following the path of the heart, guaranteed a smooth ride. Sitting on
the steps in David Earl's arms, I began to question that assumption.

He also opened a door to my awareness that offered a broader
perspective on who I was. During my days as a student, I had
reacted strongly to the divisions inherent in academic disciplines.
I pursued an interdisciplinary major, the university's "state of the
art" response to students' increasing dissatisfaction with rigidly
separated fields of knowledge. In my own budding spiritual life, I
resisted the separation of body, mind, and spirit. I wanted a learning

experience that would integrate all areas of the mind as well as the body, emotions, and spirit. The academic principle of analysis, cutting things into parts to examine them more closely, challenged my desire to think in wholes.

I spent my student days trying to sew together the separated pieces. In the process, though, I had forgotten that a larger spirit infuses the collected bits. The whole is greater than the sum of the parts. When all of the disparate bits are reconnected, something greater than simple addition of those pieces emerges. In my own life, the integration of emotions, mind, body, and spirit was possible because of a larger awareness that orchestrated all of the seemingly disparate elements. The organizing principle, the blueprint that held together all of the different aspects of myself, was the "real" me.

Perhaps, I mused, the whole point of the journey was to learn to identify with the "real" me, and to enjoy the roller coaster ride en route to that destination. Perhaps, too, I would never "arrive" anywhere, in which case I had best learn to enjoy the ups and downs.

I hoped that the roller coaster would slow and perhaps even stop when I left the Findhorn community nearly four years later. The Findhorn Foundation, like every intentional community that I have ever visited or lived in, is focused on transformation. "What you hold in mind, produces in kind"—hence, in a community focused on transformation, I was not surprised by the massive changes that erupted, or sometimes swept gracefully through people's lives. No one who stayed for any length of time was immune to the process of transformation. The long-time survivors generally endured a period of struggle, varying in length and intensity according to the individual, as they resisted the changes moving through them. Eventually the resistance wore thin, and they broke through to a new way of working with transformation. The general buzzword was surrender: learning to go with changes instead of trying to stop them. For each person, the method of befriending change varied, but the need to work with the process of transformation was universal.

Riding the Roller Coaster

I returned to the United States, sure that I would find the roller coaster ride smoother when I left the transformative vortex of the community. I should have known better. The spirit of transformation lives in people, not in a particular place or cause. The internal work goes on no matter where I am or who is around me.

Back in the U.S., I faced many major decisions, from finding a place to live to redefining my relationship with my partner to committing myself to a life direction. My partner David and I made plans to buy the one-room cabin where we had been living despite a lot of personal difficulties in our relationship. After months of internal struggle, we made an offer on the house and put down $1,000.

Soon afterward we left for the West Coast. During the journey I became extremely ill with a bladder infection. I lay in my friend Reidun's living room during an achingly beautiful week of Seattle sunshine and reluctantly listened to the messages emanating from my battered body:

"I DON'T WANT TO LIVE IN THAT PLACE. AND I DON'T WANT TO LIVE WITH DAVID OR ANYONE ELSE. WHAT THE HELL AM I DOING? GET ME OUT OF THIS MESS!"

I knew that our friends, from whom we were buying the property, desperately needed the money for a new business they were starting. We were supposed to begin making payments by the end of the week. My Goddess, how could I back out now? Even worse, could I handle the payments by myself? I realized that I was already thinking as if I lived alone in the cabin. That thought was the first warning bell that penetrated the panic in my body.

I spent a couple of days trying to decide what to do. Finally, after two days of inward-looking agony, I told David that I wanted to live alone. I wasn't sure about what form our relationship would take, but I knew I wanted to live by myself.

During the two months following the trip, I sat in front of the computer writing articles, on my bed meditating, or in a rocking chair on the porch reading tarot cards, desperately asking to be guided in my life. Everything around me was crumbling. All of my "New Age" ideas about how to live my life, to do what I love and not worry about getting paid, came to stare me in the face. They looked sweet and tasted bitter.

Searching for a house led me from a crazed hermit to houses full of students to a couple of witches living on the edge of Hadley, Massachusetts. Finally, one Sunday morning in Quaker Meeting, I prayed for a place. I envisioned it. I chose it. I took stock of my current reality and chose again. And I wasn't an inch closer to having a door key in my hand.

I stood up at the end of Quaker Meeting and announced that the house across the street was for rent. Was anyone interested in joining me there? A woman from Connecticut walked across the street with me and looked through the empty house. We both were smitten.

Within an hour I made the down payment and returned to the house to pick the luscious high-bush blueberries growing in the back field. Not until a couple of weeks after moving into the house did I realize that the house fulfilled a dream that I had had for nearly a year, of living in a place surrounded by a garden and fruit orchard.

The woman from Connecticut never moved in, but within two weeks another person did, an arborist with a passion for the Earth and a knowledge of pruning that would help resurrect the neglected fruit orchard on the property. He felt like a long-lost brother. Later, when I picked up the paper and glanced through the names of people still seeking renters amidst a housing glut in the area, I realized with what naive trust I had made my move.

My struggle to find a place taught me some important lessons. First and foremost I needed clarity about what I wanted; I had to state my desires clearly both to myself and to the Creator. Once I was clear about my needs and desires, I had to continue in my life with the absolute knowledge that my needs would be met. I was challenged to cultivate trust.

Learning How to Ask and Believe

I remembered the story of a friend who was invited to the building of a sweat lodge, or "stone people's lodge," with a Lakota elder. During the preparations, the elder watched my friend carefully tucking and folding the cover. Her whole attention was focused on the task. She looked up and met his eye. He nodded approvingly at her. "White lady all right."

When the lodge was completed around 1 a.m., everyone crawled inside for the ceremony. Afterwards the elder sought out my friend, and in halting English asked, "Lady, you know how to pray?"

"Well, I, uh, sure, I mean it's, uh . . ."

"That's the trouble with you white people," he said. "That's how you pray. You want something from the Creator, you gotta ask. Got to ask loud, strong. Got to make your prayers so the Creator can hear. That's how you pray, lady. That's how you pray."

In all of my worrying, I had forgotten that basic rule. If I want something, I have to ask, clearly and strongly. And then act and live with the knowledge that the prayers have been heard.

My ability to ask and then persevere with the firm belief that something will come has grown, though I still have periods of difficulty. I have learned to ask and then believe, to persevere with the calm assurance that the Universe (especially my own internal cosmos) is reordering itself to comply with my request.

The reordering process never really ends. Change is constant in my life. And, as my friend Reidun adds, growth is optional. Changes will steamroll relentlessly throughout my life. I have the option, though, to learn from the changes or to continue without integrating the lessons they present. If I don't learn, I continue to create the same situations, although the names and addresses may be different, until I finally create a new structure, make different choices, and walk a new path.

Changing the Shape of Reality

Like the repeating patterns in my life, my physical body also develops habits. A friend who works as an acupuncturist taught me that energy patterns in the body become entrenched. Energy pathways within the body, called "meridians" in the Chinese medical system, follow memorized grooves, creating health or disease according to how beneficial or detrimental the patterns are for the whole body. Needles inserted at key points in the body redirect the flow of energy. "I have to redirect the flow gradually," he explained. "Each session I redirect the flow of energy, but the body tends to regress to the old pattern. I have to create a new pathway slowly, over time, as the body moves out of the old trenches and establishes new patterns."

The pathways in my mind become trenches within my brain. Robbie Kendall, an Australian acupuncturist, also teaches Super-learning. He emphasizes that habits of mind physiologically manifest as deep grooves in the brain. The brain generally needs a 14- to 21-day period to move out of those trenches and establish new pathways. During the "retraining period," the mind needs regular practice intervals to form new grooves in the brain.

Daily repetition of a new habit helps strengthen the desired pattern. Each repetition causes energy to flow along the new pathway. Like a trail through the woods, the pathway becomes smoother and more clearly delineated with each repeated journey. Eventually the new trail (habit pattern) becomes more deeply entrenched than the old, and energy follows the path of least resistance—in this case, the deeper groove in the brain.

One way of befriending change is to set aside moments each day to focus upon some area of your life that you want to transform. Your planetary vision, for example, may include peace among all human beings. Within your life you may be working to embody that desired peace in your own personal relationships.

♦ ♦ ♦

You can facilitate the new pathway in your own life by setting aside time each day to visualize yourself acting in new ways.

Give yourself at least ten minutes of undisturbed time, preferably within the first hour of waking; research shows that the link between the subconscious and conscious minds is strongest during the first and last waking hours of the day. Take three deep breaths, filling the abdomen, then the stomach, and finally the chest with air. Release the breath in the same order—abdomen, stomach, chest. Allow the body to relax deeply. Feel the muscles in the shoulders, arms, back, neck, and face growing heavy, releasing any tension.

Begin to follow the breath, watching the movement of air in and out of the body. Become aware of your heartbeat and the places in your body where you can feel your pulse. Turn your attention inwards, focusing on the heart or the space between the brows (the "third eye"). Feel your attention move inside yourself.

In this quiet, inward place, focus on the quality or activity that you want to develop in your life. Acknowledge the feelings and thoughts. Allow them to pass through your mind. Observe your responses, like images passing on a screen, but don't hold onto them.

Return to focusing on the heart or brow. With your inner eye, see yourself acting in a way that expresses the qualities that you desire to strengthen in your life. See and feel yourself become those qualities. Become aware of how you can express the quality within yourself, with others, within your community. Be open to the ideas and images that present themselves—some may give you

surprising new ideas about how to express this quality in
your life.

If you are focusing on a project, experience yourself
completing the action that you envision. Hold a picture of
the final result that you desire.

When you are ready, bring your attention back to your
breath, to your body, to the place where you are sitting.
Take a deep breath and open your eyes. Record anything
that you want to remember in your journal.

◆   ◆   ◆

Remember that the mind is literal. If you focus on the process
of becoming, the mind will forever be in a state of becoming. You
will always be on your way to something, without ever actually
arriving. Focus upon the final outcome, and the mind will follow
the most direct path to the completion of that project.

Becoming Your Future Self

You also may choose to internally practice stepping into your
desired future self. I discovered the power of this sort of attunement
when I learned to visualize myself *moving inside* particular plants
or animals. At first I thought that the information that I gained
during these periods of merging into another creature and looking
out through its eyes was a product of my imagination. As I shared
the technique with others, though, I learned beyond a shadow of
a doubt that the method works. Time after time I saw people
choose unfamiliar plants or animals. After the attunement, they
would say apologetically, "Well, I really don't know anything about
the dragonfly (or whatever it was), but . . ." and then proceed to
describe perfectly the life cycle, environment, feeding habits, and
movements of that creature.

I apply the same technique to working with tarot cards, particularly the *Motherpeace* deck created by Vicki Noble and Karen
Vogel. After choosing a card or laying out a complicated spread, I
take a few moments to move inside each card with my inner eye.
I become the image in the card. Rather than reading about or
visually absorbing the card, I experience the teaching and I absorb
the wisdom with my inner senses.

Through this internal attunement, I glean the information that
pertains to my particular situation, rather than relying on a general
description. I also gain strength from particular cards by attuning

BEFRIENDING CHANGE   55

with them during my morning meditations. This past summer I worked extensively with the High Priestess and the Crone when I was trying to choose a life path. When I moved inside the High Priestess, my mind grew calm and my body relaxed. I felt ancient and wise and powerful. I could see clearly and calmly, without the fearful static that I was generating during the rest of my day. The Crone supported me in choosing as I stood alone at the crossroads and listened without distraction to the deepest wisdom inside. By becoming these figures, I was bringing their strengths and their wisdom to life inside myself, in a more tangible way than reading or thinking about them ever could.

Life Experience as Teacher

Native people know the power of merging with a plant or animal. Many of their dances not only celebrate animals and plants and the passing of the seasons, but also empower the people as they become the creature celebrated in the dance. No one explains to the children what the "symbol" of the deer means; they experience its power through the ceremony.

George Tinker, an Episcopalian minister and a member of the Osage nation, bridges the Christian and the native spiritual traditions in his community. He shares a story about leading a ceremony during an Episcopalian ministers' retreat. After carefully preparing the hilltop where the ceremony was to take place, he led the people to the site and silently "smudged" each person. When everyone was smudged, he proceeded with the ceremony.

Afterwards, as he was walking down the hill, a fellow minister began to comment on how much the ceremony had moved her. "It was beautiful," she said. "And the sage . . . can you tell me what it means?"

George was silent for a few steps. Then he began to tell her a bit about sage, the legends associated with it, and what it meant to him in ceremony.

"And that," he told her, "is more than I have ever told my people about sage. It's more than I've ever shared with my son. In fact, it's more than anyone has ever told me about sage."

Against the backdrop of her remarks, George identified part of the native culture that was so ingrained in him. Native people learn something in context, by experiencing it in its rightful place, at the proper time. George never needed to explain sage to his son. He already knew the importance of the sage and its "meaning" from his own participation in the ceremonies.

You can practice the art of "becoming" with any object or image that draws your attention. Pay attention to your fascinations. They may be teachers waiting to instruct you. The greatest teachers, however, rarely teach with words. They teach through the essence of their being. Attunement, actually becoming something, is a powerful tool to help you listen to their wordless language.

♦ ♦ ♦

Another helpful exercise to aid in establishing new habits is the "daily review."

> At the end of each day, preferably in the hour before sleep—although any time after 5 p.m. will suffice—set aside quiet time to review your day. In your mind, move backwards in time, recalling what you were doing in half-hour intervals. Observe yourself dispassionately, as if you were viewing a movie. Don't stop to analyze or "fix" anything that happened. Simply watch the flow of events. Once you have reviewed the entire day, return to any situation that you would like to have handled differently. Without criticizing yourself, decide how you could act differently the next time. With that change in mind, replay the scene. See yourself speaking, responding, and being your ideal self. Repeat the scene until you feel the desired pattern established in your mind. Instead of regretting an action, you spend your energy changing the scene before it becomes a fixed pathway in the brain.

♦ ♦ ♦

Pivotal Choices

You also can practice in the moment as well as before and after an incident. If you find yourself in a difficult situation, stop and tell yourself the truth about what is going on. Give yourself the facts without embellishment. Don't make excuses for yourself or others. Ask yourself if you want the situation to continue in the future. If not, ask yourself what you really want and then choose your desired situation.

I first learned this method as part of Robert Fritz's "Technologies for Creating" course. Although the exercise sounds deceptively simple, I soon realized that it has a lot of power. I was living in

Scotland at the time, and my partner Alan and I often spent our weekends walking and exploring in remnants of the Caledonian forest. One Sunday in late August we visited a local river where the salmon were jumping, struggling to reach their spawning grounds far upstream.

We climbed down the steep path that led to a waterfall. We sat for several minutes on the water-smoothed granite slabs along the edge of the river, watching the salmon as they leapt and then swam furiously up through the cascading water. Alan wanted to take some photographs farther downstream. We found a path that ran along the edge of the river but soon ran into a chain link fence with a "NO TRESPASSING—Private Property" sign posted on it. Alan quickly slid past the fence, and I followed. While he charged ahead, camera bag swinging at his side and tripod firmly gripped in his hand, I lingered to watch the salmon in the pool at the bottom of the waterfall.

When I looked up, I met the eyes of a woman perched on a rock in midstream. She was dressed in skintight khaki waterproofs, clutching a fly rod. Next to her stood an aging gentleman, elegant in stance as well as apparel. His woolen knee socks, barely showing above the rim of his Wellington boots, were folded neatly over the edge of his plaid knickers. He was a portrait fit for a British edition of *Field and Stream*. The woman glared at me.

"Yeeew," she called, thrusting her pole in my direction. "Go back. The path is dangerous. You might get hurt."

I stared back. If she was so worried about safety, what was she doing in the middle of the river perched on a slippery moss-covered rock? "I'm fine," I called back. "I'm a good hiker."

"But it's dangerous," she shouted. Her face grew red under her black velvet hunting hat. "You must go back."

I saw Alan disappearing around the edge of the cliff just a few meters beyond the woman. She seemed oblivious to his presence. We locked eyes in a silent battle, and I finally turned and reluctantly walked back along the cliff edge.

I sat on the rocks near the river, waiting for Alan to return. I was furious about being blocked from walking along the river by some privileged Scottish laird's daughter. I decided to try the choice-point exercise outlined above.

What's going on? I asked myself. I'm angry that the woman has the power to keep me from walking on this part of the Earth. And

I'm even angrier that she pretended to be worried about my safety when in fact she simply wants me off her property. As I looked inside my fuming mind, I discovered that I was angry that she had ignored Alan. Perhaps his expensive camera gear made him look more well-to-do, and therefore more acceptable. The truth of the situation for me at that moment was that I had come face-to-face with the niggardliness of wealth, and I found the encounter distasteful.

What did I want? To live in a world with a fair distribution of wealth, in a society that shared land rather than owning it, especially wilderness areas. I wanted to live in a world that judged human beings on the basis of their inner qualities, not their outer wealth.

Sitting on the rocks next to the stream, I chose to live in such a world. Within a few minutes, a great peace filled me. I sat enjoying the play of water on rock and the power of the salmon struggling upstream. Normally I would fume for hours about such an incident, but when Alan returned half an hour later, I felt calm and at peace with the world.

Enacting Choices

The power of change rests in the present moment. Although I may meditate and visualize and affirm and forgive and do all sorts of other important inner work, a change is not complete until I practice it in my daily life. Eventually I must enact my envisioned world.

Peace Pilgrim describes her own process of personal transformation as

> . . . a very interesting project. This was to live all the good
> things I believed in. I did not confuse myself by trying to take
> them all at once, but rather if I was doing something that I
> knew I shouldn't be doing I stopped doing it and I always make
> a quick relinquishment. That's the easy way. Tapering off is long
> and hard . . . It took the living quite a while to catch up with the
> believing, but of course it can, and now if I believe something, I
> live it. Otherwise it would be perfectly meaningless.[1]

Whether the changes come slowly or in quick, decisive bursts, our personal transformations form the foundation of societal change. We can most fruitfully invest our energy in re-educating ourselves and learning to live in a good way on the Earth.

Although causes such as saving whales or rainforests inform people about environmental disasters, they do not fundamentally change the underlying reasons for what is wrong. I've heard "activists" in the local Quaker Meeting, for example, talking at length about the terrible conditions that Latin American people endure. I've seen their slide shows and heard their impassioned condemnation of America's imperialistic actions in those countries. "Look at the cars," commented one woman as she was showing her slides of Nicaragua. "They have old, beat-up cars, and some of them don't even run."

My Goddess, I wanted to tell her, do you know how many people in India are too poor to even think about buying a bicycle, much less a car? Do you know how Aboriginal people live in the middle of the Western Desert of Australia, sweltering under sheets of corrugated iron in the 160-degree summer heat, or how Native Americans in your own country suffer on reservations, or how homeless people in Boston agonize during the depths of winter? Where have you been?

This is not to belittle the suffering of Central and South America, but the world is so much bigger, so much more complex than the politics of North and South, East and West.

Our job is to learn and then enact a fundamentally different way of living upon the Earth, one that is just for all life forms, not only human beings. To enter such a world, we must transform the basic tenets of human life on Earth. The journey may be long and arduous, but the path guarantees one companion who will steadfastly remain beside us through every step of the way—Change. We can choose to view Change as tormentor or ally. The path most certainly will be smoother if we choose to befriend, rather than battle with, Change.

> Change came a'knocking at my door
> Unbidden, but no less welcome
> than the cold that seeped into the crack
> of a mind that was left ajar.
>
> Change came unbidden, stalking
> the wayward places, finding the
> chinks in my well-laid world,
> penetrating my thickest defenses.

Change came unbidden, creeping
into the folds of my gown,
the shell of my ribs, the flesh of my heart,
the valley of my soul.

Change, you are wild and without apparent plan
save the blueprint of
the soulful need to grow.
Lie down, let us make the best
of this timely imposition.
I cannot tame, but I can befriend you.

Part Two
What You Consume

There is enough for everyone: enough to satisfy everyone's needs, but not necessarily their excessive wants. As true materialists, we can satisfy our needs with a minimum of goods and find a surplus of meaning in the process.

Five

Our Daily Bread

IN MY EARLY TEENS I read a book that changed my life: *Diet for a Small Planet* by Francis Moore Lappé. This book awakened my awareness of the social and political impact of food. Although I had done a lot of research on food and nutrition, an outgrowth of being diagnosed with food allergies, I had never been exposed to the political impact of food. In fact, I had never before stopped to think about where my food came from, or how it was grown. Green beans were good for you, and so were the bananas on special at the local grocery store. Never mind that the beans were trucked from southern California through the January blizzards of the Midwest, or that the bananas were sprayed lavishly with chemicals both during and after their growing season to stop insect pests and to prolong their ripening time during shipment. And I never considered where those Chiquita bananas were grown or who owned the land.

Some facts to ponder from *Realities for the 90's,* excerpted from *Diet for a New America* by John Robbins, which are similar to those found in Frances Moore Lappé's book:

- Amount of corn grown in the United States consumed by human beings: 20%
- Amount of corn grown in the United States consumed by livestock: 80%
- How frequently a child on Earth dies as a result of malnutrition: Every 2.3 seconds
- Number of children who die as a result of malnutrition every day: 38,000

- Amount of nutrient wasted by cycling grain through livestock: Protein 90%, Carbohydrate 99%, Fiber 100%
- Number of people who will die as a result of malnutrition this year: 20,000,000
- Number of people who can be adequately fed with the grain and soy needed to produce the meat, poultry, and dairy products eaten by the average American each year: 7
- Amount of U.S. cropland producing livestock feed: 64%
- Number of people who could be adequately nourished using the land, water, and energy that would be freed by growing livestock feed if Americans reduced their intake of meat by 10%: 100,000,000
- Amount of U.S. topsoil lost from cropland, pasture, rangeland and forest land directly associated with livestock raising: 85%
- Amount of meat imported in 1987 by U.S. from Central and South America: 300,000,000 pounds
- Current rate of species extinction due to destruction of tropical rainforests and related habitats: 1,000/year[1]

The Politics of Food

Where and how food is grown has become a hot political issue in some countries. The politics of food involves a form of oppression that is almost invisible to most people living in First World countries: economic imperialism.

Farmland in many Third World nations, cleared centuries ago to raise corn, beans, squash, and other primary foodstuffs, today supports crops of sugar cane, coffee, and cocoa. These cash crops, sold to rich nations in the North, bring in just enough money to buy food at inflated prices from those northern countries and pay for the chemicals used on the crops.

Representatives from North American and European petroleum companies ply Third World farmers with chemicals, convincing them that the insecticides, pesticides, and fertilizers will stimulate their crops. They do—for a short time. Although the application of fertilizers, herbicides, and insecticides initially causes substantial gains in agricultural yields, the ratio of energy input (gasoline, fertilizer, pesticides, and herbicides) to crop output increases dramatically. After a few years the chemicals "burn" the soil, killing the micro-organisms that help the plant rootlets to absorb nutrients. Farmers traditionally replenished this living layer of soil called humus with applications of manure or compost. Without humus the soil cannot absorb the chemicals applied to the fields. Each year the farmer sprays more chemicals, with decreasing effect. South American farmers' debt increases and they never quite save enough money to convert back to primary food production. This bondage to growing cash crops is a subtle form of economic imperialism, harder to lay a finger on than the practice of slavery, but just as crippling.

This story involves more than Peruvian or Brazilian peasants. Multinational businesses have entered the cash crop market. They buy huge tracts of land to grow, among other things, groves of palm trees to produce a lucrative oil crop. Ever wonder where *Palm-Olive* soap comes from? Or the palm oil that lubricates processed foods?

Consider bananas. Where do they come from? United Brands, a multinational conglomerate, controls two-thirds of all of the banana species known on the planet. They bought the "seed rights," a commodity invented by legislation passed in Britain in 1964 (the Plant Variety and Seeds Act) and later by the European Community in 1974. South American governments sold huge tracts of land to this and other multinationals, displacing many subsistence farmers.

Individually and collectively we can help to break this crippling relationship by growing our own food and meeting as many of our own nutritional needs as possible in the local neighborhood. We also can break our dependence on cash crops such as coffee, bananas, sugar, and the cheap beef raised in Central and South America.

Paying For What You Eat

Cattle are grazed on clearings bulldozed out of the rainforests. This denuded soil supports the cattle for about two, at maximum five, years before the soil solidifies into laterite, a hard brick-like soil, or washes away. The beef raised on these "slash and burn" fields is sold chiefly to American fastfood chains such as McDonald's and Wendy's. (After an extensive boycott in the summer of 1987, Burger King announced that it would no longer buy Costa Rican beef.)

In my own life I have chosen to forgo meat, bananas, and coffee. I try to avoid sugar and cocoa, not only to protest the way that these crops are grown, but also for health reasons. I made these choices for two reasons.

One is that in our present economy, money—or lack of it—speaks. If enough people choose not to buy certain products, the company folds or changes its policies. The boycott of Nestlé's products is an example of successful economic pressuring. Nestlé promoted the sale of its baby formula in Third World countries by hiring nurses who instructed mothers to feed their babies the soy-based mixture instead of their own breast milk. The mothers' milk dried up, and soon the money to pay for the formula evaporated, too. Mothers fed babies watered-down formula, prepared in less than sanitary conditions, in an effort to save money. A plague of malnourished infants resulted.

Warnings from the U.N. left the company unruffled (they simply sent in women dressed like nurses), but loss of revenue as a result of boycotting pinched hard. Nestlé finally changed its policy and amended its sales tactics in the Third World.

The second reason for making these choices is to maintain my sanity. I feel responsible for any communication that I receive about the state of the world, and in these times most of the information is disturbing, even shocking. When I'm faced with all of the problems, depression could easily overwhelm me. To counter the despair, I try to take action, no matter how small, within my daily life. I do so with the hope that enough other people will make the same small, daily choices that add up to an avalanche of change. I also cultivate an awareness of people and groups that are succeeding, in small and large ways, in righting the imbalances.

"In Buddhism," explains Thich Nhat Hanh,

> the most important precept of all is to live in awareness, to know what is going on. To know what is going on, not only here, but there. For instance, when you eat a piece of bread, you may choose to be aware that our farmers, in growing that wheat, use chemical poisons a little too much. Eating the bread, we are somehow co-responsible for the destruction of our ecology. When we eat a piece of meat or drink alcohol, we can produce awareness that 40,000 children die each day in the Third World from hunger and that in order to produce a piece of meat or a bottle of liquor, we have to use a lot of grain. Eating a bowl of cereal may be more reconciling with the suffering of the world than eating a piece of meat. An authority on economics who lives in France told me that if only the people in Western countries would reduce the eating of meat

and the drinking of alcohol by 50%, that would be enough to change the situation of the world. Only 50% less.

Every day we do things, we are things, that have to do with peace. If we are aware of our lifestyle, our way of consuming, of looking at things, we will know how to make peace right in the moment we are alive, the present moment.[2]

Living with Awareness

Living with awareness also means valuing the health of the land—taking only what I need and finding ways to replenish the place where I have taken. Equitable giving and taking are the basis of sustainable agriculture. The process of returning matter to the soil and developing new planting methods to ensure the health of the soil must begin now.

The failure of past civilizations to develop sustainable agriculture is marked on the planet in the form of deserts resulting from past abuse of the land; deforestation and destruction of other forms of plant cover bring about the climatic changes that lead to desertification. The United States has lost 75 percent of its original topsoil. Already we are beginning to see shifts in weather patterns as a result of huge areas of rainforest being cut and burned in South America, India, Southeast Asia, and Australia. Not only the amount and type of food we eat but also how we grow that food figure importantly in the health of the planet as a whole.

It's true that organic foods cost more than "commercial" brands. The organically grown sweet potatoes at the local market cost 98¢ while the "conventionally grown" variety costs 68¢. My hand wavers between the two bins. Being a cost-conscious consumer on a limited budget, I can hardly justify the extra 30¢ a pound. But when I stop to think about the costs not accounted for on the conventional farm, my hand swings back toward the organic bin.

When chemically based farms tabulate costs, they studiously ignore most of the environmental costs involved in the growing cycle, including soil degradation and soil erosion, the water pollution costs of fertilizer runoff, the costs of ground-water depletion, the national-security costs of over-reliance on imported fossil fuels, the health and despeciation costs of herbicide and pesticide use, the agricultural-security costs of reduced plant-species diversity, and the cultural costs of factory farming.[3] We all pay for the hidden costs involved in "conventional" farming. ("Conventional" is a strange term when we consider that after thousands of years of largely chemical-free farming, the extensive use of chemicals in agriculture only became "conventional" after World War II.)

Herbicide and Pesticide Use

Since the EPA's creation in 1970, only 26 pesticides have been banned, although the agency reports that approximately 70 of the pesticides now in use are carcinogenic in animals. In the EPA's defense, the Federal Government has budgeted just under $14 million to review pesticide use, an amount that precludes completing an adequate review until well into the next century.

Simply banning chemicals does not banish them from the environment, however. Toxic residues of a chemical may remain in the environment for decades, entering the food chain and accumulating in the tissues of animals, including humans. Although the federal government banned DDT in 1972, it is still one of the most common residues found in food grown in the United States. Residues of DDT are found in animals—including humans—in increasing amounts; DDT is stored in body fat, and therefore, unlike water-soluble residues, accumulates over a lifetime. Rachel Carson was the first national figure to spotlight the effects of DDT and other chemicals on the reproductive cycle of many creatures, especially birds.

Pesticides become increasingly concentrated in the food chain. A 1969 study of DDT, DDE and TDE residues in foods demonstrated that pesticides in fruits and vegetables ranged from .003 to .036 parts per million (ppm). Meat, fish and poultry, however, were contaminated with .281 ppm.[4] More recent figures show that 99 percent of all U.S. mothers have dangerous levels of DDT in their breast milk; meat-eating mothers have 35 times more pesticide contamination in their milk than vegetarian mothers.

Men also suffer from the effects of pesticide contamination. The average sperm count among American males has decreased by 30 percent over the past thirty years. In 1950, half a percent of male college students were sterile, but by 1978, the figure increaseed to 25 percent. Chlorinated hydrocarbon pesticides such as DDT, dioxin, and PCB's are chiefly responsible for the increase in sterility and the reduction in sperm counts.[5]

Reducing or eliminating meat from the diet is one way to decrease pesticide consumption. Other foodstuffs, however, also contain large amounts of pesticide residues. The National Academy of Sciences identifies the following foods as accounting for 95 percent of the health problems associated with pesticides: tomatoes (the most heavily contaminated), potatoes, oranges, lettuce, apples, peaches, pork, wheat, soybeans and all other beans, carrots, chicken, corn and grapes. Simply washing fruits and vegetables does not prevent ingesting pesticides. Some vegetables and fruits are coated with wax laced with fungicide to prevent spoilage and keep them looking fresh. The wax and fungicide cannot be washed off. Other poisons are systemic, meaning that they are absorbed through the plants' roots and leaves; washing the outer parts of the fruits and vegetables will not remove these internal poisons.

While we have some idea of what pesticides we are likely to consume (or avoid) in American foods, we have little or no guarantee about produce from other countries, especially from the Third World. Beware, too of produce from Hawaii. The U.S. makes many exceptions for pesticide use in Hawaii, and its fruits and vegetables may be just as contaminated as crops from Central and South America. Chemical manufacturers readily sell pesticides banned in the United States to other countries. For example, Uniroyal stopped selling Alar in the U.S. in June 1989. The company continues, however, to sell it abroad.

Although DDT is also banned in the United States, I can tell you from firsthand experience that copious amounts of DDT are sold and used in India. I have watched village women among the cashew bushes applying DDT with their bare hands, flinging the gray dust from a burlap bag with one hand while holding a child on their hip with the other. Neither mothers nor children wore protective clothing of any kind. Accumulation of DDT in one of the nearby village water supplies killed all of the fish. The villagers eyed the fish floating belly-up in the pond but made no correlation between DDT use and the fish's demise.

Some of the most virulent insect pests do not respond to DDT. Either the insect sidesteps the DDT in its feeding and reproductive cycle (i.e., DDT is applied early in the season, before the fruits actually set, and some insects prey solely on the fruit surrounding the cashew nut) or the insect develops a tolerance to the chemical. Either way, the villagers spend a great deal of money to buy DDT and invest much time and intensive hand labor to apply it. Most importantly, they sacrifice both the land's and their own health.

An example of stimulating insect tolerance through pesticide use is the spider mite:

> Only 25 years ago, the spider mite was a minor pest. Repeated use of pesticides supposedly aimed at other pests has decimated the natural enemies and competitors of the mite. Today, the mite is the pest most seriously threatening agriculture worldwide ... The irony ... is that the more effective an insecticide is in killing susceptible individuals of a pest population, the faster resistant individuals evolve.[6]

Uprooting From the Land

Many people in our culture, especially children raised in cities and suburbs, have lost the ability to listen to the Earth's wisdom. Some have even lost the ability to tell the difference between natural and artificial creations. "I once talked with my four-year-old neighbor," writes Ellen Buchman Ewald, author of *Recipes for a Small Planet,* "about a flower that my husband Doug had picked on a fall afternoon. A sunburst of yellow, it was a giant puff with a perfect green stem and a mild scent like the memory of a meadow. 'That isn't real,' she said in her four-year-old voice, 'and four-year-olds know.' It was extremely difficult to explain how I knew that the flower was one that had grown in the earth. For each characteristic of the flower might have been manufactured in a factory; every aspect, except perhaps its death, could be duplicated by a machine."[7]

I learned while working at the Aullwood Audubon Center and Farm in Dayton, Ohio that even school-aged children have little idea about the difference between natural and processed items. Aullwood created a program for the local schools to educate children about where their food comes from. Many children, before the program, were convinced that milk came from cardboard cartons in the supermarket. They had never associated *milk* with a cow. Nor had they ever connected items in the meat department with animals. Fruits and vegetables in the produce department were divorced from the seeds that they emerged from, or the Earth that nourished them. The program included a dramatization of milking a cow (complete with one of the kids dressed up as a cow with prominent pink teats) and planting a seed in soil.

"And what does a seed need to grow?" asked Abby Wilgus, one of the program's originators.

"Dirt?" said one of the kids tentatively.

"Right, soil. What else?"

Eventually the kids identified the ingredients—soil, water, air, sunlight, nutrients in the soil. This was a long way from carrots in a plastic bag sitting on ice in the produce section.

I remember, too, from my own childhood a week-long expedition with my sixth grade class to a local environmental education center. In between the sleepless nights filled with whispered giggles and poking games, we explored the nearby creek filled with fossils and the surrounding regrowth forest.

One afternoon the environmental education instructor led us on a hike to a clearing among the trees. Standing amidst the tall, dried grasses of late winter, he asked us what we thought would grow next.

Without hesitation, one of the kids yelled out, "HOUSES!"

We all burst into laughter. Although the teacher meant to give us a lesson in the succession of plant species from field to forest, our suburban upbringing had taught us another lesson: cleared land meant buildings soon to follow, not grasses followed by shrubs and then trees. We laughed, but there was a painful truth buried in the student's jest.

Support Local, Organic Foods

Despite the creeping cancer of suburban sprawl, we have alternatives to our present agricultural crisis. As consumers, we can re-educate local supermarkets about the kinds of foods we want to buy.

Once you have encouraged the local market to carry organic foods, however, make sure that you buy their organic produce. Nothing is more disheartening for a supermarket than to stock some long-demanded product and then watch it rot on the shelves. Reward supermarkets for their innovative efforts by giving them your business. Encourage friends to buy local, organic produce, too.

Support local farmers who are launching innovative marketing programs. Farmers produce plenty of food; their problem is getting the food to the right market that will pay them equitably for their efforts. Since the 1950s, most of the increase in food prices has gone to the middleperson, not the farmer. You can bypass this inequality by purchasing directly from the farmer.

One of farmers' greatest problems is stretching their income throughout the year. Most of the money comes in during the summer months, but bills continue through the winter as well. In Great Barrington, Massachusetts, local farmers banded together to address the cash flow dilemma. They formed a non-profit group called SHARE: Self-Help Association for a Regional Economy. They created "Berkshire Farm Preserve Notes," green-colored bills with hand-drawn plants and vegetables with the motto, "In Farms We Trust." The notes were sold for $9.00 and could be redeemed for $10.00 of produce at harvest time.

"At this time of year," says Martha Tawczynski of Taft Farms, "many farmers have to borrow money. We thought it would be great to give our customers the interest, instead of the bank, to encourage them to invest in us."[8]

Another innovative approach mushrooming in New England is "Subscription Farms." Local growers set a monthly rate for a family or individual, dependent on the ages and number of people in each household. In return for paying the agreed upon rate, people may visit and take whatever they need from the subscription farm's produce.

These systems benefit both the farmers and consumers. They give the farmers a market, and they provide consumers with low-cost, locally grown vegetables. In the long run, they benefit the Earth as well. Buying locally eliminates the need for cross-country trucking, saving fossil fuels and reducing air pollution. It also decreases or eliminates the need for chemicals sprayed on produce to keep them fresh during transport.

You Are Where and When You Eat

In a broader sense, eating local food also helps people acclimate to the particular region where they are living. When I eat local food, I calibrate myself to my surroundings. I am reminded of the story of a medicine man who taught his students to eat something when they went into the woods or fields in search of knowledge. Ingesting something from the area heightens one's sensitivity and attunement with the land.

Eating local produce also heightens my awareness of the seasonal cycles of my region. In New England, strawberries do not grow in January, but they flourish in June and July. Asparagus shoots push through the spring-thawed ground long before zucchini or acorn squash even blossom. Not only are the June-ripened strawberries infinitely more tasty than the sprayed and trucked California fruits of January, they also support the needs of my body in that particular season.

Consider for a moment the precision with which the growing season and your body interact. After a long winter with few greens, livers tend to grow sluggish. Through the winter months, the liver handles an increased load of heavy, oily/fatty foods that the body needs to supply warmth and nutrients during the winter. Many of the first plants to appear in the spring, such as dandelion greens and asparagus, have powerful constituents that help detoxify the liver. As the season progresses to midsummer, fruits and vegetables with high water content come to maturity. During the hot summer months, the body requires more water and less heavy carbohydrates and proteins. Although human bodies are not green photosynthesizers like plants, some people contend that humans absorb energy from the sun during the summer months, and throughout the year in the tropics. Hence, you tend to decrease calorie intake and eat "lighter" (get the symbolism?) foods in the summer.

As the summer progresses into autumn, more of the complex carbohydrate vegetables, such as winter squash, grains, and beans, come to fruition. When the days shorten and the temperature begins to drop, the body requires more fats and carbohydrates to make up for dwindling solar warmth and energy. These late season vegetables generally store well and can be eaten through the winter months. Modern canning, freezing, and drying preservation techniques extend the season for the high water content vegetables and fruits as well.

You can directly participate in this seasonal dance by planting your own garden. Even if you live in the center of New York City, you can supply a large percentage of summer salad vegetables by planting window boxes and large flower pots with radishes (one of the quickest growing vegetables), miniature lettuces, and parsley. I know a woman who lives on West 19th Street in Manhattan; she has transformed the top of her apartment building into a garden of trees and flower beds. On a summer evening I wandered through her garden, sniffing the many delicate flower scents and looking up from time to time to enjoy the view of the Empire State Building beyond. Incongruous, but beautiful, and somehow fitting in Manhattan's diverse mix of cultures and attitudes. An artist and city-dweller for most of her life, she had never planted a garden before, but her innate sense of beauty guided the creation. "And I never knew before," she told me with quiet wonder in her eyes, "that crocuses came before daffodils, and tulips before roses. I'm learning about the natural cycle of the year by watching what happens in my garden."

Grow Your Own

If you live in an apartment or have a landlord/lady who loathes gardens, consider a community garden plot shared by several families or a church or community group. Many towns now run community plots through the local town council. Some local communities even provide compost and/or leaf mold. If you fancy creating your own compost heap, consider approaching local farmers for manure—unless, of course, they use the manure on their own fields. Horse stables are another good manure source. Goats, if you are lucky enough to live near a goat farm, produce the most balanced manure for fertilizing. Remember to compost manures before applying them to your garden—fresh manure can burn young plants. If you live near the ocean, you can collect and compost seaweed as a fertilizer for the garden. A simple fertilizing method is to spread up to a foot of seaweed on the garden bed in late autumn and allow it to decompose during the winter. In the springtime, simply turn over the soil and begin planting.

For those months when your garden is not producing, look for roadside stands and farmers' markets. Ask for locally grown, organic produce. Another option for those without earth to plant a garden is "You-Pick" farms. Even those fortunate enough to have flourishing gardens can take advantage of these farms for fruits and vegetables that they don't grow.

Encourage schools and hospitals to buy local, organic food. Offer schools and hospitals your own surplus of garden produce at the peak of the growing season. While tending one of the gardens at the Findhorn Foundation, I would take crates of our surplus lettuce to the nearby hospital, where they were graciously received.

Ask your favorite restaurants to use organic produce. Pester them to serve whole grains as well. After years of persistent requests, almost all of the Chinese restaurants in Amherst, Massachusetts serve brown rice. The family which runs one of the most popular Chinese restaurants also owns a farm that supplies fresh organic produce for the restaurant.

Ask the county and state Agricultural Extension Office for organic gardening and farming information. Enquire about sources for organic meat and produce. The more requests the Extension Office receives for organic produce sources and sustainable growing practices, the more likely it is to pass the information to farmers in your area.

You may even choose to create a Seed Savers Exchange. Kent and Diane Whealy run the only national Seed Savers Exchange (P.O. Box 70, Decorah, IA 52101), and regional exchanges are forming all the time.

Wild Foods—Free for the Picking

Consider as well the abundance of wild food available simply for the harvesting. Become familiar with indigenous herbs and fruits; local ailments are often best treated with local remedies. Stinging nettles, for example, almost always grow within a few feet of the best known antidote for nettle stings—jewelweed. Seek out the herbalists and the wise elders who know the plants in your area. They may teach you how to identify plantain (practically a first aid kit in itself), where to find wild asparagus in the spring, and when the blackberries will ripen. Check the library for good field guides and remember that your reading will be vastly supplemented by a day or even an afternoon spent with an experienced guide.

Once you have considered the means of growing and/or obtaining organic, local produce, consider as well the quality that you bring to the food. Once you have harvested your food, prepare it with care. Kirlian photography, which records the subtle energy field around objects, demonstrates that each food flourishes with a specific amount of steaming, baking, or frying. Many vegetables increase their energy field during cooking, but after a certain length of time the vital energy of the food decreases and finally disappears. Err, whenever possible, toward undercooking, and include raw foods in the diet as well.

The Source of True Nourishment

When you sit down to eat the food, take a couple of deep breaths. Center yourself. All of the healthy food in the world will never benefit a distressed, tense body. Food eaten during periods of emotional tension tends to remain undigested in the stomach, causing gas, bloating, heartburn, and general discomfort.

Consider, too, that a moment's pause before eating focuses your attention on the subtle energy of the food, and the quality of nourishment. A well-prepared meal feeds not only the physical body, but also the many finer levels of your awareness (subtle bodies). Many religious traditions include the observance of prayer before eating. Grace, as it is known in the Western Christian tradition, precedes the act of nourishment. I generally envision each of the plants (and the occasional animal product) included in the meal. I see the place where it was grown and give thanks for the interaction of all of the elements—the wind, sun, rain, and soil— that supported the growth of the food. I thank the farmer who planted, cultivated, and harvested the food and every other pair of hands that touched the food before it arrived in my kitchen. I give thanks for the "Spirit Helpers and Spirit Keepers," the Elementals and Devas, who direct the growth of the plants and animals. I thank the Creator for the miracle of the food before me. Anyone who has watched a beet or carrot or cabbage grow from a seed in the raw spring earth to full maturity knows the full glory of that miracle.

At the Bear Tribe, we preceded meals with the offering of a "spirit plate" to the Creator. The cook would put a small portion of everything prepared for the meal on a plate and take it to a special place on the mountain. The food generally disappeared quickly—absorbed by the Creator in His/Her many guises, from Raven to Coyote to Mouse. We were practicing The Giveaway with the understanding that each one must give away in order to keep the circle of life connected. Raven, Coyote, and Mouse, I give away some of my food in order that your life might go on. Some day you may return my gift with the gift of your own life, in order that my life might continue.

An attitude of relaxed reverence helps prepare you for a meal. The act of eating is equally important. While a student at Oberlin, I took a day-long workshop on food with visiting teachers from the Kripalu Center for Holistic Health. At one point during the day, the facilitator passed a tray of apple slices around the room.

◆   ◆   ◆

The following exercise is an adaptation of her guided journey to the conscious eating of an apple slice.

First, look at the apple slice. Note its color and shape.

Smell the apple. Feel its texture—touch it with your

fingers, slide it across the soft part of your cheek. Take a small bite. Notice how and where you experience taste. Which part of the tongue is stimulated? What happens to your sense of taste when your throat closes? When you hold your nose? How quickly do you want to swallow? Babies usually chew for a long time before swallowing, until the solid food becomes liquid. How many chews do you usually take before swallowing? Two? Three? Maybe six? Are you comfortable continuing longer than your habitual number? Chew slowly until the apple becomes liquid in your mouth. Now swallow. Note the passage of the food down the throat. Follow the apple all the way to your stomach.

Take another bite. Repeat the process of observing yourself tasting, chewing, and swallowing.

◆   ◆   ◆

The first time I tried this exercise, I was amazed at how much difficulty I had willing myself to continue chewing after my habitual two or three chews. I felt like a cow ruminating a bale of hay. I noticed, too, that my ability to taste completely disappeared when I closed the back of my throat, held my breath, or closed my nose.

Although I had not eaten much that day and my stomach was growling, I found that thin slice of apple remarkably satisfying. What would happen, I wondered, if I ate every bite with the same concentrated attention? "Try eating a piece of double fudge chocolate cake this way," said the facilitator, smiling. "I can guarantee that you won't finish a whole piece."

The workshop recalled an important lesson that I had learned—and since forgotten, I'm sorry to say. For six months I followed a Macrobiotic diet and religiously chewed my food fifty times per mouthful. Eating a bowl of rice was a major accomplishment. I thought twice about eating a second bowlful when my jaws were tired and my stomach pleasantly full. Perhaps part of the "magic" of being satisfied with a bowl of rice was simply the amount of time required to chew it thoroughly. The stomach takes twenty minutes to signal "full" to the brain, regardless of the amount of food intake. I could eat two steaks, a salad, a baked potato and a dessert or one bowl of rice during that twenty-minute period. Either way, the stomach would wait twenty minutes to send the signal "full." Eat slowly, with awareness, and you will certainly eat less food and absorb more nutrients from the food you eat.

Elson M. Haas, in his book *Staying Healthy With the Seasons*, offers the following advice on eating, condensed into seven directives:

Seven to Heaven
1. Eat only when you are hungry.
2. Take a moment before eating to relax and breathe deeply—prepare for your nourishment.
3. Eat slowly and chew well.
4. Eat only as much as you need.
5. After eating, relax a while, then do some light movement, like walking, to help digest, assimilate, and circulate nutrients.
6. Do not eat for two hours before bedtime.
7. Eat a balanced diet.[9]

◆　◆　◆

Throughout this chapter, we have been exploring food as the source of Our Daily Bread. *The following meditation explores all of the sources of nourishment in your life. From where do you derive nourishment, and with whom do you share your bounty?*

Sit in a comfortable position in a place where you will not be disturbed for at least fifteen minutes. Take three deep breaths, expanding your abdomen as you take in air, and flattening the tummy as you completely exhale. Allow the body to grow heavy and relaxed. Follow your breath as it moves in and out of the lungs. Allow any thoughts that come into your mind to pass away, like clouds blown across the sky on a windy spring day. Let them go.

Turn your attention to the food that you have eaten in the last two days. Consider everything you put into your body, from the moment you awoke to the time you went to sleep at night. Remember how you cooked the food, how you served it, and with whom you ate it. If you ate anything away from home, recall what and where you ate. Remember the color of the walls, the decorations, the chairs, the music (if any). How did you feel in that space? Remember the taste of the food and the way it was served. Who was with you? Did you talk? Were you silent? Did you chew the food or even notice it was in your mouth? Note your body posture—were you tense or relaxed, tired or stressed? Observe your emotional response to the food, atmosphere and people around you.

For the foods you cooked and ate at home, consider the source of the food. Was it purchased from a store, harvested from a garden, or given to you by a friend? Recall where the food came from—the place where it was grown and how it was harvested, transported, and displayed. If you bought the food in a grocery store or market stand, remember how you felt shopping. What do you remember of your experience in the store? Which foods did you choose, and why? Examine your decision-making methods. What drew you to buy a particular brand or type of food? Did you buy what you came for, or something else? Remember the lighting, the layout of the aisles, the other people around you, the smells and sights and sounds. How did you feel before going into the store? How did you feel after? If the food came from more than one store, examine your experiences and note how they differ.

For the food that came from your garden, remember the cycle of planting, watering, weeding, and harvesting. Remember the feel of the soil in your hands, the warmth of the sun, or the coolness of the rain on your back. Observe the plant throughout its growing process. See yourself harvesting the food.

If you raise your own meat or other animal products, recall the lifecycle of the animal. Observe your role in providing its basic needs. Remember the feel of morning and evening air, the weight of the grain bucket, and the sounds and smells of the shed or barn. Observe yourself in the process of harvesting, butchering, and preparing the meat for freezing or cooking.

Now, step back for a moment and expand your awareness to include the entire cycle of growing, buying, preparing, sharing, and eating the food. Note which aspects of the cycle bring satisfaction, and which are sources of strain or frustration.

Mentally walk through the process again. You have witnessed what works well for you and what doesn't. This time, observe yourself incorporating enjoyment into the areas of frustration. Picture yourself seated before the ideal dinner in the most nourishing atmosphere you can imagine. Consider where and how the food was grown (pause), your state of mind when you bought or harvested it (pause), and how you prepared the food (pause). Note where you are sitting—are you having a picnic outside on the grass, sitting on a rock in the middle of a stream, or eating at a table decorated with flowers and set with silver and china? Who is with you? What are you talking about? Note how your body feels—are you tense or relaxed, distracted or engaged? Allow yourself to enjoy the most nourishing experience possible.

◆   ◆   ◆

Nourishment comes from more than food. The means of obtaining and preparing our daily bread is just as important as the act of chewing it. Nourishment comes from our relationships—with ourselves, with other humans at the dinner table, with the plants and animals that provide our food, and with our ultimate source of sustenance, the Earth. Relationship with Self is primary: I can not truly nourish another until my own needs are met. From the foundation of right relationship with my (well-nourished) Self, I can interact in a good way with my family, my community, and my planet.

Six

Energy Flow

IN ESSENCE, throughout the whole of this book, we have been discussing the management of energy—how do I choose to use my time and energy? What is important to me in my life? I have only so many hours to live; how do I want to spend them? And how many do I spend running errands, daydreaming, doodling, making phone calls, making excuses, and generally avoiding what I consider my passionate interests that I "never have time for"?

My greatest commodity, I have come to realize, is time. Like everyone else, I have a limited amount. I can invest my inheritance wisely, or I can squander it on the inconsequential. I can put my time into matters of importance to me, that will have enduring value, or I can spend my bequest on trivia. No one else's yardstick of importance can measure my own desires. I need my life vision, my blueprint of life goals, in order to make wise decisions.

When I hear people talking about what they really want to do, their first sigh is almost always, "If only I had the time . . ." and the second groan is, "And if only I had the money . . ." Sometimes the order reverses, but generally the two biggest stumbling blocks in the Western world are time and money.

Although most of my major life goals have nothing to do with money, many of my activities require financial support. Money is a concretized abstraction of energy produced or exchanged—the energy of the goods or services rendered. For most of humankind's history, energy exchange occurred through barter. Instead of abstracting the energy into the "neutral" substance of money, two parties mutually agreed upon an exchange of goods or work. The goods and services passing from hand to hand were tangible, name-able, concrete.

A barter system offers both advantages and disadvantages. Barter-ing discourages hoarding. I cannot stack up pigs with the same ease that I can stack up money in a bank account. As long as wealth is measured in goods and services, I immediately experience a strain when caring for more material goods than I truly need. On the other hand, the greatest hindrance in barter is finding someone whose services I desire, who also needs my goods or services in return.

In a world marginally dependent upon money, I focus more on *primary needs.* I could, for example, spend eight hours working at a production line to pay for the week's groceries. Alternatively, I could invest the same amount of time tending a garden, pruning an apple orchard, or harvesting and preserving slightly frosted winter squash from a neighboring field. As a production line worker, I receive money, a *secondary* form of energy, to buy food, my primary need. How often do I negate the value of the work that I do providing for my primary needs simply because I did not ex-change money in the process?

One summer I maintained a neighbor's garden while she was away. During July and August I worked twenty to thirty hours a week weeding, mulching, and harvesting in the garden. During the mornings I sat in front of my computer in my one-room cabin, writing magazine articles and book proposals. When friends asked if I was working, I told them about the writing, but I neglected to mention the garden. The activity involved more joy than drudgery, and because no money was exchanged, I did not consider the garden my work, and yet the garden provided all of my summer and autumn produce needs. In reality, I was paid richly for my garden work, more so than for my magazine articles.

When I examine things that are "free"—"free" for the picking or "free" for the asking—I find that those who tip the balance of energy at zero never counted the costs of time and energy. My own work, my own sweat, are required to pay the cost of "free" commodities.

Homework—Preparation for Success

Now, I'm about to write something that would have raised my feminist hackles ten years ago. Then, I was convinced that women's worth would increase if we performed roles that society valued. If engineers, doctors, and lawyers were respected people, then women should become engineers, doctors, and lawyers. But certainly not housewives. That would never do.

Over the years I have come to realize that the woman herself, not the role she plays, must be valued in society.

Gradually, despite my feminist dogma, I came to view the role of housewife as a powerful occupation. I became, in Alice Walker's words, a "womanist"—one who loves and values women. As a womanist, I value any woman's occupation, regardless of pay scale. In fact, I am learning that the housewife/homemaker/mother who receives no monetary compensation probably has one of the most powerful, pivotal crafts imaginable in terms of enacting planetary vision in a daily way.

Consider the household duties of a homemaker. A century ago, she played a highly esteemed role in her community. She was the "keeper of the keys," the one who carried the keys for the larder, linen closet, cupboards, storerooms, and attic. Even today, most of the financial matters of the household are her jurisdiction. Her hand is the one that wavers over the organic or conventionally grown sweet potatoes. Her sweat goes into the cooking of the meal. Her heart goes into the nourishment of the family on many levels.

I propose that a homemaker, whether female or male, actually produces more valuable work than most executives. Much of what passes across an executive's office is little more than trivia. The day is neatly scheduled according to reports, coffee breaks, and meetings. A homemaker, on the other hand, must create a rhythm from her/his own inner resources. And the work is focused mainly on satisfying the primary needs of the household: providing nourishing food, comfortable clothing, a beautiful space to live in, and an abundant garden.

Some couples beautifully balance work both inside and outside the home. In most situations, however, the reality is that the man works outside the home while the woman works both inside and outside. In my own life, I have struggled with a belief instilled during childhood: "A woman can have either a career or children, but not both." My sister has lived out our childhood indoctrination, and (so far) I as well. I will continue to live in this either/or world until I let go of the belief.

For those women and men (I know a few such pioneering men) who choose to take on the traditional role of "the keeper of the keys," may they do so with the awareness that their activities in the home are the foundation for what happens in the world. Instead of choosing a life of isolation in the home, may they take on the job of bonding neighborhoods into communities once again.

The Commodity of Time

"Time is money," say the wizards of finance. Knowing the value of the commodity of time, take a moment to consider what you want to spend your time doing. If your joy truly lies in your occupation outside the home, pursue it. In the town where I lived in Scotland, I visited the local shoe repair shop from time to time. Inconspicuously tucked into the back of an alley, the tiny shop was crammed with odd pieces of leather and bits of this and that. An aging man presided over the ordered clutter, carefully mending old, battered shoes. His worn hands passed over the shoes, pressing them into shape, scanning the footwear like a doctor preparing for surgery. At 65 he reluctantly retired. Within a week, he was dead. I sometimes wonder how much longer he might have lived if he had continued the work he loved, sustained by his sense of usefulness and daily contact with people.

I am also aware of people who spend their lives earning money for their retirement, or for the vacation home they never visit, or for the trip they never take. Obsessed with the belief that they need money to accomplish what they really want to do, these people immerse themselves so fully in the task of earning money that they never have the time or energy to do what they really want to do. I once spent an evening talking with a man who was obsessed with making money. "I want money so that I can help my family," he told me. He listed scheme after scheme, from making a video on photography to selling real estate.

"If you want to help your family," I said, "why don't you look at what they need? Do they really need money, or do they need something else?"

"Well, of course they need money. And I'm going to help them. . . ."

The end of the sentence that he failed to complete was ". . . so they will be grateful and indebted to me." He wanted to be the knight in shining armor for a damsel who wasn't in distress. From his descriptions of his marriage, I deduced that his wife needed compassion, caring, and general loving attention more than she needed money. What the man really wanted was not money but love, admiration, and respect. Perhaps, too, he really wanted to support his immediate and extended family, but he saw their needs only through the lens of money.

My friend David is a master at identifying the essence of what people want. He has a knack for identifying the most direct path to his desires. If he wants to fly to Australia to complete a project that he is working on, he goes to an airline and requests a ticket. If he needs film to complete a video production, he solicits help from the film manufacturer. They receive publicity through credits in his work; he receives the equipment that he needs. You scratch my back, I'll scratch yours. Admittedly, he has developed his contacts over several decades, but they grew as a result of his ability to identify his true needs, and not the means to procure his needs.

♦ ♦ ♦

The following meditation and series of questions are designed to help you look at the essence of what you desire in your life. Energy can flow through your life "system" in many forms. Consider money as one among many energy resources.

Give yourself at least ten minutes of uninterrupted quiet time. Sit in a comfortable position, either in a chair or on the floor. Close your eyes and take three deep breaths. Allow your body to grow heavy and relaxed. Let go of any tension stored in the face, neck, or back. Breathe into your abdomen. Follow the movement of breath in and out of your body until you feel centered and alert.

If you are meditating in the morning, observe yourself moving through the events of the preceding day. If you are meditating in the afternoon or evening, review today's events. Move backwards in time, noting your activities, the blocks of time dedicated to each task, and the amount and type of your personal energy invested in each event. "Personal" energy might include physical work—lifting, carrying, washing, digging, etc; mental work—deciding, planning, problem-solving, accounting, organizing, discussing; emotional work—worry, anger, excitement, compassion, frustration; spiritual work—meditating, praying, visualizing, affirming, giving thanks. Observe the events without judgment; simply take note and move on.

Recall the life vision that you have identified for yourself and the planet. Focus on the essence of what you desire. Look at each aspect of your vision. Ask yourself, "Is this what I want, or is this a means to something else? If I had this, what would I want next?" You may discover that your desire for a house by the sea is in essence a need for more quiet, contemplative time in your life, a desire for more contact with wilderness, or a wish for more meaningful contact with your partner or family. Examine your personal and planetary visions, considering each aspect, asking whether you are focusing on means or ends.

Ask yourself how money would (or would not) support each aspect of your vision. Do I need money, or do I need material goods to complete a project? If I were given a million dollars, how would I use it to support my vision? If I lived in an economy based on bartering, how would I fulfill my vision? If I had enough money, what would be the next step I would take? Can I take that step with the resources I have now? How can I best use the money I have now to support my goals?

Focus on one aspect of your personal vision that is most important to you at this time. Take a deep breath. Relax even more. Ask to be shown the next step in realizing this part of your vision. Be open to surprises. The Divine comes in small, humble packages. You may receive very specific ideas, but more often the information is about the quality of the work you need to do. The quality of your action may be just as important in determining the outcome as the task itself.

When you are ready, take a deep breath, stretch your body, and open your eyes. Record anything you want to remember in your journal.

◆　◆　◆

Taking Stock of Your Investments

Although money is not the only form of energy flow in my life, inevitably in today's society I am drawn to use it as a means of exchange. In Western society, money does indeed talk—often in a very loud voice. The way I choose to spend and invest my money can have powerful, long-term ramifications for the planet.

When I was a toddler, my grandparents bought me shares of American Home Products stock. I never knew about my grandparents' forward-looking gift until I was 21 and was handed a financial statement from the trust my parents held in my name. The stock had accrued in value to a moderate sum—certainly nothing extravagant, but to a college student scraping by in drafty rented rooms, it was a fortune. If I lived in a tent and ate tahini and honey sandwiches, I could survive on the dividends. The thought tempted me, but I earmarked the money to pay for further schooling.

Another six years passed before I carefully examined one of the company proxies that arrived in early spring. Besides the usual request to bless the incoming board of directors (the usual smattering of "good old boys"—I always pencil "Where are the women?" in the margin and leave the question blank), I was asked to vote on two issues that were to be addressed at the annual meeting. The first was the company's use of animals for testing drugs and cosmetics, and the second called for a divestment from all company operations in South Africa.

I was stunned by my own ignorance about the company I had supported for nearly thirty years. I had strict inner guidelines about the consumer products I would or would not buy according to numerous company policies, such as environmental hazards, infant formula scandals, animal testing, investment in racially oppressive countries, and participation in nuclear and/or military contracting. I suddenly realized that I knew almost nothing about the companies in which I held stocks.

A couple of months later I bought a copy of *Shopping For a Better World,* an excellent "quick and easy guide" to background information on products commonly found in supermarkets. Hesitantly, I looked up American Home Products. It scored "poor performance" in the areas of women's advancement, animal testing, and investments in South Africa. No surprises so far. What shook me was an entry in the "Alert" column: infant formula. I had boycotted Nestlé's products for years because of its scandalous promotion of infant formula in the Third World. The shopper's guide did not give details about AHP's promotion record, but the fact that it manufactured infant formula coupled with its other violations convinced me to sell off the stock. I found my confirmation later in another book on ethical investing, *Economics as If the Earth Really Mattered* (see below), that listed American Home Products, Bristol-Myers, and Abbott/Ross Laboratories as violators of the World Health Organization code for marketing infant formula. Grandma and Grandpa, don't think me ungrateful; I hope I can invest your hard-earned money in wiser ways.

My first attempt to take control of my investments was to give my stockbroker a list of what I did not want: investments in South Africa, the nuclear industry, military contractors, toxic waste producers, petroleum companies, etc. He patiently labored under my restrictions, occasionally complaining that my mother and I were his most difficult clients to buy for—she, too, had her moral imperatives.

I questioned some of my self-righteous decrees after attending an afternoon seminar on ethical investing. The presenter, a wealthy British businessman who had carefully cultivated an impressive investment portfolio, pointed out that most portfolios with negative restrictions had far smaller returns than those who gave their brokers carte blanche to follow the hottest market leads despite ethical concerns. "In my opinion," he drawled patiently, "I can do more good in the world by going for the best returns, regardless of the company's ethical standards, and then giving my profits to good causes."

I wavered, but just could not stomach the thought of seeing "General Electric" and "Sohio Oil" envelopes in my mailbox. I began to research alternatives to the restrictive investment approach. I knew what I didn't want but had little information about companies engaged in projects I believed in. Gradually the information began to flow in my direction. One gold mine that has provided much of the practical information I sought is *Economics as If the Earth Really Mattered* by Susan Meeker-Lowry:

> Dealing with surplus money involves *work*. The steps for doing the work involve clarifying personal needs and social values (what you are against, what you are for) and learning investment skills. Only then will you have the capacity to evaluate and make investment decisions you will be happy with. In clarifying and learning, there is an *investment* involved—using

one's surplus money to educate oneself and clarify one's values. And that is surely one of the most socially responsible investments you can make.[1]

This book covers everything from evaluating a personal loan to family or friends to choosing socially responsible investments in national and/or community-based companies. Just its extensive list of resources and bibliography is worth the price. Through contacts it suggested, I found money market funds that "screened" certain types of companies from their holdings, ones that supported positive alternatives in specific areas, and ones that combined the avoidance and support approaches. Gradually I am reinvesting my inheritance in projects and companies that I want to see prosper and flourish in the world.

Shopping For a Better World is an important tool for those who want to use their money wisely in the consumer marketplace. When you pick up a jar from the grocery shelf, ask yourself, "Who owns this company, anyhow?" You may be surprised by some of the companies that own the companies that own the companies. Conglomerates and multinationals often obscure real ownership. I remember reading the annual report of a huge multinational with chills running down my spine as I realized how many assets this one parent company controlled. MGM, a huge business in itself, was just one of its many holdings. Buying locally-made goods from small businesses bypasses the multinational tangle and keeps financial power circulating where you live.

Fossil Fuel: Outdated Energy Source

Another energy source, as finite as time, is fossil fuel. Residential and transportation use, the realm of our daily activities at home and in the community, account for more energy consumption than all of the industries in the United States. In other words, what you and I choose to do in our homes and with our cars accounts for nearly half of all of the energy this country uses.

The Earth can support twenty billion humans over the next 400,000 million years (our planet's projected life expectancy). Do we want to use all of its resources in one or two centuries or over a long period of time? The Earth has a limited supply of resources. Can we discipline ourselves to sustain a long, slow "burn" of energy resources as our ancestors did, or are we enamored with the quick flash/burn consumption of contemporary society?

Limitless Abundance, Finite Resources

Now, I can hear New Agers screaming, "But what about abundance? Prosperity consciousness? The Universe has limitless energy—what do you mean by 'limited resources'?" While spiritual inspiration is indeed limitless, physical resources are limited. The challenge of living on Earth is to bring the infinite wisdom of the Spirit into the finite physical world. Living a "spiritual" life means applying profound truths to the nuts and bolts of day-to-day living. Meditation opens me to exquisite insights. For the most part, hearing great wisdom from within myself is not difficult. The excruciating work comes in living those principles in my daily life. I can sit in meditation and contemplate the beauty of forgiveness, but when my housemate dumps floor sweepings and rotten ginger and old socks into the paper recycling bin for the second time in a week, I pray for amnesia. All of my profound insights are put to the test. I wish I could report that I triumphantly meet each challenge. I don't. I yell and bluster and hold grudges over the silliest of things. And these are people I love. No wonder the United Nations has difficulty coming to agreements and carrying out policies—our household of three struggles with agreements about how to separate the trash. Such are the weighty decisions upon which peace depends.

These simple, daily decisions affect not only my own household, but also my community and eventually the world at large. The fossil fuels that I consume deplete everyone's future supply, and the CO_2 emitted as a result affects everyone's air quality. Although Americans comprise only 5 percent of the world population, we are accountable for a fifth of the world's estimated greenhouse effect.[2]

Not every American is willing to take responsibility for these figures, however. I remember sitting in the break room at a nursing home where I was working, discussing energy use with one of my colleagues. We hashed over the pros and cons of nuclear energy, and then plunged into a debate on energy use in general. I explained America's inequitable energy consumption in comparison with the rest of the world.

"But you can't ask people to change the way they live," she said. "You can't make them change. They have a right to do what they want to do."

My foundation for evaluating resource use, I learned in the process of this discussion, consisted of assumptions completely foreign to my colleague. Resources are a planetary affair, not something to be controlled by the whim of wealthy industrialists. Simply having the power to buy resources does not mean that I have the right or the obligation to use them. Other nations, other peoples, indeed other generations, must be considered in my choices. I ponder the people in more energy-frugal countries—frugal by choice or by necessity. What "rights" do they have in deciding how energy resources are used? They were never asked if they chose to support American's opulent lifestyle at the expense of their and future generations' resources. How would she feel if she lived in a country where she didn't have a choice to squander her resources willy-nilly while other countries did?

My thinking process coalesced while I was running errands in town—driving my car, of course. I organize my trips to minimize gas mileage, and I pick up hitchhikers to share my gasoline usage. (Take a deep breath, Mom—I screen them intuitively before I let them in the car.)

Thich Nhat Hanh was the first monk in his temple to ride a bicycle. He believes in keeping his Buddhist practice in line with current times, and offers the following *gatha* (meditative focus) to use when driving:

> Before starting the car,
> I know where I am going.
> The car and I are one.
> If the car goes fast, I go fast.

> Sometimes we don't really need to use the car, but because we want to get away from ourselves, we go down and start the car. . . . It is said that in the last few years, two million square miles of forest land have been destroyed by acid rain, and that is partly because of our cars. "Before starting the car, I know where I am going," is a very deep question. "Where shall I go? To my own destruction?" If the trees die, humans are going to die also. If trees and animals are not alive, how can we be alive?
>
> "The car and I are one." We have the impression that we are the boss, and the car is only an instrument, but that is not true. With the car, we become something different. With a gun, we become very dangerous. With a flute, we become pleasant. With 50,000 atomic bombs, humankind has become the most

dangerous species on earth. . . . The most basic precept of all is to be aware of what we do, what we are, each minute. Every other precept will follow from that.[3]

Human Energy

One of the most underrated energy sources I know of is human energy. Couple human power with one of the most efficient users of petroleum oil—the bicycle—and you have a winning combination; a bicycle can travel hundreds of miles on little more than a thimbleful of oil.

Human energy can be applied in the home as well. How many electrical appliances do I rely upon to complete tasks once performed by humans? If you choose to use electrical appliances, give them the best care possible to ensure that they are running at maximum efficiency.

Take stock of all of the gadgets in your home. How many of them are electrically powered, and how many of them do you really need? Ivan Illich points out that many "time- and work-saving" devices actually create work in the home. Before the advent of electric vacuum cleaners, for example, people used carpet sweepers to clean rugs. When vacuum cleaners replaced most carpet sweepers, the expected standard of cleanliness increased, and homemakers spent more time vacuuming the floors and furniture than they ever did pushing the carpet sweeper. Washing machines developed a similar tyranny. When clothes were washed in tubs and squeezed through hand-cranked wringers, people wore clothes more often between washings and made an effort to wipe off spills and dirt to increase the wearing time. Washing machines provided cleaner clothes with less physical effort—but, like the vacuum cleaner, the washing machine set a new standard of cleanliness. People expected clothes to be cleaner, requiring them to be laundered more often.

Each moment of the day I am presented with opportunities to make decisions about energy use, including my own energy (time, money, emotional, and mental attention), renewable resources (wood, sun, wind, and water), and non-renewable energy sources (nuclear and fossil fuels). Each decision supports or undermines my vision for the world and my life. What would I do if I took my vision for the planet seriously? Can I make choices to support that vision in this moment? I just turned off the lamp next to the computer—a small step, a minor sacrifice on a cloudy spring day. Small steps, though, accumulate into a journey—if, as Thich Nhat Hanh reminds me, I know where I am going.

Seven

Bringing It All Back Home

RECENTLY, WHEN I WAS CREATING a recycling corner in the kitchen, I posted notes on the wall about how to compost food, separate paper, and clean cans and bottles. "And remember," I scribbled on the last note, "the less packaged food and other items we bring into the house, the less waste we have to send out. DON'T BUY OVER-PACKAGED PRODUCTS."

Rereading the note today, I realize that the problem is not only packaging, but the accumulation of goods themselves. Having grown up in a culture addicted to acquiring material goods, I was well trained in procuring, saving, and collecting. Part of the mania, I am aware, is an aftermath of the Great Depression. The survival mode of scraping by from day to day during the Depression became a way of life that continues to affect my parents' and grandparents' lives. "Save it—you might need it later" translated into overstuffed closets and basements. The ethic has its strengths: "Waste not, want not." Reuse and recycle and refurbish, my ancestors intoned. My great-grandfather, an Ohio farmer who lived in the late nineteenth and early twentieth centuries, could fix almost anything, using wire and a pair of pliers.

Reusing and refurbishing are honorable pursuits. My great-grandfather must have perpetuated the "fix-it" genes through my grandmother, and she through my mother and then to me. I'm probably one of the few remaining women of my generation who knows how to darn socks. Like the whooping crane, we are a tender, tenuous sort of oddity.

Hoarding is the distortion of the "waste not, want not" mentality.

When my great-aunt died, she left boxes of stationery collected over forty years of touring around the world. Three years after my aunt's death, my mother is still writing to me on yellowed note paper from a motel in Carlsbad, New Mexico. "Telephones in every room, air conditioned summer and winter. Just south of town," proclaims the 1950's letterhead. I can understand taking enough paper to write letters during a trip, but pocketing enough to supply one's descendants is too much!

Before World War II, manufacturers packaged food and other goods with shipping, not consumers, in mind. During the war, the military needed to feed millions of troops scattered around the planet. To meet this challenge, they developed a new range of food preservation techniques, including improved canning technology and the introduction of disposable beverage containers. After the war, the food industry incorporated these "improvements" into the civilian market, wooing the affluent postwar population with an increasing array of convenience foods. "Convenience," according to Ozzie and Harriet's education, means "throw-away." How many consumers, I wonder, would buy "convenience packaging" if the price reflected the true cost, including the environmental damage? You can help reduce unnecessary packaging by refusing to buy overpackaged products.

Imagine what would happen if the food industry was captivated by a trend towards "elegant simplicity"—minimal packaging that enhanced the natural, innate attractiveness of food. Imagine shopping for beautifully packaged items that could be recycled, like the jelly jars that can be reused as juice glasses. The current trend in bulk food shopping, now as common in supermarkets as in co-ops, demonstrates that consumers can forgo fancy packaging in favor of simply packaged, lower cost food.

Environmentally-Minded Shopping

Reducing consumption is a cornerstone of what the Quakers call "simple living." Simplicity is more complex than "simply" doing without—it requires effort and awareness to achieve.

"Live simply that others may simply live." For years, I have associated simplicity with "doing without." But simplicity does not necessarily mean deprivation. I can simplify my life by finding greater meaning in fewer things; thus, the deprivation approach of "having fewer things" shifts to finding more appreciation, pleasure, and respect for material things. José Lutzemburger, an environmental activist in the Brazilian rainforest, addresses the error of labeling our culture "materialistic." "A materialist," explains Lutzemburger, "would by definition revere material objects. A materialist would not create things to throw away, or things that would become obsolete or self-destruct." Living a simple life means becoming a true materialist, one who respects and appreciatively uses the objects of creation.

The Politics of Paper

I became aware of the "politics of paper" while traveling in the southwest of Australia, where I hiked and camped in the remnants of what was once a magnificent stretch of forest. The remaining Karri and Jarrah trees towered above, the tallest of Australia's native eucalyptus trees that rival even North America's sequoias. The first Europeans to "explore" (read "invade") the area struggled for two weeks and moved only eight miles through the dense undergrowth. They contented themselves with settlements on the coast and then began the systematic clearcutting of the forest that has continued to this day.

Four weeks before I arrived, a group of local people completed "The Great Walk," a month-long hike from the southwestern tip of Australia up to Perth, the capital of Western Australia. There, the walkers presented a Declaration of Interdependence that outlined ways of preserving and eventually expanding the Karri and Jarrah forest. In addition to alerting the government to possible ways of supporting the native forest, The Great Walk also transformed the participants' lives. For many participants, The Walk was their first experience of living in the forests, of spending more than a day or a weekend hiking among the trees. They came to know the forests on a fundamental level, through their bodies. They slept on the ground, walked on the Earth, sat on the forest floor, drank from the streams, absorbed the rain, felt the wind, and endured the sun. They became one with the forest, and developed a loving, supportive human community in the process. During the Great Walk they experienced the interdependent relationship that they outlined in their Declaration to the government.

Western Australia governs the territory that includes the Karri and Jarrah forest. Its environmental record is, to say the least, poor. The forests "protected" by national park designation must comply with federal law which prohibits the sale of lumber from the national park within the country of Australia. The national government, however, has no control over the sale of national parks lumber outside Australia; therefore, the Western Australian government cannot sell lumber to Australia's Northern Territory, but it can legally sell the wood to foreign countries. Most of the remaining stands of Karri and Jarrah forest are being felled and milled for woodchips, which are sold chiefly to Japan, where they are used to make cardboard. Yes, those magnificent Karri and Jarrah trees were not used for furniture or building lumber; but for cardboard boxes to protect the Sony stereo and the Toshiba tape player that you and I buy at the local electronic store and bring into our homes. My Sony stereo box is a legacy of the rainforests of Sarawak and the Karri and Jarrah forests of southwestern Australia. Ultimately I, too, am responsible for the forests' demise.

The Politics of Fiber

The clothing that I buy also may harbor "hidden costs" that are linked with foreign nations. The wool sweaters that I bought while living in Scotland are a good example. The wool industry has a bloody history in the Scottish Highlands, and the wounds are recent enough to continue to cause pain among the Scots. In the mid-eighteenth century, English lairds owned most of Scotland. Much of the land was still forested or farmed by "crofters," subsistence farmers who gave most of their profits to the lairds. The English lairds eventually realized that wool from sheep would bring more profit than the labor-intensive crops grown by the crofters. The lairds ordered the crofters to leave lands that in some cases had been farmed for centuries. During the "Highland Clearances" many Scots fled to foreign countries. Those who submitted willingly were settled in villages and taught handicrafts to support themselves. The homes of those crofters who defied the Removal were burned and smashed so that they could not easily return to rebuild them.

The sheep may have brought profits in the wool trade, but their grazing habits further bankrupted the Highlands environment. Sheep and deer chew on young tree seedlings as well as ground vegetation. The young trees never grow more than about six inches before being pruned by the grazing animals. Today only remnants of Scotland's once great Caledonian pine forest remain, scattered old "Granny pines" with no young seedlings growing to take their place. The Highlands region, photographed from the air, looks like the surface of the moon. Rivers and streams turn muddy brown in the spring from the soil eroding from treeless slopes. Many of the native animal species have disappeared or been drastically reduced because of the demise of their natural habitats.

My Arran sweater, most likely hand-knitted by one of the descendants of those crofting families, costs much more than the £56.00 marked on the price tag. The externalities, the hidden costs unaccounted for in the price, include the destruction of both the land and the human culture of the Highlands.

For years I have refused to buy or wear synthetic clothing, preferring instead the "natural" feel of wool, linen, and cotton. "Natural" clothing, though, is not necessarily the healthiest environmental choice. Cotton is one of the most heavily sprayed agricultural crops. Although most of the cotton used in the U.S. was once grown within the country, much of today's cotton comes from Central America. Pesticides banned in the U.S., including DDT, BHC, endrin, dieldrin, Phosvel and DBCP, are exported to Central America. The chemicals are lavishly applied by untrained, unprotected workers.

The "circle of poison" in which American-made pesticides contaminate Third World food imported to the United States encompasses fiber production as well. Many South and Central American countries, desperate to pay off massive debts, grow cash crops instead of primary foodstuffs to generate income.

Bernice Johnson Reagon, founder of the women's gospel group Sweet Honey in the Rock, chronicles the saga of clothing production from the fields of El Salvador to a blouse on sale at Sears in the song "Are My Hands Clean?" The lyrics are based on an article by John Cavanagh, fellow of the Institute for Policy Studies, entitled "The Journey of the Blouse: A Global Assembly."

> I wear garments touched by hands from all over the world
> 35% cotton, 65% polyester, the journey begins in Central
>   America
> In the cotton fields of El Salvador
> In a province soaked in blood, pesticide sprayed workers toil in
>   a broiling sun
> Pulling cotton for two dollars a day.

Then we move on up another rung—Cargill
A top forty trading conglomerate, takes the cotton through the
    Panama Canal
Up the Eastern seaboard, coming to the U.S. of A. for the first
    time.

In South Carolina
At the Burlington mills
Joins a shipment of polyester filament courtesy of the New
    Jersey petro-chemical mills of Dupont

Dupont strands of filament begin in the South American country
    of Venezuela
Where oil riggers bring up oil from the earth for six dollars a
    day
Then Exxon, largest oil company in the world
Upgrades the product in the country of Trinidad and Tobago
Then back into the Caribbean and Atlantic Seas
To the factories of Dupont
On the way to the Burlington mills

In South Carolina
Burlington factories hum with the business of weaving oil and
    cotton into miles of fabric for Sears
Who takes this bounty back into the Caribbean Sea
Headed for Haiti this time
May she be one day soon free

Far from the Port-au-Prince palace
Third world women toil doing piece work to Sears specifications
For three dollars a day my sisters make my blouse
It leaves the third world for the last time
Coming back into the sea to be sealed in plastic for me

This third world sister
And I go to the Sears department store where I buy my blouse
On sale for 20% discount

Are my hands clean?[1]

I wonder, too, how clean my hands are when I dust the furniture
in my living room. In my own living room, I touch a bookshelf
made of oak, a rocking chair carved from pine, and an antique
sidetable made of cherry. These are woods from the deciduous
forests of North America, not the tropical forest of South and
Central America. The rainforest activists would say that my hands
are "clean"; I, however, detect smudges. I have witnessed the scars

of clearcut slopes in New England, and the vast stretches of pine plantations in Maine. These overcrowded, single-species plantations are ecological deserts, devoid of the natural variety of plants and animals found in a native forest. Plantations are in essence tree factories, subject to producing environmental degradation as damaging as any "heavy industry." Pine trees acidify the soil, making the area unfit to support other tree species (except acid-loving shrubs like rhododendrons). The soil can recover, but the time scale of a forest is fossil-like in comparison to human lifespans.

In the rainforest, the "slow" time scale of the deciduous forest dilates to boggling proportions. The tropical rainforests' evolution spans 14 million years. As a species, we humans have succeeded in destroying most of this evolutionary time bank in twelve years. In other words, we have succeeded in removing most of the rainforest in .00008 percent of the amount of time that the planet took to create it. Today, tropical forests cover only 2 percent of the planet, but the percentage was much larger before the last ice age. The rainforests are in fact the only ecosystem that continued to evolve undisturbed throughout the ice ages, which explains why ancient, "primordial" plant species grow interspersed with "highly evolved" species. Although the rainforests cover a minute percentage of the total surface of the planet, they support over half of the planet's animal, insect and plant species.

> In a typical four-mile-square patch of tropical rainforest you
> would find: over 750 species of trees, over 1500 different kinds
> of flowering plants, 125 different mammals, 400 kinds of birds,
> 100 reptiles, 60 amphibians, and countless insects—including
> 150 types of butterflies. And only 1 percent of these species
> have ever been studied![2]

The soil that supports such a vast array of plants much be extremely fertile, right? **Wrong.** The fertile nutrients in the forest are recycled above ground through a complex system of epiphytic plants—ones that obtain nutrients from rain, air, and decomposed material that falls into their cup-like leaf structures. A common example of an epiphytic plant is the pineapple. You can grow a pineapple plant at home by cutting the green top about an inch below its base and planting it in well-drained soil. The soil, however, does not supply nutrients; it simply supports the plant's scanty root system. The pineapple absorbs nutrients through water poured into the "cup" formed at the center of the leaves. Your plant will thrive when you water the cup, but will wither if you only moisten the soil.

Farmers migrating from other regions as well as multinational agribusinesses made a classic error in assuming that the soil supported the rainforests' fertility. Instead of rooting deeply in the soil to stabilize themselves, the trees spread their shallow root systems over large areas to provide ballast. When the trees and plants are removed, the soil quickly erodes and then bakes into a hard, bricklike substance known as "laterite." Cattle ranchers clearcut the rainforest, expecting a lush crop of grass to follow. They found instead that the soil supported only a sparse covering of grass the first year which declined to nothing within three to five years. Instead of halting their folly and looking for more appropriate pasture land, the cattle ranchers continue to clearcut new sections of rainforest as the previously cleared sections wash away in hard, tropical rains and bake into laterite under the intense sun.

For what have we used this environmentally rich ecosystem? Unbelievably, much of the felled timber was not used for anything. In Brazil, for example, farmers displaced in other regions are encouraged to "homestead" patches of rainforest. The incoming farmers clear the land for planting by cutting down trees and burning them where they fall. Thousands of peasant farmers use this "slash and burn" technique. In 1987, such fires spewed approximately 518 million tons of carbon into the air, an amount equal to roughly a tenth of all the carbon emitted from fossil fuel combustion during that year.

The crops grown in the scorched earth are as devastatingly poor as the rainforest was environmentally rich. During the first year, most farmers' rice crops return less than the seed stock they planted, so that sowing 100 pounds of rice produces only 50 pounds of grain at maturity. Anyone who has planted a pack of bean seeds in a patch of fertile earth knows that this is an outrageously poor return. The second year, only a small percentage of the seeds planted even germinate. Most farmers abandon the land during the third year and move to a new section of rainforest where they repeat the "slash and burn" technique.

Although much of the rainforests are simply burned, some of the lumber makes its way to the marketplace. Many of the hardwoods revered for fine furniture making, such as teak, mahogany, rosewood, ebony, and iroko, come from the tropical rainforest. Tropical woods are used to produce pulp, wood chips, chopsticks, and matches as well as furniture. Many of these products, like chopsticks and matches, cost little and are used only once before disposal. The true price for our offhand consumption is millions of acres of rainforest. Only Japan exceeds the U.S. in the consumption of tropical woods (remember those Sony stereo boxes?). Every 16 minutes an area the size of New York's Central Park is destroyed, every hour 3,000 acres are cleared, and every year 27 million acres, an area the size of the state of Ohio, is cut. Ravaging tropical rainforests is a fairly recent "innovation"—80 percent of the planet's rainforests have been destroyed since 1980.

Third World countries generally steward rainforest lands. Among the "developed" countries, only Australia, and to a lesser extent the United States (Hawaii), have rainforests within their territories. Developed countries, however, are the chief consumers of tropical hardwood products, and their buying habits often dictate the rate at which the forests are destroyed. In the U.S., a mere 2 percent reduction in timber consumption (lumber, plywood, and furniture) would eliminate the need for tropical hardwood imports.

Withdrawing economic support, though, is only part of the solution. First World countries need to examine their own forest management policies and address the hardships of Third World countries dependent upon timber exports for economic survival. Activists in the United States are demanding that Central and South American countries halt rainforest destruction. Few people are aware, however, that the United States is involved with the destruction of its only stand of lowland tropical forest for a proposed geothermal power plant in Hawaii.

Protecting the environment is a complex affair that must be addressed globally, from an environmental as well as an economic perspective. I cannot simply point a finger at Third World countries and ask them to stop ravaging their tropical forests. My own country's economic policies are responsible for the destruction as well. As an individual consumer, I am responsible for the earth's future. My choice of furniture and building materials affects the future of the tropical rainforests. Rainforest activist groups are working with the timber industry to develop a labeling system that identifies a product's country of origin so that consumers can make informed choices.

Debt-For-Nature Swaps

Many Third World countries are driven to clearcut their rainforests. They need resources and income—how can they meet these needs and protect natural resources? Ken Rubelli, a forester by training, spent over ten years living and working as an environmental activist in Malaysia. He recently told me about a conference on rainforest destruction he had attended. A young Malaysian woman spoke about her country's need for health care, housing, and food. The forests are the islands' primary natural resource. Timber exports are the chief source of income. If the government declared a moratorium on tree-cutting, how would the Malaysian people pay for medicine and housing and food? Were Western environmentalists willing to support the Malaysian people while they created another economic base? And if they couldn't make the transition to another economic base, what then?

One brilliant scheme, devised by Dr. Thomas Lovejoy when he was vice president of World Wildlife Fund, is to "buy" these nations' debt. In return, the countries fund projects for the protection, restoration, and sustainable use of natural resources. Because the debts can be purchased at a fraction of their face value—the lending banks realize they have little chance of ever receiving full payment of the loans—one U.S. dollar "buys" several dollars worth of funding for conservation efforts. World Wildlife Fund has arranged "debt-for-nature" swaps in Ecuador, Costa Rica, the Philippines, Zambia, and Madagascar. In total, WWF is responsible for the conversion of over $200 million of developing countries' debt into conservation funds.

Other conservation groups have implemented similar programs. In 1987 Bolivia agreed to protect 3.7 million acres of rainforest in exchange for a $650,000 reduction of its national debt. The new conservation area borders the Beni Biosphere Reserve in northern Bolivia, an Amazonian region that includes thirteen of Bolivia's eighteen endangered animal species. Conservation International, a nonprofit organization based in Washington, D.C., implemented the exchange with the help of a $100,000 donation from the Frank Weeden Foundation.[3] The Nature Conservancy arranged a similar "debt-for-nature" swap in Costa Rica.

Even the U.S. government is implementing the "debt-for-nature" scheme. In November 1989, the U.S. Congress passed "The Global

Environmental Protection Assistance Act" which authorizes the use of U.S. foreign assistance funds to purchase Third World commercial debts, the proceeds of which will finance local environmental projects.

Delegates at the Fourth World Wilderness Congress in 1987 applauded the debt purchasing schemes. Former United Nations Undersecretary General Maurice Strong, though, warned that "environmentalists alone can't save the environment. This is Planet Earth, Incorporated, and we have to run it like a business." Knowing the illogical foundation of our current economic system, based as it is on the illusion of unending resources to fuel limitless growth, I shiver at his analogy of managing the Earth as a business. Several other delegates echoed his concerns and prescribed more economic development, not less, to soothe the world's woes. They called for "sustainable" and "intelligent" development. But are these concepts fundamentally contradictory, especially in the mind of an economist? Environmental studies professor Raymond Dasmann obviously shared the same concern when he diverged from his prepared speech to question the meaning of "sustainable development." "Beware of bankers bearing gifts," he warned. "When you talk about economic development, you have to ask development of what, in what way, for the benefit of whom, and at whose expense?"[4]

Scientists have warned the global community about the adverse environmental effects of rainforest destruction for over a decade, but recent studies link economic factors with tropical forest destruction as well. "The study, reported in the current issue of the journal *Nature*, showed that revenues generated by harvesting edible fruits, rubber, oils, and cocoa from 2.5 acres of tropical rainforest are *nearly two times greater* than the return on timber or the value of the land if used for grazing cattle (emphasis mine)."[5] The study banishes the idea that "the only (economically) useful rainforest is a cleared one." Instead of clearing forests for cattle grazing and crop production, developing countries shouldering huge debts can work with their forests to generate more income:

> The new study showed that 12 products, primarily edible fruits and latex, found in one hectare, about 2.5 acres, of forest at the village of Mishana, in northeastern Peru near the Brazilian border, are worth $6,330 if sold in local markets over 50 years, with the cost of harvesting deducted from the market price. The

study also showed that the same land if used as a timber planta-
tion would produce $3,184 over the same period, and that if
converted to cattle pastures, it would be worth $2,960. Dr.
Peters said people who live in the region harvest and sell all of
the products that were detailed in the study, and for many it is
their main source of income.[6]

Clearly, the human population benefits both environmentally
and economically, while the tropical forest and the planet benefit
on all levels.

Endangered Plant and Animal Species

Decisions made in the local garden center affect tropical as well
as local forests. Each year Americans plant over one billion flower
bulbs, yet few are aware that many popular garden species are
overcollected in the wild. Note that many bulbs labeled "wild,"
"species," or "botanical" may have been collected in Central Asia,
South Africa, Portugal, Turkey, or the United States. Some species
are propagated by retail nurseries and suppliers. Ask before buying,
and be aware that "nursery-grown" bulbs obtained from "commercial sources" may have been wild-collected. Among the Amaryllis
family, for example, *Galanthus elwessi* is always of wild origin,
and *Narcissus triandrus albus* and *N. bulbocodium conspicuous*
are heavily collected. Other plant families to buy with caution are
Lily (including *Trillium* and *Fritillaria*), Orchid (Ladyslippers are
an endangered species), Primrose (including *Cyclamen*), and
Rannunculaceae.[7]

Pet stores are another outlet for species collected in wilderness
areas. International law now protects many species of endangered
birds and other animals; if caught, wildlife smugglers are fined
several thousand dollars. More stringent enforcement of these laws,
however, has made the business of smuggling rare, endangered
species a very profitable business. A single bird may sell for two
to three thousand dollars. A smuggler recently caught trying to
leave Australia was carrying six tropical birds in his suitcase. Each
bird was stuffed inside a sock. Only four of the six birds were still
alive when customs officials examined his baggage before his departure to the United States.

Local species also may be endangered. In Massachusetts, for
example, wood turtles are a protected species. The Eastern box
turtle, once common throughout the Northeast, is protected on

Long Island. Leave the natives where they belong and consider adopting a cat, dog, rabbit, goldfish, or canary. The U.S. halted importation of parakeets and canaries because of problems with disease in their native countries. All canaries and parakeets now sold in pet stores are bred in captivity. Be wary, though, of pet store owners who try to convince you that their sulfur-crested cockatoo or other rare bird was bred in captivity—most wild birds refuse to lay eggs when caged. Avoid buying macaws, cockatoos, monkeys, marmosets, pythons, boa constrictors, iguanas, red-footed tortoises, poison arrow frogs, jaguars, ocelots, and margays. Best of all, check your local animal shelter for your next pet.

Sharing Resources

Educating ourselves about what we buy is an important step to responsible consumption. Even better than watching consumption, though, is creating ways to share the resources that already exist.

A group of children in Wales taught me a profound lesson about sharing global resources. I was guiding an EarthLove workshop with five children, helping them to explore their personal relationship with the different kingdoms of life (mineral, plant, animal, human, and Oneness), and to experience Oneness as a group.

Halfway through the afternoon one of the girls turned to me, her forehead creased with concentration. "The point of the game is for everybody to move into Oneness, right?"

"Yes," I replied, nodding.

"Well," she said, surveying the game board, "I have more Grounding currency than I need, and Seth has extra Loves and Jessica needs some Consciousness. Can we just trade everything around until everyone has what they need to move on?"

I sat dumbfounded for a moment. Usually I guide the workshop with adults who hang on to their currency for dear life. The children, though, quickly grasped the reality of Oneness, the unifying web that connects all of life. This little girl knew how to "paint outside the lines" and create a system to meet everyone's needs: Share. I give something, you give something, we all move on. How elegantly, profoundly simple.

"Sure," I said. "Let's see what happens."

Without saying a word, the children gave and received and traded currency until each had what he or she needed to move on to the next kingdom. I sat with tears in my eyes, moved by their matter-of-fact caring for one another. These, I thought to myself, are the peacemakers in the making.

Remember the "free boxes" that sprouted like spring crocuses in the early Seventies? The Free Box is just what it says—free, a natural resource for slightly outdated jeans and baby clothes and wool sweaters and even day-old bakery goods. You never know what might be in the box when you open it.

Food co-ops are another tool for sharing resources and building community spirit. Our local co-op meets monthly on Monday evenings to order bulk food supplies. We sip tea and share news, throw logs in the woodburning stove and tell jokes. And, incidentally, we order food. A week later the local whole-foods distribution truck arrives at the Community Church to unload boxes and pails and bags of food. Usually within an hour we divide the food according to our orders. For the investment of an hour of time unloading and a couple of hours ordering, I fulfill most of the month's food needs. Along with that bargain, I save money and get to know my neighbors. Not a bad investment all the way around.

To daily activists, the products we choose to bring back home with us—or leave on the shelf—have great impact on the health of our planet. I may not be able to see the effects of my actions immediately, but compounded with the decisions made by neighbors in community, state and country, my consumer habits are a powerful tool for change. According to James Lovelock, the scientist who developed the Gaia Hypothesis, ". . . there are so many things we do that are harmless in moderation, and malign only in excess. I find it helpful to think of the three deadly c's: cars, cattle, and chain saws. You don't have to be a puritan and ban them, just use them moderately." Lovelock offers a profound lesson that our ancestors knew well—moderation, nothing in excess. Take only what you need and leave the rest for someone else. That "someone else" may be you a few years from now, or your children, or your grandchildren. There is enough for everyone: enough to satisfy everyone's needs, but not necessarily their excessive wants. As true materialists, we can satisfy our needs with a minimum of goods and find a surplus of meaning in the process.

Part Three
What You Produce

Divine intervention usually comes in the form
of other human beings. We are the "magic,"
the "miracle," the unforeseen circumstance.
In our best moments, we are moved by the
breath of heaven here on Earth.

Eight

Garbage

"SMALL" DECISIONS ABOUT "trivial" things, I am learning, form the basis of peaceful co-existence in our house. We had a major confrontation about buying toilet paper for the house. Nothing is more disheartening than sitting on the toilet in the early morning, half-opening a sleepy eye, and seeing an empty cardboard tube in the toilet paper dispenser. The recycling corner in the kitchen is another bone of contention. Last week I blew up about someone indiscriminately dumping "garbage" in the paper recycling bag. An untrained eye might classify the paper collection as "trash." My housemate, though, has been in training for nearly eight months. Perhaps he is too old and set in his ways for paper-training.

Both issues, the toilet paper and the recycling corner, bring up one of our culture's most carefully suppressed topics—waste disposal. Trash. Garbage. Refuse. What we refuse to look at. What is "trash," anyhow? A few minutes ago the second layer of plastic on a loaf of bread was a welcome "convenience" that kept the bread fresh. Now, after the last slice has been eaten, that layer of plastic is suddenly a liability labeled "trash." Garbage is simply improperly placed waste. One woman's treasure is another's garbage. Food scraps, for example, can be a nuisance or a welcome addition to the compost heap. Garbage, quite simply, is a matter of perspective.

In the United States and throughout most of Europe, people will do almost anything to blind themselves to any sight of garbage. To avoid even glimpsing the byproducts of our lifestyle, we place waste in trash cans that are emptied into black plastic bags. The bags go into larger trash cans that are placed on the curb to be taken

away by the garbage truck. Many people are unwilling to sort
through the accumulation of discarded material to separate the
useful recyclables from the unrecoverable waste. The "garbage"
mentality is insidious—what I could hold in my hand five minutes
before lifting the lid is not "safe" or "clean" once it has passed
beyond the lip of the trash can.

Fortunately, some communities ask residents to separate garbage
for recycling. The garbage truck doubles as recycling pickup on
certain days of the week, saving residents from additional trips to
a local recycling center. Many people who were uninterested or
unable, such as shut-ins or elderly folks without cars, now recycle
glass, cans, and paper.

◆ ◆ ◆

*How often in our society do we dismiss our waste with an "out
of sight, out of mind" attitude? To increase your own awareness
of how much garbage you generate, try the following exercise.*

Beginning tomorrow morning, wear a clear plastic bag
attached to a belt around your waist. For the next week,
place every bit of garbage that you generate into bags.
Include food scraps, empty bottles and cans, food wrappers, tampons, gum wrappers, paper napkins, styrofoam
cups—anything that you normally would toss into the
trash can. At the end of the week, take note of what you
have gathered (you probably will have several bags by
this time). Separate the trash into recyclable and non-
recyclable items. What is the largest single contribution
to your garbage pile: plastic, fast food wrapping, glass
bottles? What could you easily eliminate? How many
items did you hesitate to buy or open this week, knowing
that you would have to carry the packaging with you?

◆ ◆ ◆

The exercise of carrying your garbage for a week should give
you a few clues about reducing garbage output. Some items, like
disposable cameras, are blatantly obvious candidates for permanent
removal from your shopping list. Others, like disposable diapers
or fast food fixes, may become occasional use items.

Not In My Back Yard

Thinking about carrying my garbage leads to some very valuable
information. How many items would I choose not to buy if I knew

that the offal would end up dangling from my waist? I wonder, too, how many toxic chemicals would be eliminated if the factory owners lived next to the dump site. Wendell Berry tells of the nuclear power magnates of Indiana placating local people about the dangers of nuclear power.

> A lady rose in the audience and asked the fifteen or twenty personages on the stage to tell us how many of them lived within the fifty-mile danger zone around Marble Hill (the proposed nuclear power plant). The question proved tactically brilliant, apparently shocking the personages on the stage, who were forced to give it the shortest, plainest answer of the evening: *Not one.* Not a single one of those well-paid, well-educated, successful, important men would need to worry about his family or his property in the event of a catastrophic mistake at Marble Hill.
>
> This story would be less interesting if it were unusual. My point, of course, is that it is not unusual. Some version of it is happening in this country virtually everywhere, virtually every day. Everywhere, every day, local life is being discomforted, disrupted, endangered, or destroyed by powerful people who live, or who are privileged to think they live, beyond the bad effects of their bad work.[1]

In the end, Public Service of Indiana did not build the Marble Hill nuclear power plant. In retrospect, they may be grateful. Some utility companies, including Dairyland Power Cooperative in Genoa, Wisconsin, have decided that burning coal produces cheaper energy than nuclear fission. They cannot, however, simply close the gates of the nuclear power facility and walk away. The plant still contains 33,300 cylinders of enriched uranium which continue to fission and generate heat. When the Genoa plant was constructed, the power company assumed that they would able to dispose of nuclear waste as easily as toxic chemicals—i.e., dig a hole, drop in barrels of waste, and cover with dirt. For twenty years, however, the government has failed to find a single state willing to accept nuclear wastes.

Matching Technologies with Needs

The difficulties of disposing of nuclear waste reinforce a lesson I learned while building a sweat lodge—a juxtaposition of technology that supports the universality of the teaching. A friend helped me build the lodge. We offered prayers and cut the birch tree, then stripped the limbs of their twigs. The cuttings became our lashing material that we wound around the boughs arched into a network of overlapping supports. The twigs dried into a tough binding that held the branches together. Thus far, we had relied solely on a saw, our knives, and the tree itself for construction materials. For the cover, however, we used old carpets and then a layer of discarded plastic tarps. To hold the plastic in place, we resorted to electrical tape bought at the local hardware store. "You see," said my friend Gunther, "as soon as we move to newer technology (the plastic tarp), we have to bind it with newer technology, too."

Nuclear power is the newest and most complicated energy production technology. No surprise, then, that it generates the most complicated form of waste. Complex technologies tend to produce complex problems as a byproduct. I cannot easily bind a plastic tarp with birch twigs. Similarly, I cannot dispose of nuclear waste the same way I would dump ashes from a woodburning stove. The easiest way to solve the problem of toxic wastes, though, is to not generate them in the first place. The same wisdom holds true for all types of garbage.

Question all of the household, garden, and hardware products you buy. Seek out your grandparents' wisdom. Ask them what they used to clean the house and laundry, to nourish and protect the garden. Research current information as well. Greenpeace publishes an excellent pamphlet, *Stepping Lightly on the Earth: Everyone's Guide to Toxics in the Home* (available from Greenpeace, 1436 U Street NW, Washington, DC 20009) which suggests many alternatives to common household cleaners. Debra Lynn Dadd has written two extremely informative guides, *Nontoxic and Natural* and *The Nontoxic Home* (both published by Jeremy P. Tarcher, Inc., Los Angeles). Check your library for additional sources.

Toxic Waste—Child's Play?

Plastics disposal presents many problems, but plastics production generates even more. Plastics factories emit many toxic effluents, and even children know that toxic wastes deserve special treatment. Teacher Barbara Lewis' fifth and sixth grade students at Jackson Elementary in Salt Lake City, Utah studied groundwater contamination from toxic wastes and then searched their own neighborhood for offending chemicals. They did not need to look very far; three blocks from the school they found 50,000 corroding barrels of toxic wastes. The mountain of barrels, often climbed by school children, had been leaking solvents, pesticides, coal tar, and other harmful chemicals for over forty years. Until the children discovered it, no one seemed to notice or care about the toxic chemical dump.

The children contacted the local health department, which was unresponsive. They countered by conducting their own survey of the industrial neighborhood, locating wells for the health department to take water samples, and informing local residents about the hazards of toxic wastes. Although the neighbors were unruffled by the children's activities, local reporters were impressed by the kids' enthusiasm. Students contacted the EPA, the landowner, and finally Mayor Palmer DePaulis, who promised to clean up the site within eighteen months.

The children's interest did not stop in their own back yard, however. They raised $2,000 to support other state cleanup projects, but the state health department told the students that the money legally could not be contributed to, or monitored by, the state. Therefore they wrote House Bill 199 to establish a state contributory Superfund that would help clean up abandoned toxic-waste sites. Wearing their best clothes, they lobbied in the Senate, handing out fliers with red crayon borders. The bill passed without a single dissenting vote. The students are continuing their environmental efforts, focusing now on raising money for trees. They remind potential contributors that trees inhale carbon dioxide and exhale oxygen, and one tree can save over sixty thousand dollars in pollution control over its lifespan of fifty years.

Perhaps the children's greatest lesson, beyond the techniques of lobbying, is the knowledge of self-empowerment. They have learned that their voices, their action and their concerns really matter.[2]

Ms. Lewis' students truly inspire me—empowered, effective children grow into empowered, active adults. I believe in the empowerment of children. One danger I see in the story, however, is the tendency to look to our children to save our world: "The next generation, the children, are our hope for the future." Frankly, I'm not content to wait for my unborn children to take action. I've invested too much time and energy in "growing up" to lightly pass the baton to a younger generation. I'm barely grown myself, and I'm not willing to bet on unripened sprouts to take on the job of mature trees. Hoping for our children to save the world is a cop-out. In fact, the reverse should be our focus—I am responsible to save the world, or at least some of it, for my children. "Our children are our hope for the future"? NO. We are the hope for our children's future.

Recycling

Each of our consumer decisions has an impact on the mountains of garbage awaiting disposal at the local landfill or incinerator. If each of us practiced the three "R's" (Reducing, Recycling, and Reusing), we could substantially reduce garbage output. The United States ranks as the most trash-happy nation on the planet. During World War II, Americans recycled 43 percent of the paper they used.[3] My mother also remembers having to return an empty tube of toothpaste, made of metals valuable to "the war effort," before purchasing a new one. Today, however, Americans recycle only 11 percent of the 140.8 million tons of garbage generated each year, most of which is attributed to beverage container deposits.[4] Do we truly need wars to activate our best resource management instincts?

Each of us can help reduce garbage output by voluntarily reducing our intake and participating in recycling programs where they exist.

Reusing Resources

In addition to reducing and recycling household products, consider reusing items as well. Living in India, I saw how every scrap of material habitually discarded in the West was carefully saved and reshaped into something useful. Villagers know how to cut and pound metal cans into an infinite variety of shapes to repair anything from a roof to a bicycle. Pieces of paper and cardboard form the walls of shanty houses on the outskirts of Bombay. Nothing lies fallow; everything has a use.

A friend traveling in Latin America described the same resourcefulness among the people there. Walking along the streets of a Mexican city, he stopped to watch a vendor cooking a meal. The cook squatted over an open fire, stirring the food steaming in a "pot"—made from a car's hubcap.

So when the threads on the sofa begin to wear thin, consider recovering the cushions or investing in an afghan. If you really don't need two sets of metal mixing bowls, give one to a neighbor or the Goodwill. Repair the clock radio instead of discarding it. Challenge the insurance company when they tell you the car is "totalled" in an accident. One friend fought for several months before the insurance company agreed to pay repair costs which they claimed exceeded the value of the car. Keep in mind that insurance companies usually repair and resell your "defunct" car for a decent profit.

Sharing

In addition to the three "R's" (Reducing, Recycling and Reusing), remember the Big "S" (Sharing) as well. Sharing is the foundation of most native cultures. Indigenous peoples had to share in order to survive. Young children are quickly acculturated in the art of giving and receiving. A friend who has lived and worked with traditional aboriginal people for over ten years described his cultural relearning. In the desert camps, anyone is free to use a tool left unattended. Someone might borrow a hammer and then return it, or pass it on to someone else. "When I was visiting some friends in the city one time, after I'd been living in the (aboriginal) camps for awhile," he told me, "I picked up some things that no one was using that I needed and took them with me. It wasn't until later I realized those people, in their society, call it stealing."

Sharing forges community bonds and cultivates trust among neighbors. Distributing the bounty of your garden ensures that excess food will be used and provides an opportunity to chat with neighbors and perhaps initiate friendships that will weather many changing seasons. Tools and gardening implements can be shared among several neighbors, especially occasional-use items that otherwise would be duplicated in each household. How many cider presses, for example, does one suburban neighborhood need? My father dusts off his cider press each autumn and organizes a cider-pressing party. On a crisp October afternoon, neighbors bring baskets full of apples, harvested from the trees growing in their back yards, and feed them into the press. After a potluck dinner, each family takes home a share of cider commensurate with the bushels of apples they brought.

Garbage In, Garbage Out

Evaluate the media lines coming into your home, those umbilical cords connecting you to the news and blues of the outside world. How often do you actually read the paper from cover to cover? Do you buy an entire Sunday paper simply for the joy of reading *Doonesbury* and *Peanuts* in color? Each Sunday edition of the *New York Times* consumes 75,000 trees. Go out and count the number of trees you can see from your front door. If you live in the middle of an expanse of concrete, go to the nearest park. Count how many trees you see. Now think of 75,000 trees. Imagine how many acres those trees would cover. That expanse of forest is chopped, ground and mixed with dioxins so that you and I can read the comics and the *New York Times Book Review*—maybe—before dumping the entire two-pound package of newsprint in the trash. Consider sharing the Sunday *Times* with neighbors; perhaps three or four households can read one edition. How many magazine subscriptions do you receive, and how many do you actually read? How many weekly news magazines do you actually need to keep abreast of world news? Ram Dass spoke of spending six months with his guru in an isolated area of India. Upon his return to the U.S., he was anxious to read the newspapers and magazines that had accumulated in his mailbox. "I really wanted to know what had been happening in the world," he said. "Well, in one day I caught up on six months of news." The audience erupted in peals of laughter. "Do you know how many hours up 'til then I had spent reading the news every day?"

Ken Carey, author of *Starseed Transmissions* and several other books, describes his own seven-year media fast. He and his wife agreed that they wanted to move out of the city and live on a farm, to provide a healthy environment for their children. They also wanted to cultivate their own inner wisdom, and they identified the media—in the form of television, radio, newspapers, and magazines—as the major source of distraction. The "voice of the nation" had drowned out their own inner voice. For seven years they lived and worked on a midwestern farm, tending their young children and their gardens, doing carpentry work, and making occasional trips into town. "During those seven years," says Carey, "we did hear all of the important news. We'd go into town and hear people talking about the latest arms agreements, or the presidential elections, or the death of a great actor. I realized that we were getting news the way people did a century before—information spread across the nation, from town to town and neighbor to neighbor. So we were never really completely cut off."[5]

I offer these views not so much as a call to eliminate all information channels, but rather as a reminder to select wisely the amount and type of news you want to receive. In fact, certain age sectors of the U.S. population need to read more news. Today's young Americans are alarmingly uninformed about current affairs, an inexcusable condition in our increasingly complex world society.

In these times, information is equated with power. We have "evolved" from using iron implements to wielding nuclear arms. Today, the power of the bomb has been overshadowed by the power of information, the facts, figures, and concepts that weave the fabric of our minds. Power is moving from the realm of tangibles—how many hoes, factories, intercontinental ballistic missiles—to the realm of intangibles—how many facts, concepts, contacts, computer networks. The amount of information available for mental consumption literally staggers the mind. Our Western linear mental framework quickly overloads, fouled by the conflicting tangle of details.

Evolution of the Mind

I am reminded of the wisdom of an excellent clarinet teacher who continually stretches his students' capabilities. He assigns etudes just beyond their current grasp, and moves on to the next before the first is mastered. One day an exasperated student asked why the teacher kept assigning more difficult exercises before he had mastered the previous one. The teacher smiled and turned the pages back to an earlier etude. "Try it now," he said. The student effortlessly played the etude he had struggled with a few weeks before. "You see now?" asked the teacher. "If I stayed with an exercise until you perfected it, you would not learn as quickly. I want to keep stretching you, extending the limits of what you think you can do. When you move on to another level, you automatically absorb the previous lessons."

Perhaps as a society we are undergoing a similar teaching. The increasing glut of information challenges us to expand our minds, to absorb knowledge more quickly, to think in wholes instead of in limited, linear frameworks.

The left hemisphere processes bits of information one at a time, in sequence; pays attention to detail (a straggling hair, for instance); defines cause and effect; relies on previously established codes and organized information; and divides the world into identifiable pieces. The right brain processes many bits of information all at once, creating a simultaneous, complex image; perceives the whole (the entire face); sees correspondences; transforms into new patterns; unites and connects information.

In a culture heavily dependent on "left brain functions," we quickly overload with information, adding more stress to an already harried lifestyle. Jeffrey Davidson, a time-attitude consultant, identifies five "mega-realities" that exacerbate the feeling of being out of control of time and information. The first reality is "living on top of each other" in urban centers where everyone is trying to do the same thing or go to the same place at the same time. Secondly, Davidson renames this era the "Over-Information Age." We are glutted with more information each day than we can assimilate easily in a lifetime. The third mega-reality is the media, who convince us that their information is vital to our lives, absolutely necessary to keep in touch with the world. The fourth is the deluge of paper that threatens to bury our waking lives. Every new information system promises the replacement of the old, but in truth we *gain* rather than replace technologies. The flow of paper accelerates and accumulates: We now have newspapers, magazines, books, fax machines, computer printouts, direct mail as well as electronic information: radio, television, and telephones. We are drowning in words. Finally, the fifth mega-reality is *too much* choice. We are overwhelmed, glutted with more choices and information than we possibly can assimilate.

How to break out of the "paper/information cage"? "We simply don't need most of the information we get," says Davidson. "Become a discerning consumer of news and a discriminating keeper of paper." He recommends questioning all routines. Refer to your own life vision. Examine your priorities. Perhaps that first morning hour could be better spent in quiet contemplation, accessing a completely different field of "information." Reserve time to be in wild, undisturbed areas. The Earth's cycles remind us of how time passes: in balanced patterns that we cannot control, such as the movement of light from night to day or the passage of the seasons. Being "outdoors," without the shielding, numbing influence of buildings, also stimulates all of our senses and brings us into balance, into relationship with the Earth, ultimately our greatest source of information and teaching.

Finally, throw away "paper crutches," the clutter of paper that clogs filing cabinets and camouflages desks. Be bold. Recycle bank statements from ten years ago. Sell or give away books that you haven't opened since high school. Open your mail over the recycling bin. I've stopped even opening a lot of unsolicited mail; I simply toss it directly into the paper recycling bag. You can reduce "junk mail" by writing or calling the Direct Marketing Association (DMA, 6 E. 43rd St, New York, NY 10017) and asking them to remove your name from mailing lists. The DMA will add your name to their next quarterly "do not mail" list sent to catalogue companies, and to some sweepstakes and charitable organizations. Within a few months you should receive a significantly smaller volume of junk in your mail box. To stop unsolicited pornographic mail, fill out Form 2201 at your post office.[6]

Are we being glutted with information to expand our minds, to open doors to that 90 percent of the brain that researchers tell us lies dormant? Perhaps, like the clarinet student, we are being "overloaded" so that we can make the leap to the next level and apply all of the previous input. I can no longer absorb the mass of information in a linear, left-brain fashion. To keep up with the explosion of knowledge, I must absorb through the right brain as well, reconnecting the shattered bits of logical thought into a united world view.

Internal Garbage

Choose your information wisely, whether it comes through television, radio, or newspaper. Just as you carefully choose the appliances that fill your home, ensuring that they are durable, energy-efficient, and useful, judiciously choose the contents of your inner environment as well. "Garbage in, garbage out," the computer technicians teach us. Likewise, a mind filled with garbage—worry, prejudice, fear, poorly digested information—will generate garbage. Be sure to give yourself silent spaces during the day to order information into a related kaleidoscope of meaning. Otherwise, the unrelated facts and figures accumulate like dust in the mind, a source of internal garbage that must be discarded. Meaning relates the seemingly disjointed "factoids" that fill our days and roots the mass of unrelated data in our own internal landscape.

No matter how objective I pretend to be, the truth is all that I perceive must first pass through the lens of my own mind. I must digest, assimilate, and excrete my "mental food," just as the stomach and intestines process, absorb, and discard the food that I eat. Not all information needs to be assimilated into the "bones" of my mind; some thoughts, in fact, behave more like toxic waste than nourishing food. How then to discard of the errant, destructive thoughts in our awareness?

◆   ◆   ◆

Below is an exercise from Caroline Myss, author of The Creation of Health. *Use this tool whenever you identify what she calls a "thought capsule" (thought form) that does not serve you.*

Sit in a comfortable position and close your eyes. Take a few deep breaths and allow your body to grow heavy and relaxed. Now identify your greatest fear, the most terrifying imagined (or real) situation in your life, the circumstance you most dread. Acknowledge the emotion impersonally and simply observe your feelings. Say to yourself, "I am not this emotion, I am simply observing it."

Observe this emotion's power, how it makes you feel, how it controls your body. Notice the effect on your solar plexus, stomach, shoulders, back, throat, heart. Feel its impact on your body. Remind yourself again, "I am not this emotion, I am observing the power of this fear in motion, and I am choosing to let it move through me rather than attaching to me. This is simply an emotional current going through me, not attaching to me."

Take a deep breath, and move the emotion through your body with your breath. Imagine your body as porous and permeable. Use the power of your breath, your *prana,* to push the emotional current out, like wind moving through a cheesecloth.

Now mentally replace it with a powerful thought form. Say to yourself, "I am stronger than that thought. I release it. It does not control me. This feeling is simply an emotional current and does not control me. I release it."

In its place create an image of exactly what you want. Immediately hold the image there. See what you want—a harmonious family life, a partner, a clean environment, cooperative co-workers, a supportive community, financial and/or material support for yourself, whatever it is that you deeply desire in your life. Plug in your vision.

Say to yourself, "I choose to honor this vision. I align my thoughts and emotions with this vision." Create this thought form inside yourself. Then ask each thought form in your mind, body and spirit that interferes with the creation of your vision to enter your awareness so that you can see it and release it. Invoke every thought, every fear that interferes with the creation of the vision of yourself as a whole and happy and loving being.

As you take the next breath, ask for the courage to see these fears so that they can come to you directly and not through your cell tissue. Unacknowledged, unreleased fears take residence in the body and create disease. Ask to see the fears immediately, before they express themselves through your physical body.

When you are ready, take a deep breath, become aware of your body and the place where you are sitting. Stretch your arms over your head and gently open your eyes.

♦ ♦ ♦

This is a form of visualization. Be aware that it has "post-traumatic effects," similar to taking homeopathic medicine; a small dose has a large impact. You have asked your unconscious to produce information about all of the areas that block you from fulfilling your vision. If you want to practice this technique, remember that you are invoking the information and experiences that will help you identify your blockages. Information will come. Pay attention to the subtle as well as the blatant movements of your life. Note thoughts, dreams, and "chance" encounters. Take time both morning and evening to listen inside. Close your eyes and ask, "What am I feeling, what am I fearing, what's coming up?" Pay attention to data from your interior. You have invited this information; the least you can do is pay attention to it once it has arrived! Welcome the new insights. Continue to say, "Speak to me. What fears control me? What am I working with?" Every single time your fears come up, reduce them to wind through a cheesecloth and send them out of your reality. Send them out. Don't let them take up residence. Get them out, and ask for anything and everything that is affiliated with them to come out. Use your breath to send them out. (Adopted from a talk by Caroline Myss.)

Becoming aware of and breathing out destructive beliefs, using my own breath/life force to move them out of my physical body, is a much healthier alternative. I can safely release those patterns that no longer serve my health. Again, like the toxic materials brought into the home, the best preventative for a healthy mind is not to buy the garbage in the first place. Keep an open mind, fill it with healthful information, digest and assimilate it wisely. Share the good fruits of your internal labor in the form of songs and poems and thoughtful discussions with neighbors. Share your internal peace in the form of healthy relationships, an attitude of reverence for life, and spontaneous, hearty laughter.

Cleanliness, both inner and outer, is next to godliness. The road to cleanliness, however, is littered with garbage: the things we "refuse" to look at, the "refuse" of our lives. Take heart—all of the superfluous elements of our lives have the potential to become rich compost, a fertile bed for new growth. Legs do not become strong from years of sitting in one place; they become strong by climbing mountains. So, too, a human cannot strengthen without challenge. Are our legs strong enough to climb the mountain of garbage awaiting us? Our arms limber enough to turn the compost of our discarded waste? Our hearts open enough to let go and forgive? Our souls flexible enough to change? We have the choice of transforming misplaced garbage into useful resources—bombs into plowshares, rotting vegetables into fertile soil, and damaged relationships into healthy families and communities.

Nine

Relationships: Home Is Where the Heart Is

"ALL THE FAME IN THE WORLD will never warm my bed." The thought came to me as I sat in front of my computer one day, sweating out an article for the local paper. I had spent the previous week laboring over the story, collecting data and transcribing interview tapes and struggling to meld facts with an artful writing style. Intent on developing my career, I had chosen to overlook personal relationships in my life. Most of my days were spent sequestered in my office, although I occasionally ran errands or visited friends in the evening. I wanted to establish a firm financial foundation so that I could avoid manipulative power games with a partner. I had to admit to myself, too, that I needed a successful career to boost my self-esteem so that I could relate to a lover as a whole person, not as a half-baked personality in need of constant reassurance. Sitting in front of the computer, though, with an early spring breeze teasing the mound of unkempt papers on my desk, I remembered that money was not the primary currency in a relationship—the basic tender in any sort of relationship exchange is love.

"All the fame in the world will never warm my bed." Diplomas and awards offer no heat—they sit in cold leather binders on my bookshelf. Books, magazine articles, and cassette tapes, the measure of my "success," would crumple under the weight of my limbs if I tucked them under the covers. Trophies gather dust on the dresser or lie wrapped in tissue paper in the closet. Accolades spoken from a podium disperse like pollen on the first spring-warmed breezes. Fame is ephemeral—it cannot nourish me day-to-day.

Only flesh and blood and bone will warm my bed—and heart. When all other outer measurements of recognition fall away, all the yardsticks to assess the progress of my journey, I will have only relationships, the intangible connections that bond my life with another's, to judge the wealth of my life. My world will be richer or poorer according to the presence or lack of love in my life.

Taking a Stand—Without Knocking Someone Down

Recently I was forced to ponder my relationship to silence. Living at the Findhorn Foundation, we often included periods of silence in any sort of gathering or celebration. Silence created the possibility for a group of very diverse people to join together, to approach spirit in their own way, without the potentially divisive labeling of the experience. But in many other situations, silence was equated with "death." Were there areas of my life in which I endured a deathly silence?

The night before I left for my college reunion, I had a long discussion with my parents. In essence, my mother shared her pain and frustration that I had chosen not to reveal certain aspects of my life to them, but had written about them in a book that was about to be published. She asked that I edit out the sections she found offensive. The penalty: she would pretend that the book did not exist. "And it will cause a great rift between us that I do not think will be easily healed."

Over the next few days I felt queasy, aching in my solar plexus, panicked by the thought of losing my parents' love. I knew they would still love me, but they would no longer respect and approve of me. I studied my dreams and talked with friends who simply listened without giving advice. "What I'm hearing," said one friend, "is that you want to publish the book and maintain a good relationship with your parents. Do you believe you can do both, have a 'both/and' solution instead of an 'either/or' one that will make both of you happy?"

I had forgotten that basic tenet of conflict resolution. "Winning" an argument never settles the underlying issues. Both parties lose in the end. When I arrived at my parents' house, I asked my mother if she believed a "both/and" solution was possible. "It's a nice idea," she said, "but things don't always work out the way you want them to."

At that point I turned inside myself, asking what "being true to myself" meant in this situation. One of my basic values is to speak honestly about my life. Another is to maintain loving relationships with my parents. The two values seemed diametrically opposed. For much of my life I had altered plans to placate their distress over my "moral" standards. Perhaps the lesson in this situation was to take a stand for who I was, to speak my truth at last, to break the silence that had maintained my parents' incomplete image of me.

I pondered and prayed. Finally, I chose to keep the sections they found offensive. But, to my discredit, I did not tell them of my choice. I let two weeks slide by until the editor's message arrived that the book was at the printers. By default, it seemed, the sections would stay in place. I had made a choice to speak, to break the silence surrounding certain areas of my life, but I still played the victim with my parents. I was unwilling to address them directly, to inform them of my choices.

Playing the Victim

Victimization nullifies my ability to connect with people. I can grovel and blame and manipulate, but I cannot truly bond. As I learned with Edith, the German woman in the EarthLove workshop, victimization has its own perverted sort of power, just as oppression does.

Many people left the White House in Abraham Lincoln's time saying, "Well, I certainly could be President!" Lincoln had the ability to make anyone feel like his equal. He truly believed in equality, as expressed in the U.S. Constitution. Lincoln allowed no one to stand beneath him, and conversely, he allowed no one to stand above him. In his eyes, we were all created equal, and he chose to enact that belief in his own life. As a student, I spoke passionately about equality. I believed in equality in my mind, but had not yet translated that belief into the daily experience of my life.

While working with the EarthLove game, I was challenged to look at my own pattern of self-victimization. While moving through the human realm, I drew a card that read, "Putting someone on a pedestal gives away your power and denies intimacy." I knew immediately that the card referred to a relationship with a man whom I had placed on a pedestal by exaggerating his gifts and denying my own. I had placed him on a pedestal and yet raged inside because he was unattainable. I had made him unreachable and blamed him for the distance.

Later that night I asked in meditation for my guide to help me understand the dynamics of placing people on pedestals. We walked into a garden, and she climbed onto a marble pillar and stood up.

"How do you feel now?" she asked. All I could see were her knees. Instead of communicating with her face-to-face, I was speaking face-to-foot. She was not a person to me, but rather a pair of knees with an unreachable head and heart looming somewhere far above. I didn't have a relationship with her; I was preoccupied with her knees. At first I felt silly but then grew angry at her separation.

"Come on up," she said, pointing to a column nearby. I clambered up the marble pillar and stood facing her. We were now on the same level, seeing eye-to-eye, but we couldn't reach each other. In fact, we couldn't move at all. We were marooned in mid-air on our stone perches.

"How do you feel now?" she asked.

"Frustrated. I can't move at all. I have to stay in one place."

She smiled patiently. After a few moments she slid down the column and motioned for me to follow. When I stood beside her, she wrapped her arm around my waist, and we strolled along the garden path. "Now how do you feel?" she asked.

"Relieved. I feel like I'm relating to you as a person. I can feel you, touch you, interact with you. I like having my feet on the ground. Two people on a pedestal are no better than one. I couldn't reach you then, either. I can feel you in my heart now, like a sister spirit. I like you much better this way."

My guide was teaching me how to take a stand—without knocking down other people; how to stand beside them and walk side by side. Keep your feet on the ground. If you take on "airs," you may find yourself marooned far above the ground, elevated but unable to move. Approach others from a solid foundation of self-esteem and love.

When I approach my parents from a base of love, my "stand" becomes inclusive. Yes, I want to assert myself and I want to maintain our love. Can I be in my power without denying your own? Love *includes* people. Being "in one's power" without love is divisive. Loveless power is like muscle without connective tissue—it stands alone, lacking the bonding needed to effectively express its strength.

Forgiveness

Edith Stauffer, in her book *Unconditional Love and Forgiveness,* points out that resentments and grudges that I hold toward other people not only block the flow of love to that person, they also block the flow of love and wisdom into myself. She uses a term from Aramaic literature, *naphsha* (pronounced NOFFsha), to describe "our connection with the Source of life, with that higher intelligence that directs the orderly flow of all life. . . . Naphsha is in contact with all universal laws and communicates these laws to the personal self. The messages will register if the personal self is open and receptive."[1] Those messages might come in the form of feelings, sudden insights, or dreams. When I choose to ignore naphsha, when I am in conflict with the source of greater wisdom in my life, I experience stress, anxiety, uneasiness, warning dreams, and discontent. When I separate myself from other people through anger, resentment, or fear, I shut down the flow of love and understanding between us. When I block my love for another person, I halt my own energy as well. I cannot disconnect myself from any aspect of creation without unplugging myself as well. I stand apart from others; I stand apart from myself. Each inevitably leads to the other.

How can I re-establish my connection with Self and others? Forgiveness is the key. For years I considered forgiveness a weak, passive act. My only role model was the Virgin Mary, who seemed weak and ineffective. Even Jesus had been bleached blond and softened into a dewy-eyed, suffering wimp in the hands of the Church. "Forgive them, Father, they know not what they do," he uttered from the cross. If ever I needed the image of a victim, I had it. Or so I thought.

Soon after arriving in Scotland, I participated in a workshop called "The Game of Transformation." Unlike Monopoly or other board games, the purpose of this game is self-examination and transformation. I wanted to examine my blockages to creativity. When I entered the Love Realm, I drew a card that read, "You are a midwife for Forgiveness." Immediately I thought of my ex-fiancé John. Our separation years before had plunged me into the deepest, longest dark night of the soul I have ever known. For months I tried to meditate on release, to surround him and his new love with light, but the effort reduced me to tears every time.

In time, John and I were able to patch together a loving friendship. I knew as I looked at the game card in my hand that I had not generated the love that allowed me to forgive him. Love loved through me; I simply served as midwife for its expression. The love had always been there, but I had blocked its flow.

Well, I told myself, I know the meaning of that card. However, I didn't know that the game has a way of continuing after the board is packed away, becoming real in one's life. Two nights later I lay in my bed, wracked with the same pain I had known years before. I went for a walk with a friend the next day, still agonized by the terrible weight in my heart.

"Look," said my friend, "are you willing to try something with me?" I nodded my head. He continued, "I used these three steps to forgive someone who suddenly left me. The first step is to stop seeing yourself as a victim. Look at your own part in ending the relationship, take responsibility for your role. Second is to forgive that person. Speak it, write it, communicate that forgiveness to them. And third, do something for that person to express your love. I made a collage for this woman of all the animals I knew she loved. I left it in her room and never said a word about it. Do you think you can do those three steps?"

Engulfed as I was in the all too familiar sea of pain, I hesitated. We sat down on a hill overlooking Findhorn Bay. "Yes," I said finally. "I can forgive. I can let go of this pain."

That night, for the first time in years, while composing a long, forgiving letter to John, I felt a rush of love for him. After years of blaming him for our separation, I saw my own contribution to the relationship's demise, and that awareness uncovered another level of our love. "Love is never wasted," I often tell friends undergoing a difficult separation. "Love continues, love endures. You never waste the energy of love. It always returns."

Completing Relationships

A couple years later I experienced another level of letting go. In meditation I saw all of my former lovers before me. I was sitting on a wall built across a dirt road with a cord connecting my solar plexus to each of theirs. "You must let go of these connections," my guide instructed, "before you can move on in your life."

I imagined myself jumping off the back side of the wall and trying to walk away from them but realized that the cords would tangle hopelessly. If I pulled hard, the places where the cords were inserted might tear, leaving gaping, bloody holes. No, I could not move on with all of these dangling connections. I must sever them once and for all.

"Don't yank or cut them," warned the guide. "Unscrew them. That's the safest way."

I looked down and saw that the cords were indeed screwed into fixtures embedded in my flesh. One by one I unscrewed them and watched the cords drop to the ground below me. When my abdomen was completely free of fixtures, I stood on the wall and gazed at the assemblage below me. "I love you all," I said, tears welling in my eyes, "and I have to get on with my life now." I jumped from the wall, unencumbered, and continued to walk alone.

I learned from that experience the importance of completing relationships on an energy level. Connections from heart to heart do not drain life force, but attachments to the lower chakras (energy centers in the body) siphon vital energy. In addition to grieving, forgiving, and letting go, I also need to detach my life energy from theirs. Again, this does not mean denying love. I simply need to "clear the channels" before I can open myself to new relationships and new experiences. Nurturing too many old connections depletes my present energy sources.

♦ ♦ ♦

Here's an exercise for completing relationships.

Begin by gathering all of the material objects that remind you of the person you are separating from. Pick them up, remember, let memories and tears flow freely. Grieve for the loss of this person in the inner circle of your life. Tears, like rain, cleanse the air (mind) and nourish the soil (body).

When the flow of tears diminishes, sit in a comfortable position and close your eyes. Take a few deep breaths and concentrate on your breathing. Bring yourself into the here and now. See your former partner before you. Allow yourself to journey back in time, remembering both the joy and the pain associated with your relationship. Simply observe the passage of events, like watching a movie roll before your eyes. Note both of your contributions to the development of your relationship. Ask yourself, "How did my actions support or undermine our connection?" Resolve to take the wisdom gleaned from your answers into your next relationship.

Take a few moments to acknowledge how you would have preferred to be treated. Acknowledge that this is your preference, your expectation of "how things should be."

Focus on your stomach, your solar plexus. Anger and resentment often pool in this area. Visualize yourself drawing light or clean, pure water up through the base of your spine and then passing it out the solar plexus. Feel the light or water sweeping away all of the anger and any other emotional garbage littering that area of your body. Note whether or not there are any "cords" still connecting you to the other person. Unscrew any cords that are still attached. If you feel congested in other areas of the body, such as your heart, abdomen, or throat, pass the cleansing water or light through those areas as well. Identify and release the cords in any other area of your body.

Finally, visualize a stream of pure white light pouring into the top of your head and cascading down through your entire body. Feel any remaining debris being washed down and out through your feet (or the base of your spine if you are sitting cross-legged).

Visualize yourself taking a step back from the other person. Acknowledge them for both their strengths and weaknesses. Ask that their life may continue unencumbered, without any entangling strings from you. Set that person, as well as yourself, free.

When you are ready, bring your attention back to the place where you are sitting. Take a deep breath, stretch, open your eyes. Take one object from the pile that you have gathered (preferably something biodegradable) and symbolically release it—take it to the ocean or a stream and cast it into the waters, asking that each of you, like this object, may move on with the flow of life. Or give it away to a friend, recycling center, or the Goodwill.

◆   ◆   ◆

Recently I sorted through all the old letters I had saved, dating from the time I was six years old. I placed them in stacks according to their writer, and then began to unfurl the long-folded pages. The largest stack was from one of my dearest high school friends. I had not heard from her in years.

My first impulse was to try to find her current address, to write, to re-establish connections. But I had the same feeling with each letter I opened. As I sat surrounded by stacks of letters, I realized suddenly that I have a finite amount of attention that I can give to relationships. I have only so many hours in the day to write letters, make phone calls, take long walks. My friends are scattered around the planet. So many people have passed in and out of my life that I have to trust that those who take permanent residence in my heart will stay in touch. Trying to tend too many fires disperses my energy. The reality, sad as it may be, is that I must pick and choose the handful of friends to whom I can devote my time and energy. Reluctantly I drop letters into the recycling bin. Others I reserve in a "get in touch!" pile. These people parade through my dreams. I reach out to hold their hands. You still live in my heart, and will always find a welcome home.

I sort through old boxes filled with books and dusty soccer trophies and Barbie dolls. As I discard an item, I think, "I am letting go. I bring all of the energy from my past into the present." Living either in the past or the future drains energy from the most power-ful time—the present. Here and now is when change happens, when transformation occurs. I want to bring the best of my past with me and then move on, unfettered. Healthy relationships re-quire that I weave time together, bringing past, present, and future into a pleasing design. I carry the triumphs and errors of the past, I am with you here and now, I have my vision as a compass for the future.

Conflict Resolution

Letters generally recall the sweetest of times—or perhaps I have saved only the pleasant ones. What of the times when I seethe with rage over a mishandled financial agreement, argue with my family, fume with a lover? Edith Stauffer identifies these periods of disharmony as being out of touch with naphsha. How do I return to harmony when my gut is churning and I want to move across the country to avoid someone?

Hawk Pope, principal Chief of the Shawnee Nation United Rem-nant Band, reminds us that leaving a problem does not solve it:

If you have brothers and sisters, if you live in a family, you can't undo the fact that your brother is your brother. Maybe after you're grown up, maybe after you've gone away, but while you're under the same roof, you're gonna have to figure some way to live with him, no matter what he is like.

It's the same thing in a tribe, except there never comes a time when you can move away from it. So you have to figure some way to change—yourself a little, and the offending person a lot. You have to work on it. You can't move away from it. You can't just leave it. That's the easy solution. But it destroys a society. That kind of solution, easy as it is, destroys a society. It destroys the culture. You can't have a society that continues through thousands of years if you keep moving away from your problems. This is what the Europeans have consistently done for thousands of years. They came to this continent to move away from their problems. And brought them along.[2]

As a Western European person, I have acquired few tools to work with conflict. Acknowledging discord automatically means resolving it, generally through taking action: fighting, shouting, threatening or leaving. I was taught either to "turn the other cheek" and leave, or fight back. I knew no middle road.

Danaan Parry, a long-time worker with conflict resolution, teaches that "Conflict IS." Our initial duty is not to fix or alter or mend a conflict; it is to acknowledge conflict. Simply observing a situation as it really is can be liberating. We no longer expend energy in projecting how things should or could be, or trying to bend the situation to fit expectations. When we allow ourselves to see the true picture, we are more likely to take appropriate action.

During a seminar one participant verbally attacked Danaan. "I'm bored," he shouted. "I could lead this workshop. I mean, hell, anybody could do what you are doing."

The other participants sat stunned, looking from one to the other, waiting for Danaan's reaction. "And you think I'm responsible for your boredom?" asked Danaan.

"Yeah. You're making me bored."

Danaan nodded and continued talking.

I felt terribly uncomfortable. Other people shifted and coughed. Someone finally interrupted Danaan. "Aren't you going to say something to this man?" she asked. "Aren't you going to clear it?"

"Clear what?" asked Danaan.

"Well, the conflict. I feel very uncomfortable sitting here," she said.

Danaan smiled. "One of the first lessons in conflict resolution is that conflict is. It simply is. I don't need to fix it or change it. Conflict is a state of being. In our society we haven't learned to just be with conflict. We always want to fix it, make it go away. That's why conflicts between nations are such a big deal. We scramble to fix them instead of acknowledging that we are in conflict. So we are in conflict," he said, nodding to the man. "That's all there is to it."

Suddenly the tension left my shoulders. I gave myself permission to listen to the lecture without worrying about the other participants' response. For the first time, I gave myself permission to acknowledge conflict without the need to "fix" it.

Danaan offered a model of conflict, reminding us that all models are simply constructs to keep us occupied until "the truth" finally dawns. He drew a triangle and labeled the corners "conflict," "intensity," and "intimacy." "Most people," he explained, "move from intensity through conflict to arrive at intimacy." His finger traced two sides of the triangle. "They need conflict to be intimate, like a couple who has a fight so they can make up and go to bed early, all of that. You can, though, choose to move from intensity directly to intimacy." His finger moved along one side of the triangle, connecting the corners labeled "intimacy" and "intensity." "You don't have to go through conflict to arrive at intimacy."

The man who had confronted Danaan earlier raised his hand. His eyes were filled with tears. "That's what my wife and I have always done," he said. "Actually both my wives. One finally left me. And now I realize that's what I was doing earlier. I wanted to feel close to you, so I picked a fight. That's the only way I know how to be close with people."

Codependency

Using conflict to create intimacy will not solve family problems, nor will moving to the other side of the continent resolve difficult situations. In fact, we are likely to establish new relationships that mirror the old problems. New addresses, new faces, same garbage. The wife who divorces an alcoholic soon marries another compulsive drinker, or gambler, or sex addict. Unless she changes inside and reorients the magnet of her life, she will continue to attract the same situations.

What draws us into the same destructive situations over and over? Melodie Beattie, author of *Codependent No More,* describes the behavior and attitude patterns that keep both addict and support person "hooked" in a destructive relationship. Codependents are so absorbed in other people's problems that they are unable to identify and solve their own. Codependents are so deeply concerned about taking care of other people that they forget how to take care of themselves. They try to control events and people because their own internal and external world seems so hopelessly out of control. Codependents feel responsible for everything because the people around them take responsibility for so little. They suffer from low self-esteem, repression, obsession, denial, dependency, and poor communication. They have trouble setting boundaries, saying "no," and making decisions. Codependents are like marionettes, and everyone else pulls their strings. They dance and move according to the whims of other people, even though they try desperately to control everyone else's movements.

The analogy of the puppet provides some clues about how to abandon codependent behavior. Instead of trying to control the people pulling your strings, disengage the strings. Walk on your own. Identify what you want in your life instead of fulfilling other people's desires. Set about fulfilling your own life vision; you may need to search for a period to find it, since other people have provided guidelines for so long. Stop taking care of other people and take care of yourself. You will have a lot more energy to fulfill your own visions, and you may find that the "helpless" people you have supported for so long miraculously stand and walk on their own. Perhaps your "strong," controlling presence excused them from taking responsibility for themselves.

After reading Beattie's book, I sense that almost everyone suffers from some degree of codependency. I see my own codependency in my attempts to rescue not only people, but also the planet. (If I'm going to fulfill a pattern, I'll fulfill it in a big way.) I have the woes of a whole planet to fulfill my sense of being needed, of being a model caretaker. I can easily expend all of my energy trying to "rescue" the planet, just as a codependent pours time and energy into rescuing an alcoholic.

The problem with the scenario, however, is that when I identify the planet as "sick" and in need of rescuing, I reinforce the belief that the Earth is ailing. "I don't know what all of this talk is about healing the Earth," said one native man. "As far as I'm concerned, the Earth is still healing me." His comment does not deny the pollution and degradation of the planet. He simply puts into perspective my role as a human on planet Earth. Who am I to take credit for healing the Earth? A good doctor knows that the patient heals him- or herself, either aided by the treatment or despite it. Yes, I may be able to facilitate the climate for the Earth to heal itself, but I cannot claim responsibility for the cure. The most helpful action I can take is to stop destructive human behaviors. But there I am, caught in the trap of trying to control other people. Ultimately I need to follow my own vision for a healthy planet, fulfill it in my day-to-day life, and allow other people to choose to join me if they want to.

Cultural Awareness

"There are many ways to love and many ways to live . . ." sings Cathy Winter in her song "Long Time Friends." I learned the truth of this song while organizing a "Wimmin (Women) Take Back the Night" demonstration and march in Oberlin. We envisioned the march as an act of empowerment for women, saying "yes" to being respected and walking safely wherever we pleased at any time of day or night. These marches take place annually in large cities, and the organizers typically choose the poorly lighted, "rough" sections of town to walk through, the areas where most women would be afraid to walk alone. Living in a small, Midwestern college town, we selected all of the poorly lighted, unfriendly back alleys and side streets and put together a route for the march.

We marched right through the black neighborhood in town. We had never stopped to consider who lived in the houses that lined the streets where we planned to march or why the streets were so poorly lit (the town designates less money for street lights on this side of the tracks). We were a crowd of mostly white students, unwittingly broadcasting a message to that neighborhood that "Black Men Rape White Women." A car full of black men stopped to jeer, retorts broke out among the women, and the organizers struggled to move the women along the last block to the Community Center for our post-march "celebration" with cookies provided by the local men's group.

One of the women was a brilliant facilitator. "Look," she said, "there are a lot of feelings here, and I think we should get them out in the open, talk about what's happened, what's going on for people. Let's talk one at a time, and give our attention to whoever's speaking."

The shit flew, and all of it was justified. "I'm one of about four women of color here," said one woman, shaking her head. "When we walked through that neighborhood, I just had to believe they didn't know how that neighborhood would react to what they were doing. I tried to talk other women at African Heritage House into coming, but they said it was just a bunch of white feminists, and they weren't interested."

The discussion continued with a lot of painful, honest exposés of the racial problems on campus. I spent the rest of the night walking around the campus, my stomach churning, trying to find meaning in the classic mistake we had made. I decided that night that I could never organize a demonstration again until I had examined my own racism and grappled with my "white feminist" roots.

Weekly discussion groups followed the march, as white women and women of color groped across painfully deep separation and mistrust, trying to see and honor one another. I had never considered myself *prejudiced,* but during that period I saw myself as racist, an unconscious supporter of racial discrimination through my thought patterns and actions. I also learned not to expect the oppressed to educate me, the oppressor.

During one of the discussions between white women and women of color, someone mentioned the small number of students of color involved in the student cooperatives. One woman breathed an exasperated sigh and explained, "Cooperatives are not a part of Black culture. We don't want to be part of a cooperative. We have our own community."

I finally got it. After two years of eating in a student cooperative, I was a "true believer" and could not understand why students of color shied away from community living. From the discussions, I learned that most minority groups grow up in extended family neighborhoods and form tight, supportive communities; that's part of their culture. I realized suddenly that I expected people of color to jump at the chance to take part in an artificially created version of a natural part of their growing up.

Another black woman continued. "Maybe it's hard for you to understand that we look at things differently. Take makeup, for example. All of the white feminists I know think wearing makeup is a sign of submission. Well, for me, it's a sign of power. My mama and grandma, all the women in my family worked cleaning houses or at factory jobs, and they never could grow their fingernails long or wear nail polish. But I can. I don't have to clean houses. I can paint my nails. That's a sign of power. We take pride in dressing up, looking good. That's important to us. That's part of our culture."

I was learning, slowly, that what one culture considers "good manners" may be offensive in another. Travel taught me that social customs change from place to place. The Tamil people in the south of India, for example, generally do not use the words "please" or "thank you" except for an extremely important act, such as saving someone's life. Living among them, I first found the lack of verbal "closure" in an act of giving unsettling. After a village woman taught me to draw the intricate, overlapping designs typical of Tamil Nadu, I asked my host to translate "thank you" for her time and effort. "You don't need to say 'thank you,'" he reminded me. "She wouldn't do it if she didn't want to." I began to wonder how often I gave presents or did something for people simply to hear "thank you." Here, people interacted without ulterior motives. I could assume they did things because they wanted to, and they could make the same assumption of me.

In Australia, I found a similar attitude among the Martujarra, traditional people of the Western Desert. Gifts or supportive actions passed between people without comment. "You give someone something, and they won't say a word," explained a friend who had worked for years with the Martujarra. "But some day they might walk up to you in camp with a gift. They remember. They always give in return, but maybe not right away."

The Martujarra also dispense with "hellos" and "good-byes." Time, as they understand it, is a continuous weave of past, present, and future. No one really "goes away." Even those who "die" return to the desert. If all time is *now*, why bother laboring over arrivals and departures? We always have been and always will be in touch.

Relationship with All of Creation

Understanding other cultures requires that I step outside my own social conditioning to perceive the validity of another way.

Understanding another species also challenges me to abandon my human acculturation and step into much richer, more varied forms of communication. Plants, rocks, animals, and streams all have the ability to communicate. They do not, however, speak in words; they communicate through feelings that enter the heart and translate into "words" in the human mind. They communicate through a posture, a glance, a buzz, a "thought/feeling" transmitted to another receptive creature.

Fortunately, some humans have retained or rediscovered the ability to communicate with other inhabitants of the planet. *The Secret Life of Plants* explores one researcher's adventure in discovering the sensitivity of plants. Working for two years as a gardener, I, too, learned the communicative ability of plants. I took on the garden at midsummer. The beds hadn't been weeded for at least a month, and no one had planted late spring seeds. I waded into the knee-high weeds and began to excavate the beds. Within a couple of weeks, I could discern pathways and plants once again. One bed, though, remained weedy. I focused my distress towards the previous gardener and the mess she left on that bed.

One morning I knelt next to the bed and found cabbage green seedlings struggling amidst the weeds. Insects had gnawed away most of their spindly leaves. They looked like miniature trees in midwinter. I pondered whether to release them from their misery and take them to the compost heap or try to nurse them back to life. Well, either way I'll have to weed the bed, I told myself. Might as well give them a chance.

After clearing the weeds, I spread a thick layer of compost over the bed. Each morning when I arrived in the garden, I took a few moments to notice them. I stood beside the bed and sang "You are so beautiful to me" to them. Within a month, those cabbage greens had grown into two-foot-high plants with elephant ear-sized leaves. A harvest of a leaf or two from each plant filled a wheelbarrow.

The cabbages taught me an important lesson—plants, like humans, thrive on positive attention. Spite will kill them. Loving attention combined with action (common sense deeds like weeding and applying compost) will help them thrive.

The minerals, plants, and animals all are my kin. We are formed from the same dust and water and air. We are relatives. We live in relationship with one another. Coyote, in Peter Blue Cloud's collection of contemporary coyote tales, aptly summarizes our relatedness in a short piece entitled "Relativity":

> "Coyote, do you understand the theory of relativity?"
> "Yes, yes, I do. It's much easier that way. When I'm hungry I just stop at anyone's place and get a meal. Yes, it's really good to know that all creatures are related."[3]

Recently I heard the word "Kin-dom" replacing the traditional "kingdom." I always have chafed at the patriarchal term "kingdom" to describe the realms of life on Earth, and "kin-dom" speaks of relationship, a commonality of experience rather than carefully guarded territories and domains. Kinship implies connection of a loving family sort. I like to think of the "kin-doms" bonded in an extended family neighborhood. The sweet gum tree outside my window is part of that neighborhood family. She lives closer to me than the nearest "human" neighbor. Who is my "next door neighbor," anyhow? The answer to that question determines my ability to interact as a responsible citizen in my community.

I encounter "the other." Within the commnity, how do I interact with "other" from this point of "self"? I allow my center to connect with the center of this other being. I say "being" because the other may be in the form of rock, human, plant, or armchair. Our connection makes us whole.

Another description of "self relating in wholeness with others" is the concept of attunement. We choose to resonate together, to connect with something deeper (or "higher" or "greater") than our individual selves. Attunement is like tuning our inner orchestra before playing a symphony.

The symphony itself is like the environment as a whole, and the self (the violinist) relates within the environment. I am in harmony with myself (I have tuned my violin). I chose the oboe's "A" for the basis of my tuning (attunement with other), and now I co-create music to form something larger than myself or my relationship to the oboe, even larger than my relationship with all of the other violinists in my section (the human species) of the orchestra. I am making music in the context of a unified whole. Once the performance begins and the music rolls forth in a continuous unity, I forget about the hours spent in rehearsal when the music was practiced in bits and pieces, a viola section melody here, an oboe-clarinet duet there, a tricky interaction between the bass viol section and the timpanist.

Analogous to the bits and pieces of music being rehearsed, before the music of co-created life spills effortlessly forth, are the "boxes" that we as a society have created for different aspects of life. These boxes generally take the form of "-isms," like socialism, communism, conservatism, feminism, etc. Academic fields (generally separated by barbed wire) also create boxes, such as economics, biology, chemistry, political science, social studies. This is the mind breaking apart, analyzing, a very necessary process in the rehearsal as described above.

In life I am sitting in a rehearsal for wholeness, listening to the economist practice a difficult run with the politician (the oboe and the clarinet), the activists for a non-racist society rehearsing a tricky rhythm with the feminist (the bass viol section with the timpani), and the physicist making sense of the Buddhist conception of world order and becoming active in Green politics (the whole string section rehearsing interweaving countermelodies). I have a sense that the performance date is approaching and the rehearsals will end soon. The more "sectional rehearsals" we perfect, with several parts playing in harmony, the closer we come to the full performance of the symphony.

Ten

Neighborhood

> Little boxes, on the hillside, little boxes made of ticky tacky
> Little boxes, little boxes, little boxes all the same.
> There's a green one and a pink one and a blue one and a yellow
>   one
> And they're all made out of ticky tacky and they all look just
>   the same. —*Malvina Reynolds, "Little Boxes"*[1]

AS I SIT HERE AT MY DESK, thinking about my neighbors, I am aware that the computer glowing in front of me, the birch tree shimmering outside the window, and the crickets thrumming in the late summer grass are much closer "neighbors" than the nearest humans living in a trailer across the field. Who are neighbors, and what do they mean to me?

The dictionary provides a few clues. *Neighbor,* or *nyebour,* is from Middle English. Even earlier is the Anglo-Saxon word *neahgebur.* The prefix *nigh* means "turning or looking toward" or "near" the object of the prefix—in this case, *gebur,* freeholder, peasant, farmer. Together, then, *neah'gebur* means "turning towards, or near, freeholder or farmer." The definition highlights two important points. One is that "neighbors" are people associated with the land. They are dwellers in the country, with a relationship to the land. They do not, however, dwell in isolation. A neighbor is a person who works with the land with an awareness of other humans nearby. They are fellow occupants of the land who look towards each other. They move and act and think, taking into consideration those around them. The important twist is the *turning* or *looking toward.* Being a neighbor means keeping an eye out for those who share my surroundings.

In this age of "expanding consciousness," I would venture that my neighborhood includes far more than the nearest humans and their dwellings. Included in my home territory is a flock of catbirds who devour the blueberries just ripening in the field behind the house. Another neighbor is the owl, an occasional visitor to the hedgerow on the south side of the yard. A week ago, while I lay awake long past midnight, the owl perched in the birch tree outside my bedroom window and "who who-who who-*whoooed*" for over an hour.

Crickets hop unannounced into the kitchen. Tomatoes ripen in the withering August heat. A fox cries in the evening. Wind sings in the gnarled boughs of the neglected apple trees behind the house. The begonia on the kitchen windowsill unfurls delicate pink blossoms. They and many others are my neighbors. When I act with an awareness of kinship, I automatically begin to treat these fellow beings, these neighboring creatures, with respect.

Cultivating neighborhood means sowing seeds of respect, of deference. I make room for you to step onto "my" ground; you make room for me on yours. Many species are very territorial, establishing clearly delineated homesteads, but for the most part territories exist within a species.

Bioregions

For humanity, those territories take the form of continents, nations, states, towns, villages, and "properties." For many ages, the contours and features of the earth determined the shape and size of these territories. The Alps create a natural division between northern and southern Europe. In North America the Appalachian and Allegheny mountains form a barrier that contained the European invaders on the eastern seaboard for a couple of centuries. The oceans are both a medium of transportation and insulation between the continents. Some indigenous peoples feel that the continents were meant to be separated. Each had a race of people specifically adapted to that place, spiritually and culturally as well as biologically.

Today this ancient awareness of the efficacy of local identity has been translated into a new movement, Bioregionalism. Instead of defining states by artificially drawn lines, bioregionalists advocate delineating territories by naturally occurring boundaries. The seashore and a neighboring mountain range might determine a bio-region. Another might be defined by the natural spread of the bristlecone pine, the range of the wolf, or the migratory route of the Canada goose.

A bioregionalist acknowledges the inter-relatedness of all the species in a bioregion, including the human inhabitants. Humans must work in harmony with naturally occurring ecosystems, with the other inhabitants of the neighborhood, to ensure a sustainable future—indeed, to ensure any sort of future at all. Gary Snyder suggests examining a particular area of land to determine what it does best, be it growing coniferous forest or prairie grass, and then working with the land's natural inclination. Working from points of strength is a basic tenet of restoration ecology, the science of rebuilding damaged environments. We can apply the same discriminative skills and then work with those points of strength before damaging an area. Deserts were not made to grow cabbages; swamps cannot support cacti. Honor the basic tendencies of the land and you will reap an abundant harvest.

Each bioregion grows a different sort of human being. Admittedly, that may sound strange in a anthropocentric culture accustomed to gauging our impact on the land and dismissing the environment's impact on us. In overt and subtle ways, we are shaped by the land around us. Folklorist Alan Lomax studied the dances of Africa and Scotland and found that the terrain in each area heavily influenced dance styles. The African plains dwellers dance with a shuffling movement that mimics their walking gait over relatively flat ground. Scotland, in contrast, has many mountainous slopes, and the indigenous dances include high-stepping maneuvers that imitate the Scots' hillclimbing technique.

Our interaction with the land shapes our basic conception of the world. In Africa a forest-dwelling tribal group was taken to the edge of a vast grasslands area. Having lived among closely spaced trees, the people were overwhelmed by the open territory and could not accurately judge distances. They felt nauseous and afraid. Living in a land dominated by ice and snow throughout most of the year, the Inuit have dozens of words for snow. The Martujarra of the Western Desert in Australia, surrounded as they are by the effects of heat and light, have many names for the subtle stages of the return of light each day, many more than the simple terms "dawn" and "sunrise" in English.

Although I concede that generalizations can always be disproved, I note that different regions in the United States produce different sorts of dispositions. New England, like its namesake, still supports local character—small towns, local dances, and heated town meetings. Friends from neighboring towns ask how "our" autumn colors were, twenty miles down the road. The weather moves in microclimates, as do the people, who form local pockets of attitude and disposition. The Northeast has not succumbed to suburban sprawl, perhaps because the mountains, unlike the open stretches of the Midwest, prevent it. Like the villages hemmed in by mountains, the people are contained, reserved, slow to open to newcomers. And like a mountain valley sheltered from the wind, a small ray of sunshine makes them radiate with warmth.

Texans are known for telling "tall tales;" I can attest to their love of stretching stories to the snapping point. And after driving through parts of Texas, I can understand their love of exaggeration. You need to expand a bit, to fling yourself out into the landscape, to feel that you have any substance at all. The vast, wide open places threaten to yawn and swallow you. Nothing could be too big to fit into that expansive, unwavering landscape. No tale could be too tall to find a comfortable place to lie down in Texas. Even words expand in Texas—they stretch into a lazy drawl, as if calculated to fill the empty expanse of cattle-stamped plains. Besides, the sun is too hot to hurry in Texas, or anywhere else in the South. Save the frantic pace for the North, where the chill of autumn can soothe feverish heads. Air conditioning has allowed some northern dwellers to adapt to the swelter of the South, but they are forever out of place, like parsnips in the desert.

Which brings me to another heresy—not only do places shape people, certain areas actually draw people to them. Those who have refined the art of "deep listening" will know what I mean when I say, "I heard a certain place calling to me . . . I knew I had to go." When humans are able to listen deeply to the Earth, they are drawn to places that need their particular qualities and skills, just as certain plants and animals root and evolve in specific areas. Bioregions thrive on people who are able to listen and commit themselves to living in that place. Once you have found your place, dig in. Apply yourself to learning as much as you possibly can about your region. Develop a sense of local loyalty—not parochialism, but a feeling of belonging. Glean a part of your livelihood from the land, like "spotting downed trees for next year's firewood, gathering mushrooms or berries or herbs on time, fishing, hunting, scrounging." Living in one place sharpens our ability to listen and eventually to hear the voice of the land.

> The nature spirits are never dead, they are alive under our feet, over our heads, all around us, ready to speak when we are silent and centered. So what is this "voice"? Just the cry of a flicker, or coyote, or jay, or wind in a tree, or acorn whack on a garage roof. Nothing mysterious, but now you're home.[2]

Deep Listening

A friend of mine moved onto a piece of property in New Hampshire and built a home from bales of hay. He began to work the land in a swampy section of the property. "And one day, it was like that place was talking to me. I had this sense that I was standing in a sacred place, and it desperately wanted to be opened up again, to have the water drained, to let the light pour into it." For months he hand-dug drainage ditches and pulled stumps from the boggy land. Five years later he had nearly two acres of land under cultivation, growing organic vegetables that sustained him through most of the year.

He told me about his first house as well, a story that left me speechless with laughter. "I chose a spot down by the creek to build my house of hay, and one of the old-timers came along and shook his head. 'Not a very good place,' he told me. 'Too close to the creek.' 'Ah, it's all right,' I told him. 'The creek doesn't come up this high.'

"Well, I made it through the winter just fine. I built one big structure and then divided it into two. My horse lived in one room, I lived in the other. The combination of the horse and the wood-burning stove kept me warm at night. Oh, and the ducks lived with me on my side of the house, too. The goats lived with the horse."

Everything went well until the spring rains started. "One night I woke up, and the ducks were swimming around the bed. I heard the horse neighing in the next room, and realized in my sleepy state that the creek was now in the house." I laughed hysterically while he described his exploits getting the horse and goats and ducks out of his flooded house.

Although I laughed with my friend about his misadventures, we both recognized important lessons in the story. First and foremost, build houses only in appropriate places. In order to find an "appropriate" spot, you must develop the ability to *listen to the land* in that place. Note where the land slopes into a bog. Observe the wind patterns and avoid building in a natural wind tunnel. Locate the best drinking water supply; build close enough to utilize it, but not pollute it. The list of subtleties is endless—the point is to let the land speak. Listen with respect.

The suburban subdivisions made by bulldozing old cornfields flat and dividing the land into neat squares completely ignore the natural inclinations of the land. My parents' basement regularly floods during heavy rains. The backyard naturally holds the downpours in an impromptu pond. If the builders were astute and had watched the land before building, they would have left this property as a runoff area for the surrounding houses.

Allow the land to dictate the most appropriate designs. An adobe brick house blends with the land in the Southwest (in fact, the building materials come directly from the Earth), but fares poorly in New England. The Long Houses built of wood in the Northeast could not be duplicated in the desert; trees grow sparsely there. Allow wind, water, and sun exposure to determine where to build. Let soil quality determine location of road and garden and park. Save "good" land (the tillable, fertile sort) for growing food, not houses. Shopping centers and houses cover some of North America's richest farmland. Meanwhile, the government offers subsidies to encourage farmers to till marginal land, such as steep hillside slopes in semi-desert regions of Colorado. Where are our priorities? Why not make the fragile hillsides into wilderness parks, leave the farmland to grow food, and build houses on marginal land elsewhere?

Individual landowners can apply the same logic on their own acre. Save the richest land for the garden. Locate the house on marginal land. Don't build the access road by bulldozing a creek. Work with the natural strengths of the land, take the time to listen, and you will avoid many problems in the long run. And let dreams, the quiet funnel of the Creator's will, and the revelations of meditation guide the flow of creative application in that place. Ideas imposed upon the land are just that—impositions.

The Bear Tribe lived in a makeshift shelter for a year before they touched the spring welling from under a tamarack tree. They offered tobacco, listened, and prayed to be guided about where and how to build. You may not have the luxury of living in a tent for a full year on the land before beginning to build. You could, however, visit the land every month or two to listen to the changing rhythms of the land. Note where the water pools during the spring rains, where the winter winds lash the land, where water-loving plants congregate during the summer, where the owls nest, where the land grows parched and dry in late summer. Listen to the land for a full year, and solicit the advice of the oldtimers in the area as well.

Cultivating a Sense of Place

My friend's story reminded me of the importance of befriending the long-time residents in an area. Oldtimers are one of the most sadly overlooked "natural resources" we have. They are storehouses of information about the history of an area—everything from who married the mayor's daughter to the expected first frost date. They can tell you where to find elderberries to make jam, which section of the creek to fish in, and which beans grow best in that region. The *Foxfire* series of books is one example of a community's attempt to preserve its endemic wisdom. Started by a high school English teacher who wanted to make writing come alive for his students, the Foxfire books are a compilation of interviews and stories written by the students, based on their experiences with some of the long-time residents in their community. "This book is dedicated to the people of the mountains," writes editor Eliot Wigginton, "in the hope that, through it, some portion of their wisdom, ingenuity and individuality will remain long after them to touch us all." The books provide a wealth of information on "hog dressing, log cabin building, mountain crafts and foods, planting by the signs, snake lore, hunting tales, faith healing, moonshining, and other affairs of plain living." Collecting the material for the book reintroduced the students to family members. They talked, really talked, with their grandparents and great aunts and uncles and cousins, some for the first time. They were learning about their roots, their culture, their heritage. Those students were acquiring a sense of place.

After having studied and lived in several "intentional" communities, ones that join together for an agreed upon purpose, I would say that developing a sense of place is one of the key factors in any sort of sustainable community. Humans cannot live off an idea or an ideal, no matter how profound. A sustainable community will not come together solely from idea/mind. There needs to be a heart connection, a common linking, and a sense of rooted purpose that binds them. Ideas change; people's conception of what is "true" and "right" alters over time. If you want a long-term, stable community, look for people who are first committed to place, to living in the best way possible on that part of the Earth.

Neighbors, as defined at the beginning of this chapter, are those living nearby. They may or may not share interests or a common vision of life. My neighbor is as much a matter of chance as design. Our commitment to place, to living on that part of the Earth, is the common denominator. Community, on the other hand, is "a group of people living together and having interests, work, etc. in common . . ." My ideal is to meld these two aspects—connection with place and the recognition of common interest—to create neighborhood communities. In such a living situation, the inhabitants are committed to each other as well as all the other aspects of creation in that place—the land, animals, minerals, and plants.

Cohousing

"Cohousing" is one contemporary approach to what I call neighborhood communities. In a society with a large transient population, in which (according to the Census Bureau) one person in six moves every year, many people are hungry for a sense of place and the supportive bonding of community. They are not eager, however, for the restrictive social expectations of a tightly knit village or urban neighborhood. "Cohousing offers the social and practical advantages of a closely knit neighborhood within the context of twentieth-century life," write Kathryn McCamant and Charles Durrett in their book *Cohousing: A Contemporary Approach to Housing Ourselves.*[3]

The common factors shared by all cohousing developments are:

• *Participatory Process:* Residents participate in the planning of the community, from inception to construction, and take responsibility as a group for all final decisions.
• *Intentional Neighborhood Design:* The physical design encourages community interaction.
• *Extensive Common Facilities:* "'This is what makes cohousing particularly special. Common dinners have proved overwhelmingly

successful, with more than half the residents participating on any given evening.' Cohousing can also include a large functional workshop, common laundry and teen-age room."

• *Complete Resident Management:* Residents are responsible for the ongoing management of the development through decisions made at community meetings.[4]

The emphasis on common facilities and community decision-making draws from the best of intentional community living. Unlike most "intentional" groups, however, cohousing residents do not necessarily share the same views on politics, childrearing, or spirituality. In this respect, cohousing developments are like neighborhoods: people joined together by the common factor of place, and not necessarily ideological persuasion.

Neighborhood Support Systems

For those already living in a "traditional" neighborhood, whether in an urban center, suburb, or rural community, consider creating support systems to help link residents. Community organizers know, for example, that the most successful agitators for social change begin by addressing the fundamental needs of the community. A friend who worked with the Communist Party in Los Angeles in the mid-sixties explained that they first identified what they perceived as the real needs of a poor community. They helped organize a daycare program for children, then lobbied for city funds to build a playground in this poor, mostly Black and Hispanic neighborhood. Similar playgrounds already existed in more affluent sections of town. Deaf to the needs of its financially struggling neighborhoods, City Hall did not respond. The organizers arranged an appointment with the mayor to discuss the needs of local mothers and children. Dozens of women and children arrived for the meeting. After surveying the crowd, the secretary announced that the mayor was "out of his office." The mothers and children patiently waited for the rest of the day. After a couple of similar appointments, the city government agreed to build the playground.

Community organizing need not have the ulterior motive of "training the masses to do war with the capitalist machine" in order to be successful. Thoughtfully examine the needs of your community and take steps to create the sort of environment you want to live in. Urban neighborhoods, often lacking in tillable land, might choose to turn an empty lot into a community garden. The produce from the garden could be preserved in a local "canning co-op" with equipment and kitchen space shared by the whole community. Food buying co-operatives, mentioned earlier, are a way of meeting food needs with a minimum of expense while simultaneously strengthening community ties. Health care may be an important need, especially with a large infant or elderly population. Many communities have successfully organized "Meals on Wheels" programs to feed elderly shut-ins, but our elders need more than physical food. You may choose to develop a home visiting service for elderly residents to keep them integrated in the vital life of the community.

Mothers also need extra support. Some women's centers provide both regular and emergency babysitting services to give mothers a needed respite from their children. The service helps defuse potentially abusive situations between young children and over-loaded, distressed mothers. In an extended family, many people watch and nurture the children; no one person is expected to carry the full burden of disciplining and caring for a child. Only in recent times, with the advent of nuclear families living in isolated suburbs, have mothers raised children in isolation. I have seen babysitting cooperatives successfully organized in small towns and neighborhoods, but the children's parents generally organized and staffed the service without participation from the wider neighborhood. The older generation is a natural ally of the younger. Consider engaging senior citizens in the babysitting cooperative. In addition to giving purpose and meaning to an older person's life, the inter-action can expose children to the wisdom of their elders. This exchange was and is cultivated in many native societies, and our contemporary culture could benefit by the example.

Decision-making, Visioning, and Community Development

Participatory decision-making strengthens any collective—assuming that members have acquired the skills to conduct a good meeting, and are able to think with the needs of the whole in mind. Unfortunately, in many communities these skills do not exist. We have only the democratic model of voting, but not necessarily the human skills necessary to facilitate an honest discussion and then empower a collective decision. Check the Bibliography for books to help hone these skills.

People who have invested themselves in the decision-making process are likely to support its implementation. Decisions imposed without participation are likely to incur resentment and generate little support. Community decisions strengthen a sense of neighborhood and empower residents to shape a collection of people and buildings into the kind of community they want to live in. Attend town meetings; they are a wise investment of time. Hour for hour, working on a local level often has more impact on our day-to-day lives than any other stratum of governance.

The decision-making process also provides a forum for neighbors to share dreams and concerns. Just as an individual needs a vision to guide his or her life, so, too, a community needs a vision to shape its development. Viewed from the air, cities built without planning, without an organic vision for their future, sprawl in unrelated patterns. Peter Russell, author of *The Global Brain,* points out that an aerial photograph of a sprawling urban center closely resembles the pattern of malignant cancerous tissue viewed under a microscope. The macrocosm (the city's development) mirrors the microcosm (malignant cell tissue). Older European and even early American cities mimic the pattern of healthy cell tissue. They were conceived and built by residents in touch with themselves and the wider community. Healthy bodies generate healthy cell tissue; healthy communities generate integrated, supportive structures.

Ritual in Communities

Rituals can bond a group of people in ways that no business meeting ever will. Rituals are not all candles and incense; they are any repeated set of actions that carry meaning for a group or individual. The daily routine of arising early, making coffee, and reading the paper is a ritual. This morning rite centers and prepares the "celebrant" for the demands of the day.

Rituals have a larger function as well. They can carry me beyond my sense of self to root me in place and simultaneously expand me outward to commune with all of Creation. (To commune—the root of community.) The Christian faith thrives on the use of ritual, chief among them being the celebration of Communion. By eating the body of Christ, represented by bread, and drinking His blood, represented by wine or grape juice, I become Christ. I connect with a spirit and wisdom greater than my personality. We commune. I am opened, at least for a few moments, to the immensity of spirit and creation.

Every community I have lived in, both neighborhood and intentional, has practiced some sort of ritual behavior. The Bear Tribe shared what is probably the most outwardly visible form of ritual—a ceremonial life. Every Sunday morning we came together for a sweat lodge ceremony to cleanse and pray for ourselves, our community, and the whole of Creation. Following the ceremony we ate brunch together and then spent the remainder of the afternoon in a Council Meeting to discuss tribal business. Every week we gathered for a pipe ceremony. We celebrated the solstices, equinoxes, and full moons as well.

The Findhorn Foundation in Scotland welcomed all spiritual traditions, recognizing each path to God, or the Creator, as valid. Our chief ritual of communion was silence. How else could a varied collection of spiritualists come together? We gathered in sanctuary three times a day to commune in silence. In addition to joining with those present, we focused on the world at large and sent light and love to the whole planet through the "Network of Light," an energy grid that covers the entire Earth. I personally found the noon meditations too human-oriented. After becoming a member, I guided the noon sanctuary once a week and focused attention on the mineral, plant, and animal realms as well.

The town of Wendell where I lived in western Massachusetts participates in a community ritual every month—the Full Moon Coffeehouse. Held in the Town Hall on the Saturday night closest to full moon, the gatherings are a time for neighbors to chat and reconnect, to share songs, poems, and announcements, and to hear visiting artists perform. Especially in the winter, when snow and ice fuel cabin fever, the Full Moon Coffeehouses provide a focal point for the life of the community. Through poetry, music, and skits, we share our views and visions and dreams for the community. The Coffeehouse also provides what every community needs—an excuse to be together, just to be who and what we are.

Cultivate inclusive rituals in your community. Organize neighborhood picnics or potluck dinners to celebrate the equinoxes and solstices. At midwinter, gather to share songs and drink mulled cider. Take children for walks under the cold, clear full moons of winter and then gather around a fireplace to tell stories. Dance together under the midsummer sun—step to a variety of music, from homespun folk to African drums to rock 'n roll. Meet to press cider and barn dance for the autumn equinox. Organize "astrological" birthday parties every month—celebrate the Pisces birthdays in March, the Aries babies in April, etc. All of the above are ritual celebrations, with the potential to bond neighbors as friends, to develop a sense of place, and to reawaken our awareness of the earth's cyclical changes from season to season.

Rites of Passage

In Chapter Two, I mentioned our culture's lack of rites of passage. Some vestigial ceremonies remain—First Communion in the Catholic Church, Confirmation for the Protestants, Bat and Bar Mitzvahs in the Jewish Temple. For a culture rapidly abandoning outmoded religious orders, what methods remain to recognize and affirm change? Here again the community can become a supportive element. Graduation from high school or college is often likened to a rite of passage, but it is an accomplishment of the mind, the successful completion of someone else's requirements. It does not celebrate the discovery of one's own vision, or one's growing sense of power. In a community lacking in such celebrations, kids create their own tests and rites of passage—drinking bashes, drag races, drugs, sex, anything that requires cunning and a certain element of danger to accomplish. What if the community provided healthy tests of strength, like hiking alone in wilderness areas, apprenticing with the local fire department or hospital, breaking and training a horse, or running the town government for a week?

Kids need challenges, and they need recognition for successfully meeting difficult situations. Rites of passage prepare both the community and the individual for change. They strengthen the individual in preparation for a new life, for the shouldering of greater responsibility. The ritual of passage readies the community to accept the individual as a new person. In communities without such rituals, an individual must literally leave the limiting expectations of the collective in order to change. Rites of passage provide a safety valve for change, both for the individual and the community.

Adults need rites of passage as well. Women especially need rituals to celebrate the changes in their physical bodies. The beginning of menstruation is an important passage from childhood into adolescence. Many women in our culture today no longer honor the monthly cycles of their bodies. The only models we have for recognizing menstruation are negative ones—outcast from the tribe, forbidden to touch food or hunting gear, dismissed for our emotions and dreamy wateriness, ridiculed for "being on the rag." We have no positive rituals to celebrate the moon-time passage of blood. At best, we try to ignore the "imposition" of bloody panties and bloated bodies and carry on with our "important," busy lives.

We can find, however, positive explanations for the "censure" traditionally imposed on women during their bleeding. In cultures dependent on hunting, everyone knew that any strong scent on hunting weapons would alert the animals to the hunters' approach. Because menstruating women exude a strong scent, they stayed away from both hunters and weapons. Instead of "banishing" women from the tribe, some traditional Native American cultures built Moon Huts, situated away from the daily business of the tribe, where women gathered during their bleeding times. Because the menstrual cycle is affected by exposure to light, and most women in traditional cultures would have been exposed to roughly the same amount of light (not supplemented by artificial lighting), most women bled at the same time each month. Monthly gatherings in the Moon Hut became fertile times to share wisdom, stories and back rubs, to dream, paint, and plan. They received and recorded visions not only for themselves, but also for the whole tribe. A menstruating woman draws power. Empty, cleansed, like the Void, she sucks power into herself. She is immensely powerful in her emptiness. Thus, her dreams are more potent during this time, her inner voice stronger, and her attention focused more on visions than on shopping lists. No wonder contemporary women become frustrated and "bitchy" during their moon times. I find I have little interest or patience for the tasks of the mundane world. I want to be left alone to dream and vision, to weave and sing, and paint.

Facing the demands of earning a living and raising children, and satisfying a partner, few women have the luxury of spending four to seven days each month in retreat. I would counter, however, that our culture cannot afford the luxury of losing the visionary power once provided by the revelations in the Moon Hut. We cannot afford to lose the watery, dreamy side of our existence or we will become parched and loveless, mere apparitions of our full-bodied selves. I offer some compromises to help balance the need for quiet, visionary times with the demands of a fast-paced life.

No matter when your bleeding starts, give yourself at least three or four hours of alone time. That may mean leaving work early or arriving late, skipping classes, or hiring a babysitter. If you work with a supportive circle of women, you can alternate taking each other's children for a few hours or a day. During their moon time, you can return the favor.

Consider sleeping alone during your menses. When I first heard this suggestion, I dismissed it as propaganda from men who were afraid of making love with a bleeding woman. One woman, though, a student of a native herbalist, reported that during her menses she began to notice her partner stumbled when he got out of bed in the morning, or slashed his finger while cutting bread, or badly nicked himself shaving. He seemed to have lost his balance, part of his "power," after sleeping with her during her moon time. In addition to "pulling" or absorbing a mate's power, I find I have less patience with a partner. I need nurturing and alone time and am frustrated by having to meet someone else's needs. Perhaps the current "epidemic" of Premenstrual Syndrome (PMS) results from women ignoring their needs during their menstrual cycle, trying to override their desire for solitary, dreamy spaces in their lives.

Birthing is another female rite of passage. The act of giving birth to a child is a passage through the joint tunnel of life and death for the mother. "Women are closer to the Mystery," the mother of four once confided to me, "because they know what it is to be out of control. The mysteries of life are chaotic, uncontrollable, and a woman knows that once the birthing contractions start, she is no longer in control. You simply have to surrender. You face your own death. There's no other way. Men don't know about that. They don't go through anything like it in their lives. So they have to create all kinds of artificial things, like religions and battles, to test their fear of death, to try to understand the Mystery. But women know it already. We know it with our bodies."

One of women's least celebrated passages is menopause. In many native traditions one did not become a wise woman, an elder of the community, until one had passed beyond the fertile years of motherhood. Many contemporary women mourn the passing of their fertility and have no elevated status as an elder to assuage that loss. Molly Scott, a singer and educator, decided to celebrate her own passage into full maturity with a "Croning." In the Celtic tradition, the Goddess is known in three aspects: the Maiden, the Mother, and the Crone. The Grandmothers, the Crones, are the wise women who advise, teach, and work for the good of the whole.

On her fiftieth birthday, Molly's women friends gathered to ritually bathe and dress her. They sang and danced and celebrated her into a new life as Crone, Wise Woman, and respected Grandmother.

Men need rites of passage as well, perhaps even more so as they have fewer dramatic biological cues to mark their development. The growth of a beard, hair on the chest, and the first ejaculation of sperm mark the journey from childhood into adolescence. As with girls, though, physical maturity alone does not qualify a boy for adulthood. Men, too, must face their mortality and discover their life vision. And curiously enough, men and women seem to face the same issues at different ages. Gail Sheehy, in her book *Passages,* outlines the likely ages for both men's and women's life crises to occur. The predictable crises of our lives are noteworthy only in so much as we are able to engage them, meet the danger, and glean the opportunity camouflaged in the disruptive situation.

Death is our final rite of passage. Many people plan their funeral but few envision their own death, the actual process of crossing over. Although death is similar to the process of birthing in that it is uncontrollable, those with a long, slow illness have the (questionable) gift of being able to decide where and with whom they want to die. Elisabeth Kübler-Ross has pioneered the work of re-teaching our culture how to work naturally with death. She relates a story from her own childhood in which a neighboring farmer was hurt in the fields. His family carried him home and put him in bed. Knowing that his injuries were fatal, they called the local community to say goodbye. Neighbors stood around the bed, holding his hand, recalling times they had spent together. Kübler-Ross, one of the children present, kissed him and said goodbye. No one screened the children from the inevitability of his death. They were included in the process. When his time neared, the farmer asked all but his immediate family to leave the room. They talked about what to do with the farm and his possessions, expressed their love, and said goodbye. He died quietly, with the support of his family and community.

Ghost Sickness

In cultures lacking in community rituals and individual rites of passage, many people contract what David Winston, a Cherokee teacher, terms "Ghost Sickness." Unlike diseases of the body, Ghost Sickness is an illness of the spirit. One of the chief symptoms is repetition of the phrase, "I don't care." Those suffering from ghost disease have lost heart; their spirits are ailing. They have lost connection with themselves, with their community, and with the Earth. The Cherokee understand that the spirit is not immortal, but that only the individual can kill his or her own spirit. The remedy for Ghost Sickness involves more than pills or herb; it requires a completely new way of living.

Those suffering from Ghost Sickness tend to be self-indulgent; thus, the medicine person might send them to work in an old folks' home or an orphanage. They are encouraged to look at the wider woes of the world. Part of the "cure" is to spend time with disadvantaged people and learn to serve them. The medicine person arranges a series of ceremonies over a period of three or four months to help reconnect them first to their family and then to the community. The whole family and then the entire community participate in the ceremonies. Their presence builds a strong expectation that the person will heal. The ailing person wants to fulfill those expectations. Many in contemporary Western culture indulge in illness to gain attention. "I'm so sorry you are sick," we say to one another. "What can I do for you?" Among the Cherokee, friends and neighbors emphasize the healing process. "I'm so glad you're *well*," they say. "What can I do for you?"

Community as Insurance Policy

A society dependent on insurance companies and medical doctors would never diagnose a patient as having "Ghost Sickness." A doctor might diagnose a chronic loss of interest in life as "depression," "chronic fatigue syndrome," or "stress." Ironically, those same societies suffer from an epidemic of Ghost Sickness. They do not recognize the need for families and communities to participate in the restoration of health. In fact, insurance companies excuse families, friends, and neighbors from the healing process. We no longer depend on one another in times of need. Such dependency is seen as weakness. We don't want to "burden" our family and friends. Better to suffer alone, with the support of an anonymous insurance company. Unfortunately, we have become so dependent on the insurance companies that we literally cannot afford to live without them. Insurance, while making us less dependent on our community, has encouraged us to be more dependent on the medical world. People see the doctor more often and request more tests, knowing that the insurance company will cover the visits and exams. The over-use of medical care has increased costs, even for those who want only minimal emergency coverage.

Communities that do not depend on insurance companies to care for their own encourage what has become a swearword in contemporary society—obligation. The town of Wendell in western Massachusetts recently rebuilt one resident's house. Charles was a loyal worker at the local Recycling And Transfer Station (R.A.T.S., otherwise known as "The Dump"). When his house burned to the ground, he had no insurance policy and no money to replace it. The town banded together and built him a new one. "That's extraordinary," I said when I heard his story. "No, it's not," said Charles. "I didn't have any insurance. I didn't have any money. The town had to build me a new house."

"And what do you do for the town?" I asked.

"I work at R.A.T.S.," he said without hesitation. He also actively supports the local church, organizes Passover Seders, and supervises food co-op deliveries. He is obliged to the community, and they to him. Both seem to thrive on the mutual dependency.

In too many towns, though, residents do not have the same sense of obligation to care for one another. We are terrified of obligation, of being "obliged" for help rendered. "Very much obliged," say the British—but most North Americans are terrified of being obliged. They do not want to feel responsible or beholden to anyone else. While independence is to be commended, separation is not. The fear of obligation, if taken to extremes, is a fear of bonding with others.

Brother David Steindl-Rast speaks of our uprootedness—from ourselves, our communities, and the Earth—and suggests cultivating gratitude and obligation to remedy our disconnection. He mentions the tradition of giving gifts upon entering a new community. When a host accepts a gift, a bond is established. You are a guest, and no longer a stranger.

> That establishing of bonds actually happens when you say
> "thank you." You enter into obligation . . . People will say, when
> they move into a new neighborhood, "Let's not start this gift-
> giving with our neighbors." Your neighbor may be already
> there with tomatoes from the garden. Beautiful gesture. It
> happened to me once. But most people would say, "Please, let's
> not enter into this gift-giving, it just creates obligation," as if

this was something unpleasant. Most societies live on obligation, but we want to be independent. But if we say "Thank you," and really mean it, we have said "Yes" to our being together . . .
When we cultivate that gratefulness to life, we practice saying "Yes," again and again, to our limitless belonging to this Earth household, and that roots us. That makes us at home.[5]

Obligation, in the sense of mutual dependence, is a quality to be cultivated. Neighbors, those who look toward one another, are needed in a society of alienated, ghostly people. Let us look toward one another, and truly see each other. Let us laugh, hug, and sing together. Let us cry, mourn, and grieve with one another. Let us celebrate the fullness of the moon, the abundance of the fields, the building of a house, the birth of a baby, the passing of an elder. Let these ties unite but not bind, support but not strangle. Let us stand together, each beside the other—not leaning, but standing—and enjoy each other's presence. Let us enjoy our kinship, with other humans and with the land. Those rooted in place are more likely to hear, and therefore act on behalf of, their community. May we send roots into this place, and bless the Earth with our presence.

Eleven

Right Livelihood

... our life is more than our work/
And our work is more than our job.
   —song by "Bright Morning Star Arising"

We cannot do great things in life: we can only do small things
with great love. *—Mother Teresa*

One little person giving all of her time for peace makes news.
Many people giving some of their time can make history.
   —Peace Pilgrim

RIGHT LIVELIHOOD HAS much more to do with right living than
it does with a particular occupation or career. Relationships with
friends, family, neighbors, Creation, and Self all weave together to
form the fabric of right living. The work that you perform, though,
is one of the major ways in which you "take your show on the
road" and apply the inner work of vision and choice. The way you
support yourself in the world is a major part of enacting your
vision for yourself and the Earth.

   Discovering right livelihood requires a vision for the kind of life
you want to live and the sort of world you want to live in. I'm
assuming that you already have found or created your life vision,
or at least begun the process. If not, I encourage you to reread
and answer the seven questions in Chapter Two on vision (p. 26).
Give yourself time to dream and think, to take long walks and bake
bread and swim in the sea. Allow your vision to form unhurried;
let it settle into your bones. Let it breathe inside you. Feel and
follow its rhythm; then befriend your vision. Acknowledge this

babe growing in the womb of your soul. Know that you have always been impregnated with its power. Welcome its growth in your life.

The growing vision, like any child, will give you very clear feedback about the food that you are giving it. Action feeds vision. Not all acts, however, provide nourishment. Some cause colic.

In my own life I've come to realize that I am not suited for certain work. "You can do anything you want," my mother used to tell me. "You just have to put your mind to it." I've learned, though, that having the desire to do something is not always matched with the ability. One autumn I took a job as a nurse's aide in an old folks' home. The pay was good enough to work part-time and still pay the rent while I continued to write. I also wanted some medical experience to test my decision to study naturopathic medicine—was I really cut out for such work?

I endured the initial three-week training and collapsed in bed on the weekends. I hadn't had a cold in two years, but I sneezed and wheezed every Saturday morning. Early warning signs. I ignored them. After my first full week of regular work, my grandmother died. Morbidly enough, I was glad for the reprieve. I returned to work, determined to "toughen up" and make a go of it. By the middle of November I had reduced my hours by half. In mid-December I succumbed to a terrible bladder infection. My body was waving the white flag. I finally surrendered. Christmas was my last day—a present to myself that year.

Nursing is a fine profession. I have great respect for those who choose it. But I learned that I do not have the skills to succeed as a nurse's aide. I'm too thin-skinned to work in an institution.

Listening to the Heart

I am learning, too, that my life consists of more than the "jobs" that I perform day-to-day. Fulfilling my life contract, the agreements I made before entering this body, involves more than my vocation. My "work" includes the people I am scheduled to meet, the words I am meant to speak in a "chance" moment, the conflicts I am meant to resolve, the love I am meant to share. One of the key indicators for judging the accuracy of my actions and decisions is my heart.

Immediately after graduating from college, I bought my first car, a yellow Mazda GLC, and christened her "Sunflower." Within a week I was on the road, traveling west to Spokane, Washington to live with the Bear Tribe. "Don't pick up hitchhikers!" my mother warned as I rolled down the driveway in Ohio. For most of the journey I drove alone, passing through the cornfields of Indiana, then Illinois, and into Missouri. The second day I entered Kansas around midafternoon. Just as the sun was setting, I drove past the intersection of I-70 and I-135, approximately halfway across the state. I saw a man standing by the side of the road with a khaki duffel bag at his feet, thumb stuck out, waiting for a ride. As I drove past, my heart started to pound. My mother's words—"Don't pick up hitchhikers!"—echoed in my ear, but I knew from the signal of my pounding heart I was meant to do something for this man.

The next exit was about ten miles down the road. I turned around and headed east on I-70, heart still pounding. I took the wrong turn and found myself driving south on I-135. I made an illegal turn in the middle of the highway and finally got back to the westbound exit for I-70. *OK, Creator,* I prayed, heart still pounding, *if that man is still standing there*—after nearly half an hour—*I'll know I'm supposed to pick him up.*

He was slinging the duffel bag on his back when I finally reached him. He was a shadowy outline in the deepening twilight. I jammed on the brakes and pulled the car off to the side of the highway. "Hello," I called, opening my door, trying to sound confident. "You headed west?"

He paused, then turned around with the duffel bag still perched on his shoulder, and eyed me. He looked incredulous. What single woman would stop for a lone hitchhiking man at night? He walked slowly to the car. "Yeah, I'm heading for Denver," he said.

"Well, the car is pretty crowded. Maybe you can put your bag in the trunk."

He eyed the clothes and boxes jammed in the back seat. "That's OK, I think I can get it in here."

He slung the bag on top of the boxes and sat down in the passenger's seat. I took a deep breath and swung into the driver's seat. *Okay, Creator, you'd better take care of me. I did what you asked.*

During the drive, James told me the story of the past few years of his life. He had married four years before. On their honeymoon, they discovered his wife had leukemia. The following years were full of pain and hope and anguish. The trauma had brought him to God, and her into "remission."

"That's what the doctors say, but we think she's cured," he told me. They battled with his wife's ex-husband for custody of the children. He struggled to find construction work in Florida, "but they don't trust outsiders very much. I had a hard time finding jobs."

Finally, in desperation, he pocketed half of their last $200, packed a duffel bag, and set off to hitchhike west to Denver. "Why Denver?" I asked him.

"I hear there are jobs out here. I just want to find a room to live in, get a job, and earn enough money for them to come join me."

He pulled out my guitar and sang old bluesy songs. We talked about God and cancer and relationships and our dreams. The car rolled along the flat pavement of Kansas. The sky bent to touch the earth at the horizon, so distant that I imagined I could see the curve of the earth reflected in the starlight. The land is so flat and open that I could see thunderstorms raging to the north and south, but no rain touched us. I drove until about 1 a.m. My eyelids began to droop, despite our conversation, so I took the next exit marked "campground." I smiled as we turned onto the gravel driveway—I suddenly realized I had camped here a year before on another cross-country journey. We pitched a tent in the dark and curled into sleeping bags for the night.

In the morning, I stood outside the ladies' bathroom, waiting for someone with a key to come by. A kind, white-haired lady held the door open. "You forget your key, honey?" she crooned. I nodded and followed her inside. "You and your husband all right?" she asked. I covered a smile. "Yes, we're fine."

"Well, you know, we were out late last night, too. They had us in those shelters from ten o'clock onward . . ."

"Shelters?" I asked, eyes widening.

"Yes, the tornado shelters. We were in there for well onto two hours before they let us come back."

"Tornadoes?" I repeated.

"Yes, two of 'em passed just to the north and south of here."

I swallowed hard. The "thunderstorms" we had driven through last night must have been tornadoes. Holy shit. *Thank you, Creator,* I silently prayed, *for looking after us.*

James and I piled our gear in the car and headed for Denver. We spent the afternoon driving around town, putting in work applications and finding him a room in a boarding house that cost less than $100 a month. When he unloaded his duffel from the car, we stood in the street for a long time, just looking at each other. He gave me a hug and then strode across the street, turning only once to wave.

"We are each other's angels," said a friend when I told him the story. Unlike an angel, I have no idea what happened to my earthly charge. But I know that I am glad that I followed the promptings of my pounding heart. Many times since then, people have helped me when I was in a precarious situation. We are each other's angels—that's part of our contract, part of the "work" that we have come here to do. Angels have no job descriptions; they don't interview for work. Time and circumstances spontaneously elect them for jobs that need to be done. We are all itinerant angels. Divine intervention usually comes in the form of other human beings. We are the "magic," the "miracle," the unforeseen circumstance. In our best moments, we are moved by the breath of heaven here on Earth.

Right livelihood is based on claiming our angelic roles. My experience in Kansas taught me to listen to the promptings of my heart. The heart guides us along the path to right living, the root of right livelihood. The heart can guide me to the most appropriate form of service I can render for my fellow angel-humans.

Service

A few years ago I would have shouted "Blasphemy!" at anyone who claimed that doing what one loved was service. For me, service meant doing the most distasteful, difficult work I could find. Clean toilets. Hammer nails under a blistering hot sun. Take care of infants when you have no patience for humans under the age of eighteen. The less I enjoyed the work, the more I was "serving." Eventually, though, I had to ask "serving whom?" I was burned out and disillusioned. I dreaded getting out of bed in the morning to perform my "great service."

Right livelihood does not mean finding the most distasteful work and forcing yourself to like it. Elephants were not made to fly. Fish will never climb trees. Aspen trees will not survive in the rainforest. Judith will never thrive on nursing work. Forget about molding yourself to fit an unsuitable occupation. Trust that love will magnetize you into an area where you can shine and give of yourself in a fulfilling way. Trust, as well, that there truly are other people who enjoy doing the work you find so distasteful. I know people who enjoy nursing and others who thrive on housework. They truly like performing the tasks I abhor. Thank goodness we all have different passions and interests—these indwelling preferences, and sometimes prejudices, help guide us to our most appropriate vocation.

Danaan Parry, whom I mentioned in Chapter Nine, tells a story about visiting Mother Teresa in Bombay. He was on his way to the airport to leave India when his guide casually asked if he would like to meet Mother Teresa. Danaan eagerly agreed. The man stopped the car, and Danaan walked into a building crammed with dying people. He did not walk out again for four or five days. "I walked into Love," he explained. "That's the only way I could describe it. I didn't want to leave. But after a few days one of the nuns came to me and said, 'It's time for you to go.'

"'Go?' I said to her. 'But I want to stay here. There's really nothing else I want to do.'

"'It does not matter what you do,' she told me. 'You can drive a bus, you can rob a bank, you can ride a tractor . . .'

"It took me a while to understand about robbing banks," said Danaan laughing, "but I understood that she meant I could do anything, so long as I did it with love. That is what is important. Doing it with love."

Danaan had learned one of Mother Teresa's primary teachings: "We cannot do great things in life: we can only do small things with great love." Her work, taken step by step, is not extraordinary—hugging a child, spooning gruel into an old man's mouth, dragging pallets into an empty room for workers to sleep on. The "smallest" acts combine to form a masterpiece—a painting, a book, a life worthy of our living. A painting is a series of masterfully applied brushstrokes. A good life is a series of lovingly enacted moments. When Mother Teresa won the Nobel Peace Prize, she waived the usual gala dinner celebration and insisted that the money be given to the poor. Her message when she climbed to the podium: "Love. Love until it hurts."

In some of my most open-hearted moments, I have known the pain she speaks of. Completely opening one's heart means being vulnerable to both the pain and the beauty in the world. In such moments, my heart aches for all of humanity. My heart hurts for the damaged areas of the world. My heart throbs for the beauty of an ancient oak tree. My heart beats into the soul of the world. We merge and commiserate and celebrate all at once.

Life Vision and Right Livelihood

Following your heart is one way to find the most appropriate vocation. Peace Pilgrim offers two other guidelines for "finding your place in the divine plan":

> The first one is to put yourself into special inspirational circumstances. Do something that will inspire you, and lift you up, and awaken your higher nature, so that you will know what your life pattern is. If you like, and feel inspired by beautiful music, listen to beautiful music. If it inspires you to read beautiful words, maybe poetry, read beautiful words. If it inspires you to walk amid the beauties of nature, walk amid the beauties of nature.
>
> The other way, since you probably had some awakening, possibly even when you were a child, is to ask yourself, "What do I really like to do? What do I really feel is right for me to do?" It's more likely to be a well-recognized useful task in society than something unusual. It's more apt to be a number of things than just one thing.[1]

Be careful, too, not to confuse life vision with right livelihood. Right livelihood is a way of supporting your life vision, not a substitute for it. For many years I have prayed to be shown my "life work." My petitions, however, ignored the fact that I already had a life vision. My search for the "perfect life work" excused me from getting on with fulfilling that vision.

Right livelihood means fulfilling personal needs in a way that supports the whole. Thich Nhat Hanh offers these guidelines for choosing a vocation: "Do not live with a vocation that is harmful to humans and nature. Do not invest in companies that deprive others of their chance to life. Select a vocation which helps realize your ideal of compassion."[2] I personally could not work for General Electric or Shell Oil Company, but each person must decide for him- or herself what "depriving others of their chance to life" means. So long as you harm none, do what you will, say the ancient Celts. Go forth and follow your bliss; otherwise, you are harming yourself. Grinding at a job pulverizes your spirit as well. Work that you love consumes time, but generates energy. You tire from physical exertion, not from boredom or strain.

Right livelihood offers a twin paradox: Find the work that you are most suited for, and any work is appropriate so long as you do it with love. Both the what and the how of work are important. Discover the most appropriate work and then strive to keep a loving attitude in performing it. Look carefully, too, at just how much you actually require to satisfy your personal needs.

◆   ◆   ◆

The following exercise will help you discover the needs and wants in your life.

Sit down with a large stack of (scrap) paper. List those items that you need weekly and monthly to lead a satisfying life. Do this without judgment. Don't block yourself from writing "10 Snickers bars per week" if this is truly part of your life satisfaction at the moment. You are listing on paper, not stone, your needs of the moment. You are creating a baseline which can be altered as you change. The needs of a twenty-five-year-old are different from those of an octogenarian. Be specific. List the amount as well as the type of product needed. "Dish detergent" is not as specific as "one quart of Ecover dishwashing liquid every six weeks." Write down everything, from bobby pins to buckskin, that is essential to your well-being.

Next, evaluate how much money you actually spend. You may want to carry a notebook and write everything that you spend for a full week or even a month until you have a sense of your average spending. Note sodas bought in a vending machine, dimes deposited in parking meters, car payments, utility bills, the works. Create a realistic picture of how much you spend and what you buy. This information provides an important snapshot of your current needs and wants.

Sit down with your list of "needs" and compare them with your actual spending. You may have written "10 Snickers bars per week" and bought only six. You may have estimated one quart of dishwashing liquid every six weeks yet bought a new bottle after only four weeks. Adjust your "needs and wants" list according to this new information.

With the revised list in front of you, return to your life vision. Remember the important goals in your life, the values that you espouse, the dreams that you wish to realize for yourself and the Earth. Examine each item on the list and observe how it supports or undermines that vision. Choose whether to keep the item on the list according to your answers. Be honest with yourself. You may not be ready to delete Snickers bars, but you are willing to reduce the clothing budget from $100 to $50. You may choose to remove one item in favor of one you hadn't listed. When you are done adjusting the list, tally the estimated value of each item and record the total.

◆   ◆   ◆

This list, if you are honest with yourself, will provide a baseline to evaluate just how much money you need to earn to support your personal needs and wants. The exercise should also give you some idea of the difference between your needs and wants. You may not actually need Snickers bars, but you want them because they improve the quality of your life when you eat them.

Discerning Quality

Robert Pirsig, in *Zen and the Art of Motorcycle Maintenance,* reminds us that the evaluation of quality, to be of any worth, is an individual matter. When he refused to set guidelines for college English class compositions, he forced students to examine their own personal definition of "quality." They were frenzied, writing and rewriting compositions many times, floundering for the fulfillment of their own hazy definitions. They rebelled. They wrote. For too long, teachers, parents, and everyone else had supplied the yardstick to measure their efforts. Some surrendered the task, completely overwhelmed by the responsibility of evaluating their own work. Others struggled and finally discovered their own quality. They could never be fooled into accepting outside evaluation again.[3]

Honor, too, that "enough" for one person may be opulent for another and Spartan for someone else. Only you can determine what and how much you need to feel fulfilled in your life. Christine McNulty, a very successful business consultant, tests and evaluates populations according to their value systems. She divides the population into three broad categories: "survivors," "prestige-seekers," and "inner-directeds."

Those operating with a "survivor" value system constantly

evaluate their situation according to their perceived lack. I say "perceived" because a multimillionaire can operate with survival values, as can a welfare mother. Prestige-seekers make choices based on their image. They choose a violin for its price, not its tone. Inner-directeds make choices based on their own satisfaction. They do not need or want approbation from outside sources. Any one of the three can perform the same action for very different reasons.

A survivor, for example, might choose to lose weight because his clothes are too tight, and he does not want to spend money on a new wardrobe. A prestige-seeker might diet in order to look good in her bikini when she goes on vacation at a posh beach resort. An inner-directed person might diet in order to feel better. He knows that his body functions best at 165 pounds, and he wants to keep his body in top form.

Only you can decide how much money will satisfy you. One friend decided that $12,000 a year ought to be enough to support any human being. He works as a furniture maker and lives in Boston. He is content with his work and his life. On the far side of the spectrum is a relative who sold his last piece of land about five years before he died. The last corner of his once-expansive holdings sold for five million dollars. He worried that his wife and children would not have enough to support them when he was gone. Enough what, I always wanted to ask. In my eyes he was wealthy; in his eyes he was worrisomely close to financial collapse.

The Value of Money Over Time

Identify exactly what you truly need to support yourself; the truth may set you free. Jerry Ropp, a resident of Cincinnati, describes his own journey to right livelihood, although I doubt that he would use that term, or even claim that he was in search of a different way of living. "I find it downright embarrassing to tell people that I'm so wealthy I don't have to work if I don't choose to," says Ropp. "This remark usually elicits comments such as, 'Did you win the lottery?' 'Did a rich uncle die?' 'Do you live like a monk in somebody's garage?' My answer is, 'None of the above.' I work part-time and make about half as much money as other people I know. The secret to my success is that I've learned to distinguish between what I want and what I need."

Circumstances in his life forced him to reconsider the importance of work and money in his life. His wife left him, he lost his home, and his business venture failed. He found a job, was fired, and couldn't find another. "I realized then that I had absolutely nothing to lose. So I decided at that point that I would do only the things I liked to do and would attend only to my needs." His needs, he discovered, cost only eighty-five dollars a week—this included food, clothing and shelter. He worked part-time as a self-employed contractor doing home repairs and made two or three hundred dollars a week. As he gained experience and improved his skills, he had more requests than he could possibly fulfill.

> That first year I discovered two things: that I had made twenty thousand dollars and that I still continued to live on eighty-five dollars a week. I had close to fifteen thousand dollars in the bank. It was at that point that I became interested in learning more about the "value of money over time."

For the next three years he continued to work and put the majority of his earnings in the bank. His savings account increased to fifty thousand dollars, "for which the bank was paying me interest . . . about forty-five hundred dollars a year. I suddenly and pleasantly realized that by keeping my needs simple and my wants under control, I had become financially independent and happy."[4]

Ropp still continues to work—when he wants to. A financial planner might criticize his plan for overlooking losses due to inflation. Ropp could balance such losses simply by depositing more money—an amount he could easily earn—in his account each year.

Your needs may not be as streamlined as Jerry Ropp's, but you certainly can practice the same realistic evaluation of your own life. Admittedly, children and dependent relations complicate the picture. Here again you will need to set priorities—will you save money in a retirement account or buy a new hot tub? Will you work forty hours a week to finance a trust fund for your children's education or work half days and have more time at home with your children now? You can choose how to spend your money and time. Both are precious, powerful commodities. Let money serve your needs so that you don't need to serve money.

Fulfilling Primary Needs

Consider, too, that you can choose to invest more time procuring your primary needs (food, shelter, clothing) so that you require less money to buy things. Many people spend so many hours "working" that they have little or no time to plant seeds or weed in the garden. They have neither the time nor the energy to sew clothes or catch brook trout or gather raspberries in July. Too often our society defines "working" people as those who earn money. Much of the "real" work, however, the activities that fulfill our most basic needs, earns no salary. A part-time worker may be able to grow most of her food in a half-acre garden, can or freeze the surplus, and "earn" a year's supply of food for the time invested. "How can I best spend my time?" you may ask yourself, "working for money or working to fulfill my primary needs?"

A note here on "abundance." For many years I have shied away from "prosperity consciousness" workshops, in large part because I viewed them as panaceas to soothe people's guilt about having lots of money. I was pursuing a "spiritual path," and money certainly had no place of importance in my life. Gradually, I have discovered the folly in both of these approaches.

Prosperity consciousness teaches that "money is energy, and the Universe has a limitless supply of energy, so I don't need to worry about my dollar diminishing someone else's supply." The assumption is partially correct. Energy exists in limitless supply, but physical material does not. Money is a form of energy that represents physical goods. As such, it is not limitless. The dollar's worth of mahogany that I take from Central America has a real impact on that part of the world; it diminishes the tropical rainforests of the Earth. The goods that I stockpile reduce the material resources available to my neighbors, whether they be human, plant, mineral, or animal. Is the money sitting in the bank an "abstract" form of energy? Are stock dividends from an investment in Exxon purely "energy," untainted by conscience?

On the other hand, "poverty consciousness" has its own brand of tyranny. "It is easier for a camel to go through the eye of a needle than for a rich man to enter into the Kingdom of God," I was taught in Sunday school. I've spent most of my life apologizing for having any money, or pretending I didn't have it, or struggling to be "downwardly mobile." One woman of color damned this strangely white, middle class woman's dilemma as a copout. "You've been given money; now, instead of wallowing in guilt about it, or trying to give it away, take responsibility for it and do something good with it. Get on with it, woman! Don't pretend to be moneyless and powerless when you are not."

All of my life I've been bombarded with schizophrenic messages from a Puritan-based society: "Don't go after money; that's greedy and immoral," intone the purists. The Pilgrims in the bleachers, though, are chanting, "I want lots of, I want lots of, I want lots of money, money, money." When I looked at possible careers, I internally censored any consideration of financial gain. I wanted to make a "pure" decision, unswayed by the dastardly lure of money. I've begun to learn, though, that ignoring finances is irresponsible. Neglecting to take care of myself is as feckless as abusing other people. If I want to accomplish the "real work" that I came for, I need to fulfill my basic needs. Work and money are just as "spiritual" as any other aspect of my life. The Creator breathes through dollar bills and paper clips as surely as apple blossoms and oak trees. Neither hoarding nor ignoring money works; I need to grapple and make peace with this "energy" in order to successfully integrate it in my life.

Leisurely Work

Now that you have established your needs and evaluated just how much time you want to devote to money-earning ventures, consider the importance of how you go about work. Brother David Steindl-Rast advises learning to integrate leisure in both work and play.

> Leisure is the balance between work and play. Really good
> work is playful work. Now that sounds terrible to our ears, like
> fiddling around, and don't you ever dare do that! When you
> really look at how you achieve your best results in work, it is by
> leisurely work, and that means by work that is done playfully. In
> other words, by work that is quite purpose-directed, but you
> add to this narrow purpose orientation what is best in play,
> namely that you do it for its own sake . . . If you work leisurely
> in that way, life becomes so much richer. . . .

How often do you perform a task simply to get it out of the way? Your mind spins hours or days ahead or behind the fulcrum of the moment. You lose the present, and that is a tragic gift to discard. While you wash dishes, dust furniture, or perform any "monotonous" task, the clock seems to freeze in place; the second hand atrophies and finally succumbs to rigor mortis. When I am not engaged, actively involved in the task at hand, moments drag into hours. Passionate, consuming interest, however, roots me in the moment. Hours pass unnoticed; time is fluid, a cascade of smoothly jointed moments.

You can befriend dreaded jobs by acting as if you are interested in the activity. As an experiment, try frowning for two or three minutes. Note how your feelings change. In the midst of a stressful situation, stop and smile for three or four minutes. Remarkably, your feelings generally follow body cues. Body postures affect the mind and vice versa. So, the next time you find yourself involved in a tiresome task, act as if you are engrossed in the activity. Lean into it. Smile. Engage. Follow your breath, note its passage in and out of your body. Say to yourself, "Now. Now. I am here now, washing dishes. Breathing. Now. Now. Warm water on my hands, slant of evening sunlight outside the window. Here. Now. Now." Within five minutes, you may find yourself enjoying the task. This sort of work is as much a meditation as an activity—the reason that meditation feels so good is because it roots us in the present moment, a luxury in a world sprinting hellbent on a course to nowhere.

Practice this sort of mindfulness during enjoyable tasks as well. Consider taking what Thich Nhat Hanh calls a "slow motion bath":

> Allow yourself 30 to 45 minutes to take a bath. Don't hurry for even one second. From the moment you prepare the bathwater to the moment you put on clean clothes, let every motion be light and slow. Be attentive of every movement. Place your attention to every part of your body, without discrimination or fear. Be mindful of each stream of water on your body. By the time you've finished, your mind should feel as peaceful and light as your body.[5]

Moving with mindfulness imbues a task with artfulness. Taking a bath becomes art. Stroking a cat bespeaks beauty. Touching a lover's face is artistic expression. Someone once commented that Mexicans make everything they touch beautiful because they live so fully in the moment. Every act has the potential to become art—"good work" may become "genius," the outpourings of a genuine spirit, if we are rooted in the here and now.

According to Gary Snyder,

> We have been hoodwinked somehow into believing that creativity is in a separate category from the simple acts of daily life. Art is something you do in a crafts studio or a writer's workshop. We dispatch our housework as swiftly as mechanization and frozen dinners will let us so that we can hustle off to the Y to get recharged with a few hours of "creativity." Meanwhile, to support this pattern of life, we Americans are consuming the lion's share of world resources, and time is ticking out for the poor people of the world—and, just a little more slowly, for ourselves. Surely our "creativity" need not have so high a price.
>
> Why compartmentalize our lives so that art is a thing apart? There is an artistic way to carry out even the simplest task, and there is great fulfillment to be had from finding out that way and perfecting it. That is the silent message that comes to us in the village handicrafts we value so. A culture that gives priority to speed and greed and multiplicity—well, it is not culture, it has no culture. To lead lives of artistry, we have only to slow down, to simplify, to start making wise choices.[6]

As a child I volunteered to paint the fence surrounding the flower garden. Unlike Tom Sawyer, I relished the task. For days I patiently scraped the peeling posts and crosspieces and then began the task of applying two coats of paint. Three times in all I touched every inch of the fence. I was in love with that tiny patch of the world. I can still tell you how the pink-red coral bell flowers danced in the afternoon winds, the roses dropped petals, the bees visited blossoms and the sun slanted across the yard in golden plumes at the end of the afternoon. Reluctantly, I sealed the lid of the paint can, cleaned my brush, and went inside for dinner. I had entered fully the world of the garden.

"You've inspired Mrs. Herrnstein (our next door neighbor) to paint her fence," my mother told me one day. I looked over at our neighbor, enthusiastically scraping paint from her redwood fence. "Inspired someone?" I thought to myself. "I'm just doing this because I love it!"

The Power of Daily Acts

Years later I learned that doing something simply because I love it, or happen to be doing it as part of my daily life, often inspires others much more than any sermon or self-righteous demonstration.

Although our Western intellectual leanings favor books and lectures, our body/mind learns from example and experience. This experiential sort of learning impresses and influences long after the intellectual arousal has passed.

When I was eighteen, I flew from Los Angeles back to my family's house for a visit. Having recently left home, I was just beginning to eat a purely vegetarian diet and did not know that I could request a special vegetarian meal during the flight. The meal arrived—chopped beefsteak, mashed potatoes, cherry cobbler, and a wilted salad. I picked at the salad and the cobbler. I hated to see the food go to waste, but I did not want to eat it, either. Finally, I turned to the man sitting at the end of the aisle, and offered him my steak. "Thank you," he said. He seemed surprised that someone would give up her steak.

"You're not hungry?"

"No, I just don't eat meat," I said.

"Why don't you eat meat?" he asked between bites of steak.

I launched into a long explanation about rainforest destruction and water pollution from cattle ranches and additives in meat and economic imperialism. He chewed and listened with interest. When the plane landed, he thanked me for the information. "That was very interesting," he told me. He seemed genuine in his appreciation. We shook hands before he sprinted into the terminal, bound for another connecting flight.

Our encounter taught me several things. One is that "small" actions really count, not only in their immediate impact on resources but also the secondary example that they offer. One person choosing not to eat meat may not significantly reduce the nation's cattle herd or prevent rainforest destruction, but that one example can affect many people. Even if the action touches only one other person, they in turn may touch another and another. That is the ripple effect, like a stone cast into a still pond. The movement travels outward and eventually affects the whole of the pond. Admittedly, such actions are slow-paced, but they are also deep-acting in their effects. They stimulate fundamental change.

I believe that part of the reason the man listened so intently, besides the fact that he obviously had an open and curious mind, was that I was not judging him for his choices, simply offering him my own. That gave him the freedom to listen without feeling judged. I also waited until he asked a question before offering any explanation. An evangelist never waits for an invitation; he plows into others' minds uninvited. I wasn't seeking a convert, though, and perhaps that is precisely what attracted his curiosity. Like painting the fence as a child, I was doing what I chose to do, without thinking about how my actions would influence others. Simply by being myself, enacting my choices in a daily sort of way, I become an example—one that probably has more effect than a carefully contrived role model of exemplary behavior.

The point is, follow your bliss. Follow the promptings of your heart. The paradox is that you will have a much more profound effect on the world by being yourself than by trying to be what you think you should be, or acting how you think a proper, socially aware, spiritual (add your own adjectives) person should act. Chuck the expectations. They are unnecessary baggage on your journey to right livelihood. Your destination is to become your authentic self—and that is who will most profoundly, unselfishly affect the world.

Part Four

The Daily Activist

An act of love draws people—all people—
together, in a way that anger never will.
The most impeccable, "politically correct"
actions mean nothing unless they
arise from a core of love.

Twelve

Piecework/Peace Work

HEAT SHIMMERED IN WAVES over the blacktop road. The leaves on the trees lining the road were gray with late-summer dust, limp in the wilting August temperatures. One p.m., August 6, 1983—the anniversary of Hiroshima. With sweat running down the nape of my neck, I stood outside the Fernald Nuclear Reprocessing Plant outside Cincinnati, Ohio. I wondered if I would survive this afternoon without succumbing to heat stroke. How appropriate, I noted inwardly with a wry smile, to worry about a sunburn—on this day in 1945, the power of Sun exploded on Earth and changed Her forever.

On the edge of the road among the rolling fields of southern Ohio, a knot of local organizers stood around a tiny wooden platform strewn with cords and microphones. The massive gray cement buildings of the Fernald plant, set two miles back from the road, looked out of place amidst the orderly rows of cornstalks and the cows in the surrounding fields. The P.A. system whined as someone stepped forward to tap the microphone.

"Good afternoon, everybody," said a willowy woman with long black hair drawn into a single braid. "Thanks for coming. As you can see," she says, nodding to the lone photographer from a local newspaper, "not many press people showed up, but we're glad you're here."

The afternoon was filled with impassioned speeches about the atrocities of nuclear war and startling evidence about the dangers of "peaceful" nuclear power. The organizers recounted an impressive list of unreported safety violations perpetrated here at Fernald, including radioactive emissions into the nearby river, the major source of water for the community ten miles downstream. In the mid-seventies, Fernald accidentally emitted a radioactive cloud that settled over downtown Cincinnati on a busy weekday afternoon. The plant's management never reported the accident, much less warned the hundreds of thousands of workers and shoppers in the city.

The list continued, sickening in its detailed account of accidents and violations. I wondered why the well-researched reports of these blunders never appeared in the press.

During the speeches and the songs that followed, I became aware of a black smudge approaching our knot of demonstrators from the Fernald plant. As it moved closer, I realized that many separate bodies made up that black smudge, all moving in perfect rhythm. At a mile, I could see arms swinging in unison. At a half-mile, I saw the glint of light from reflector sunglasses. At a quarter-mile, the outline of billy clubs swaying beside hips and rifles slung over shoulders came into focus. I tightened my grip around my friend's waist and reached out to take someone else's hand. We swayed harder and sang louder. I'd never faced a riot squad before, and I was scared.

At the end of the road leading into the plant, two battalions of riot-squad police came to a halt. They crossed their arms and stood at attention while we finished singing and speechifying. I marveled at their composure as they stood in their black and blue polyester pants and shirts, certainly as hot as ovens. Nothing—no songs or words or gestures, not even the tearful eruption of one of the organizers at the end of the singing—ruffled them. Their refusal to respond spooked me. I wondered what they had beneath their hats and underneath the buttons of their shirts. Maybe nothing— just empty, non-reactive space.

"OK, it's time for the civil disobedience now," announced one of the organizers. "Anyone wishing to participate can meet over there," he said, pointing to a small cluster of people on the far side of the road. "I warn you that you probably will be in jail until Tuesday next week, that you will miss a couple of days of work or school. And be aware that we do have lawyers ready to assist, but we can't guarantee bail . . ."

Prominent in the knot of protesters was a woman in her seventies who had given her life to such acts of disobedience. She proudly announced the number of her arrests and criminal charges, like a boxer declaring the number of rounds and bouts endured and won.

About eight other people joined her when she faced off on our side of the road leading into the plant. One of the organizers stood beside her and yelled to the implacable riot squad. "We want to give you this chance to come join our side," he shouted, "to come over on this side of the line, while you have a chance."

Fifteen feet away, on the other side of the property line, a snicker passed among the ranks. The officers shifted and guffawed, and then fell back into rigid attention.

The protesters squared their shoulders and walked across the invisible property line, the grass-lined crack at the end of the road. The chief of the riot squad moved forward and declared, loudly enough so that everyone could hear, "I give you this opportunity to go back across the line before I arrest you for trespassing."

"We're here to stay," said the old woman, chin up, defiant.

"Then I'll have to arrest you."

Officers stepped forward to escort the protesters into a paddy wagon waiting nearby in anticipation of the arrests. No one collapsed so that the guards would have to drag their limp bodies across the pavement. They walked calmly to the truck. As doors slammed and the engine roared, the organizer shouted which prison they would be detained in, reminding us to keep these people in our hearts over the coming days.

The crowd of around eighty demonstrators slowly dispersed. My friend Marty and I walked back to the car. The seat was so hot that I sat on my backpack to keep my thighs from burning. The heat, though, didn't penetrate the terrible numbness that I felt inside. I had done my "duty," I told myself, by coming to the demonstration and taking action to change the world. I came to add my presence and make a statement about nuclear war and nuclear power, but I was left feeling empty. What had we accomplished? Who, besides the handful of people who came to endure the blistering August heat, knew any more about Fernald than they did yesterday? Who cared any more about the consequences of nuclear power and armaments than they did when they awoke this morning?

I had learned, but that knowledge was a burden. It weighed heavy in me. I felt isolated in my knowing, like the child whose information is discounted because "if it was important for us to know, it surely would have been on the news." But nobody wanted to hear news like this, spoken from the mouths of angry, passionate protesters. The only mention of the demonstration in the *Cincinnati Enquirer* newspaper the next day was a single column, two inches in length, on the back page.

"Too volatile, not reliable. Inflammatory, that's what they are." I could just hear every Harold and Millie, my imagined archetypal American couple, commiserating while they watch the six o'clock news, talking about the leftover hippies from the Sixties who still insist on having these demonstrations. But in this case, we didn't even make the news. And the illegal emissions and dumps at Fernald would continue indefinitely while the protests fell on deaf ears. What's the use, I asked myself as I shrank from the melting vinyl seats, what the hell is the use, anyway?

The memory of the demonstration stayed with me for a long time. I had left every other demonstration with some sense of accomplishment. If nothing else, at least the act of sheer defiance satisfied me, and a certain smugness that I was willing to put myself on the line while others quietly agreed but stayed at home. Maybe I was upset with myself because I wasn't actually willing to cross the line. After a lot of soul-searching, I decided that something else was bothering me, but I couldn't place the uneasiness.

Public Acts of Love

In 1985, while living at the Findhorn Foundation in Scotland, I met a woman named Ruth Traut, a native of the Cincinnati area, with whom I had an immediate rapport. Besides having lived in the same region, we also shared an interest in Native American spirituality. As we compared stories about Cincinnati, I began to tell her about the demonstration at Fernald on that sweltering Sunday afternoon. At the end of my story, she drew in a sharp breath, and leaned forward.

"I have a story to tell you," she said, eyes alight. "Those same people who organized the demonstration you went to asked me to help them create a demonstration the following year—last year. They wanted to incorporate a more spiritual aspect, and they knew that I was involved with Native American ritual, so they invited me to some of their organizational meetings."

After attending a couple of meetings, Ruth told the group, "You know, from what I've heard, I get the sense that what you really want is a healing for this place."

The organizers nodded their heads in agreement.

"So I suggest creating a Medicine Wheel, that involves prayers for all aspects of creation, at the site. The Medicine Wheel is a way of bringing healing to a place."

On August 6, 1984 a large crowd gathered again outside Fernald. All of the local television and radio stations sent reporters, as did the local newspapers. The group of "demonstrators" gathered in a circle and began the ritual to create a Medicine Wheel by offering a prayer for the Great Spirit, represented by a large stone in the very middle of the wheel. They offered a prayer and a song in honor of the Creator, the spirit that runs through all of creation. One by one a stone for each different aspect of creation was placed with a prayer and a song.

During the ceremony, the black smudge appeared again on the horizon and moved like a solid wall toward the demonstrators. When the riot squad reached the end of the blacktop road, they stood in formation facing the demonstrators. After awhile, though, they realized that no one was resisting them. In fact, no one cared whether the police were there or not. The "demonstrators" were standing in a circle, their attention focused on the creation of the Medicine Wheel.

Eventually some of the guards left the ranks and joined the edges of the circle. They began to move into the circle to see what was going on. Later, a few of the guards came forward and offered stones and prayers for the Medicine Wheel.

At the end of the ceremony, reporters flocked around the organizers. Ruth was interviewed and appeared on the six o'clock news that evening. The story of the demonstration and the violations at Fernald were reported on the front page of the newspaper the next day. After twenty years of organizing demonstrations without much effect, suddenly everyone knew about Fernald. The story exploded in the local press and eventually found its way into the national press as well (*Time,* October 31, 1988).

When she finished telling her story, we were both in tears. After sharing my experience, we both knew how fruitless a demonstration could be, and therefore how much more miraculous the success of the Medicine Wheel was.

For me, the power of the Medicine Wheel demonstration was that it was an act of love. The people were gathered to express their love and concern for the Earth and to focus the best of their healing abilities on that place. Because the demonstrators were focused in a circle, on an act of healing, there was nothing for the riot squad to resist. There were no lines, visible or invisible, to cross. There was no "us" or "them" to struggle against, to defy or blame. There were only people under the blazing August sun, people who were gathered to bring love and caring to a damaged, irradiated part of the planet. And it was the love, not the righteous anger, that finally opened people's ears to hear about Fernald.

Four months after our conversation, on August 6, 1985—the fortieth anniversary of Hiroshima—I stood again at the edge of a road under a muggy summer sky. This time, the "road" was a four-lane highway circling the Pentagon. Along with several thousand other people, I had come to participate in The Ribbon Demonstration. Unlike many demonstrations that seem to be scheduled nearly every weekend in Washington for one cause or another, the Ribbon Demonstration was the outgrowth of one woman's vision.

Justine Merritt, a devout Catholic, felt that her mission in life was to serve as a missionary in South and Central America to help bring about world peace. She was ready to quit her job and move to South America, but wanted to check her inner promptings first.

> In February (1982) . . . I went on a retreat to pray—literally— for guidance for my life. I had been travelling and writing for a couple of years, but something seemed out of focus. I prayed, I realized later, with a divided heart: half of my heart was very earnestly imploring the Lord to guide me, and the other half of my heart was saying, "and make sure you send me to South America" where I thought I wanted to go.
>
> But something happened. One morning, again in prayer, the poem "Gift" was given to me, and even the stubborn, frightened child in me could understand that the path I was to follow led not to South America, but toward working for peace at home . . .[1]

For months—
or is it years?
I have carefully,
I have silently prayed to the Father to spare the ocean's shells;
for the sake of one lovely shell, I've prayed,
do not let the world be destroyed.

For months—or is it years?
I have prayed carefully

I have prayed silently to the Father to spare the earth's blossoms;
for the sake of one lovely rose, I've prayed,
do not let the world be destroyed.

For months—or is it years,
I have carefully prayed,
I have silently prayed to the Father to spare the earth's birds;
for the sake of one grey sparrow's song, I've prayed,
do not let the earth be destroyed.

And for all those months of all those years,
since an August day in a far away Japan,
I've prayed for shells and roses and birds' song
and hid,
because I could not bear to see such a secret sorrow,
hid the image of a baby's ear,
curved, soft;
not as hard as an ocean's shell—a baby's ear—
no protection at all—a baby's ear—
against the wind of a nuclear holocaust.

Hid the image of a child's fingers curved around an adult's hand;
trusting that the adult would take the child safely across a busy
    street;
a child's fingers,
stronger than the petals of a rose,
but not strong enough to ward off the vaporizing heat of a man-
    made sun.

Hid,
for thirty-seven years, the sound of children's laughter caught
    in a blinding blast;
laughter—no protection at all against a hydrogen bomb.

The shell, the rose, the bird's song
deliberate disguises to hide the babies, the toddlers, the
    children from the unspeakable.

No wonder we have terrors in our nights,
hiding a planet's extinction in our dreams;
no wonder we wake exhausted at dawns,
unable to comprehend an end
not just of Mozart's melodies but—of ring-around-a-rosie;
unable to comprehend and then,
unable to grieve an end to the Mona Lisa as well as hide-and-seek.

Symphony, rock musician,
Michelangelo and motorcycle racing,

jungle, Antarctica,
beloveds—and enemies all changed to something we cannot
    glimpse,
nor dare to.

So, I have prayed for four hundred and forty-four months
for shells and blossoms and birds' songs
and only yesterday was strong enough to pray for all the little
    ones.

We too are the little ones,
asked to protect children from more than busy streets.

We are called,
we are chosen to spread the word;
we are chosen,
we are called to bring the peace. Amen.[2]

What emerged during that time was a realization that she could give most by focusing on peace at home, in the United States. She saw that piecework—an American folk term for needlework and quilting—could become an expression of peace work. A couple of weeks after her vigil a vision emerged of circling the Pentagon on the fortieth anniversary of Hiroshima with a ribbon made of many sections, created by individuals and groups to depict what they could not bear to lose in a nuclear war.

She wrote down the vision and sent it to everyone on her Christmas card list. During the next two years, her vision was passed through mimeographed posters, letters, and word-of-mouth until by August 6, 1985 enough people had responded to her vision to circle the Pentagon and stretch an additional fifteen miles to include the Washington Monument and Lincoln Memorial. The banners came from people all over the world expressing what humans love about this planet. Many of the banners depicted the planet Earth, children, forests, air, water, and music. Some banners had papers pinned to them that told of the despair that individuals had endured in coming to terms with nuclear war, and the power that had come with choosing life and creating "piecework" as an expression of "peace work."

While waiting for the final link-up of the chain at 2 p.m., I chatted with friends from Connecticut who had ridden all night on a bus to be here for this moment. I had walked behind a group of woman-identified spiritualists, arms linked, singing joyous songs. Now they joined brown-robed Franciscan monks who were quietly viewing the banners. Housewives from Iowa were talking about their year-long project of creating a banner together.

"Where's your banner?" I asked. "Is it the one you're holding?"

"Oh no," answered the woman. "I came here to help hold someone else's vision and to share my own."

My eyes filled with tears.

At 1:50 p.m. we moved into a line along the four-lane highway just north of the Pentagon. The people passing in cars slowed down, waved, honked. A man riding a bicycle stopped in front of me. He looked dazed. I stepped forward and touched his arm. "Are you okay?" I asked.

Tears began to stream down his face. "It just got to me," he said, his voice cracking with emotion. "I've ridden around all fifteen miles of the banner route and just there, at that corner back there, it got to me." I reached out and hugged him while he cried. After a couple of minutes, he stepped back on his bike and continued on, tears still streaming. My heart as well as my eyes overflowed.

Two p.m. Balloons rose from the Pentagon lawn. I half expected a thunderclap or a sudden rainshower to bless the moment. But only a low rumble of cheering along the line marked the moment of linkage.

Something quiet, though, had linked within my heart. At first I couldn't articulate the new connection—it was understood in the language of the heart, the "inarticulate speech" that is not easily translated into words.

Over time, the teaching of the Ribbon Demonstration penetrated my mind, too. I had never participated in such a beautiful demonstration. The police had nothing to contain nor resistance to push against because the whole impetus of the demonstration was love: to express and claim our love of life, the planet, and a peaceful world. The Ribbon was my first personal experience of a public act of love. I knew the tug in my heart and the tears that would well in my eyes and tighten my throat at a friend's wedding, when two people made themselves vulnerable and declared their love for one another, but I had never experienced a group declaration of love.

The thousands of people gathered for the Ribbon Demonstration were participating in a public act of love, aimed at the planet. I felt the power of that love and knew once again, at an even deeper level, that acts of love are powerful, even irresistible. An act of love draws people—all people—together, in a way that anger never will. The most impeccable, "politically correct" actions mean nothing unless they arise from a core of love. Although I had thrown out my Christian religious background, along with many other things, during my rebellious student days, I had a sudden understanding of the biblical quotation, "Though I speak with the tongues of men (sic) and of angels, and have not charity, I am become as sounding brass, or a tinkling cymbal." (1 Corinthians, 13:1) Speaking and acting out of anger produce a cacophony that no one can understand. People may physically listen to my words, or try to, but the manner of speaking will always evoke a defensive stance, and the listener will never fully hear my meaning.

Speaking From the Heart

Some of my greatest lessons in speaking from the heart came while living at the Findhorn Foundation. During lunch one day in the dining room at Cluny Hill, I was talking with a group of friends. Katarina, a German woman with whom I had had many discussions about our own growth as well as about planetary affairs, sat next to me as I talked about the "unconscious" decisions that the community's food buyer was making.

"But Judith, we can't tell people what they can or can't eat. They have to make their own decisions," Katarina reminded me.

In the Findhorn Community, the emphasis is upon letting each person find his or her own way on their spiritual path, free of dogma. The same laissez-faire attitude has extended to nearly every decision in the community. Choosing not to buy coffee, tea, sugar, or other cash crops from the Third World would be an imposition upon those who still want them.

As Katarina spoke, my thoughts wandered to a scene earlier in the week. While waiting in line at the community's book store, I listened to a guest commenting on the coffee in the community center, and the oranges from South Africa and bananas from Chile in the food shed. Did the people in this shop know, the guest queried, that the apples in the cooler were from South Africa and that the store could sell coffee from Nicaragua instead of Chile?

I stood in line, smiling quietly to myself. I'd been asking myself and others the same questions for years. I wondered how Michael, the focalizer of the shop, would respond.

"Well," said Michael, "the most important thing here in the community is to love each other. We're not here to tell each other what to do; it's really up to each person to make their own decisions. In the end, the most important part is to accept each other. That's what Eileen (one of the community's founders) talks about in her guidance. Are we able to really love each other—that's the most important question."

The answer did not satisfy the man. He continued offering information about why the coffee and other foods were important to consider. Michael was soothing but firm that these "political" issues were not among the community's concerns. We were a spiritual community, not a group making political statements.

As the man turned to leave, I touched his arm. "I empathize with you completely. I've been asking the same questions for years."

"And what answers have you come up with?" he asked eagerly.

"I don't have any, really." He looked disappointed. "All I can say is that decisions about food and other basic things around here seem to move to the least common denominator of consciousness. It's frustrating, but that's how decisions tend to be made. And anything people don't want to confront they can label 'political' and drop it from the discussion."

"Why are you still here?" asked the man, perplexed.

"I often ask myself the same question," I replied, laughing. "It would be a lot easier to live in a place where everyone thought and cared about the same things I do. But here I learn about tolerance and acceptance, and do my best to plant seeds where I can."

The man shook his head, picked up his bag of books from the counter, and walked slowly out the door. The droop of his shoulders told me how disappointed he was that the Findhorn Community, the place of perfection that he had dreamt about, was far from perfect. Like everyone everywhere—and we were, after all, a microcosm of what happens in the world at large—we were learning, sometimes painfully, about the world and each other. The only difference here was how we went about the learning.

These thoughts raced through my mind as Katarina spoke. I dropped my shoulders with a sigh. "Look, Katarina, what we buy as a community is important. And the food buyer is using my money to buy things I don't believe in. When I lived in a co-op at Oberlin, we always made the most conscious use of the collective money. Then, if people still wanted to buy sugar and coffee and white flour, or whatever, they could do it with their own money. So we used the greatest amount of consciousness in deciding what to buy."

I continued with a tirade about why buying bananas—from Third World or First World countries—was so terrible. Katarina's face grew red as she chewed on a forkful of lentil loaf. When I paused for a breath, she seized the moment and banged her clenched fist on the table.

"Judith, I really can't hear you when you talk like this!" she sputtered. "You may be right—everything you say I agree with— but you make me so *angry.*"

I barely heard her. I was on a roll about the injustices of most Western European people's consumption, reveling in my sense of righteous anger. I was indiscriminately flinging that anger at the closest possible target—in this case, Katarina.

I continued for another sentence or two, overcome by the momentum of my tirade, before her words registered. When they did, I threw a wall in front of them, but the anger backwatered in my throat. I sat staring at my plate, nostrils flaring, breathing hard.

Katarina touched my arm. "I agree with you. I just can't hear you when you talk like that."

I attributed Katarina's reaction to the anti-political streak in the community. *They just don't want to hear about these things, I told myself. That's why nobody can hear me.*

A few days later I was asked to join an Experience Week group, the introductory program in the community, to share about my experiences with Nature. Although I had spoken many times in groups outside the community, this would be the first time at the Findhorn Community, and I was worried about being able to communicate in a way that would reach people here.

I pondered what I could say about the Earth in sixty minutes that would be inspiring. What kind of experience could I create to open people to listening to the Earth? I rehearsed the presentation many times in my mind, both anticipating and dreading the meeting.

I arrived early and waited for the group sharing before my part of the evening to end. I sat in the hallway meditating, praying for inspiration. Fifteen minutes passed, then thirty. I could hear someone crying and talking in the room. *Must be a heavy sharing,* I thought to myself. *Creator, please help me to say what these people need to hear.*

The group sharing ended at 9:10. I had twenty minutes, instead of an hour, to create some sort of experience for these people.

When I sat in the circle, my heart was bursting, pried open by nerves as much as by meditation. I spoke of my experiences with the Earth, the great challenges and lessons that had come with learning to listen to Gaia. In the last ten minutes, I led a meditation with stones and shells and tree seeds that I had brought with me. Through the whole presentation, my heart felt like a generator producing far more warmth than it could ever distribute. I was overflowing with love.

Afterwards many people lingered in their seats. One man, an Italian in his early twenties who knew only a few words of English, wrapped his arms around me and then pulled back, groping for words.

"I know . . . not so much . . . English, but I . . . what is the word . . . feel it here," he said pointing to his heart. "I understand you, but not words."

Months later, when one of the guests in the group returned to the community, he told me that his whole relationship with the Earth changed as a result of that twenty-minute presentation. "You set me off on a path that I never knew existed," he told me. "I mean, I was aware of the Earth, but I'd never experienced it that way before."

From that time on, I knew that people could hear my love but not my anger. The words were not as important as my inner attitude. I could give the same information, but if I was angry, people became defensive. If I felt my love for the planet when I spoke, they were transformed.

Every Act Is a Political Act

The first lesson for the daily activist is to realize that any act is a political act. The great challenge is to make the small, the daily, and the mundane acts of life into a statement of how you want the world to be. Wendell Berry, in his book *Standing By Words,* examines how much of the communication in our culture is designed to avoid taking a stand. The writing texts provided for teaching college English emphasize communicating in the most innocuous way possible. In other words, don't stand out, don't rock the boat, and don't say anything important, especially if you mean it. Taking a stand is impolite, if not downright dangerous. According to Berry:

> My concern is for the *accountability* of language—hence, for the accountability of the users of language.
> My standpoint here is defined by the assumption that no statement is complete or comprehensible in itself, that in order for a statement to be complete and comprehensible three conditions are required:
> 1. It must designate its object precisely.
> 2. Its speaker must stand by it: must believe it, be accountable for it, *be willing to act on it.*
> 3. This relation of speaker, word, and object must be conventional; the community must know what it is.
>
> These are still the common assumptions of private conversations. In our ordinary dealings with each other, we take for granted that we cannot understand what is said if we cannot assume the accountability of the speaker, the accuracy of his (sic) speech, and mutual agreement on the structures of language and the meanings of words. We assume, in short, that language is communal, *and that its purpose is to tell the truth.* (italics mine).[3]

Berry continues the essay with several quotes from college textbooks intended to teach the fundamentals of written composition. The emphasis in the examples is on avoiding any statement that might offend. Better to bury your meaning in unnecessary verbiage than to offend the professor, much less the public, with a forthright statement. In other words, avoid taking a stand. Aim to please; barring that, say nothing in as many words as possible. The attitude is rooted in the U.S. political system as well. Our politicians fight for the middle, trying to offend as few as possible instead of winning votes by clearly addressing issues and proposing policies. Taking a stand seems to have gone out of fashion, along with miniskirts and bell-bottom jeans. Those stands, though, need not be flashy, media-hyped affairs.

I know a man who is a gutsy activist. He doesn't go to marches or carry banners. Instead, he takes a stand for the environment by consciously disposing of his own waste—and I'm not talking about the contents of his compost bucket. He has decided not to use indoor toilets. Instead, he chooses to save his urine until he finds a spot that really needs it. With his feces, he has single-handedly rebuilt an eroding slope outside the school where he teaches bicycle repair to a group of delinquent boys.

The Governor of Maryland recently acknowledged the value of people who have chosen to work for their neighborhood in quiet, daily ways. One recipient of the Governor's award for service is a retired postal worker who decided to pick up groceries for shut-ins in his neighborhood. He didn't think much of it—he said he had to go out to buy his own groceries anyway, and the errands filled his spare time. But the neighbors noticed, and his fame as a reliable support during times of crisis spread quickly through the community. Each person has the potential to make a difference in her community, to take action for the good of the whole. Small- or large-scale actions make no difference. The act of giving to others on a consistent basis is the important factor.

Local Decision Making

Look for ways, too, to use the existing structures to bring about change. In New England, for example, town meetings are a vital part of the community's decision-making process. Most of the towns are small enough that every person's vote matters. Issues from garbage collection to taxes to zoning ordinances are decided within these town meetings. Local decision-making has the most potential for change for the hours invested.

Befriending the Media

The media can be a powerful arm in reforming opinions. Any successful action, whether inside or outside the political system, eventually gains media attention. Masunobu Fukuoka, for example, organic farmer and author of *The One-Straw Revolution,* which outlines a method of sustainable organic agriculture, was chosen to represent his area in NHK television's "Outstanding Farmer of the Year" competition. He had developed his system without desire for recognition, but had succeeded to such an extent that his methods were noticed and rewarded.

During the screening process for the award, Fukuoka was asked why he didn't give up growing winter rye and barley. The Ministry of Agriculture had an ongoing campaign encouraging farmers to abandon winter crops and "modernize" their methods. He acknowledged that going against the will of the Ministry could ruin his chances of receiving an award, but believed that being true to his farming methods was more important.[4]

Fukuoka cares more about his work than about recognition. Yet doing something well, especially something that is part of an answer to a growing global need, eventually will attract media attention.

A word of caution, though. People in the media can only "see" organizations and events that they can understand. For example, the National Organization for Women (NOW) is probably the most visible and widely quoted organization devoted to women's issues. Not surprisingly, NOW closely mimics the bastions of male-dominated power structures in this country; it has a constitution, forms caucuses, elects delegates, and holds a yearly convention. The press recognizes NOW because it understands its methods and structure.

One radical feminist who found NOW's tactics too patriarchal nevertheless appreciated the group's existence. "They form a smoke screen behind which the real work of transformation can go on," she commented. And the "real work," for the most part, escapes the detection of the media because it does not follow the structure of most of the organizations about whom they write stories.

Herbalist Susun Weed, in her description of the Wise Woman tradition, offers several reasons why the tradition is invisible.

> Nourishing is an invisible process. The Wise Woman tradition is based on nourishment, a basic process generally taken for granted, not considered worthy of much note. Nourishment through giving suck and gathering and preparing food is presented as background by anthropologists who are fascinated by the occasional dramatic hunt. Wise women nourish in invisible ways, helping others to empower themselves without saying, "Hey, look at me healing you. Look at me teaching you!" . . .
> There's no visible structure in the Wise Woman tradition. There is no hierarchy in the Wise Woman tradition: no difference between above and below, no order of authority, no sense of "man" as better than all other forms of life. There's no president, no guru, no chairman of the board. There are no rules to follow. You can't get a degree or certificate in the Wise Woman tradition. You can't be tested on it, because there are no right and wrong answers.[5]

Imagine, for example, a reporter writing about a cooperatively run grassroots organization. "Who's in charge here?" asks the confident reporter.

"Well," says Gladys, looking through the notes from the last meeting, "Harold will be facilitating this week's meeting."

Scratch. Scribble. "So Harold is your chairman?"

Gladys furrows her brow. "No, he's not a chairman, he's a facilitator for tonight's meeting."

"Yeah," says the reporter, visibly irritated. "Who runs this organization?"

"Well," says Gladys, shuffling the papers into a neat stack, "we all do."

The reporter stares for a moment. "Can you give me some sort of official statement about this group's purpose?"

"Here's our charter," explains Gladys, unruffled by the questions. "And I can tell you what the group means to me and how it has affected our family. But each person would probably have his or her own interpretation of its importance in their lives."

"So does everyone have an equal vote in the meetings?"

"Of course," says Gladys, "but we don't vote."

"How do you make decisions?"

"By attunement," Gladys explains. "We discuss an issue and then we have a time of silence when each person goes inside, lets go of his or her personal desires, and then asks to be shown how the situation can be handled for the greatest good of the whole."

"What happens if you get, ah, well, different pictures of the solution?"

"You'd be amazed at how often the same answer comes to everyone. Sometimes when people's attunements vary, they are actually different aspects of the same solution."

"Well, thanks a lot, Gladys," says the reporter, retreating towards the door. "I have another meeting to report on tonight. Thanks for your time."

In this case, the group's methods of working together are completely foreign to the reporter, who is likely to dismiss the group as an illegitimate gaggle of quacks. Its structure is based upon shared power and responsibility. They are, in fact, synonymous. Taking more responsibility leads to an increase in power.

Self Responsibility

Ultimately, the daily activist strives to take more and more responsibility for his or her life. In *The Psychology of Achievement,* Brian Tracy describes why delegating responsibility to others, whether those "others" are co-workers or the federal government, backfires in the long run.

> There are several areas in our society today where irresponsibil-
> ity is encouraged in wholesale amounts. The first area I think of
> is in the area of political economy where men and women have
> been encouraged now for several decades to try to get the
> government to assume responsibility for things in our life that
> are not satisfactory to us. All of the attempts to get the govern-
> ment to be responsible, to make the government do some-
> thing—"The government oughta pass a law"—always end in
> frustration because the government simply takes more and
> more control, but it always leaves us with 100 percent responsi-
> bility and 100 percent accountability for our lives. That is why
> the larger governments grow, the more frustrated and more
> unhappy their populations grow.[6]

Sun Bear, a Chippewa teacher, reminds those who come to his lectures that self-responsibility is the key to self-sufficiency. Take care of your own food needs—don't wait for government handouts. Take care of your own shelter needs—salvage building materials, share the construction work with community members. Take care of your own health—avoid giving your power away to medical authorities. Learn how to mend your clothes instead of throwing them out and buying new ones. Share. Look out for yourself and each other. Put nickels in expired parking meters. Reduce your monetary needs so that you are no longer a slave to the monetary system. And don't expect Big Brother to hold your hand—he charges dearly for the service.

Evaluate Funding Groups

Perhaps you cannot "vote with your feet" and be directly involved in every cause that you support. Tithing can be another method of working as a daily activist; however, look closely at the purpose of groups which ask for your money. Are they working to change the root causes of a problem, or are they single-issue lobbyists who have forgotten the whole picture?

Attending a conference at Smith College, "From the Arctic to Amazonia: A Conference on the Industrial Nations' Exploitation of Tribal Lands," I learned how complicated single-issue campaigns can become. I listened to speech after speech about the destruction of native peoples' lands. Several people spoke passionately about the denial of hunting and fishing rights, the backbone of many tribal peoples' cultures as well as their day-to-day means of survival.

One example involves the Cree of the St. James Bay region in Canada. Animal rights organizations have joined the Canadian government in trying to deny the Cree people the right to hunt geese in the autumn. For centuries these people have "harvested" the geese, a major source of winter food. They take only what they need for their own survival. Animal rights groups questioned the Cree's right to hunt as an ancient cultural tradition, yet they did not examine "sport" hunting farther south along the geese's migration route. The reduction in the population of migratory birds is blamed on indigenous people, who are expected to pay the price for European immigrants' polluting the land and over-hunting the game. The issue is more complex than saving endangered geese (as presented by the animal rights groups); an endangered human population, an oppressive social structure, and a polluted environment must also be considered. When you consider supporting a cause, *get the whole story.* Make sure that they have their facts straight and that they address the entire issue. You may have to do a bit of research yourself, checking primary sources, before you make a decision.

Another factor that I consider when deciding which activist groups to support is their basic approach to an issue and their publicity tactics in soliciting new members. The Native American Legal Rights Foundation, for example, serves as a legal advocate for Native American people. I support their cause wholeheartedly, but their mailing campaign offends me. I am asked, as a white European, to pay for the guilt of my ancestors. This statement is not far removed from the actual wording of their mailing. I agree that my ancestors committed atrocities that native people never should have been forced to endure, but I have no interest in being swayed for a cause on the basis of guilt.

The Friends of First Nations, on the other hand, is "an alliance of people who share a concern for the economic self-sufficiency of American Indian Tribes ..." They provide funds for leadership development programs, craft industries, and purchase of tribal lands. I am happy to support these people because they are working towards a positive vision for native people. They do not prey upon white guilt. Unlike government handouts that are designed to increase dependency, The Friends of First Nations are concerned with supporting their people in immediate, concrete ways that will lead to self-sufficiency.

Some groups learn over a period of years that they need to address the larger picture in order to be effective. The World Wildlife Fund (WWF), for example, began its campaign solely on the basis of saving cute, furry animals. In many ways it preyed upon sentimentality and the public's guilty conscience. In the last decade, though, WWF has shifted the focus of its campaigns from saving individual creatures to protecting the natural habitats of endangered species, both animals and plants. (After all, what are the cute, furry animals going to eat and where will they live if their habitat is destroyed?) It has moved away from the zookeeper mentality that says, "As long as the orangutan is safe in our cages, it is saved for posterity." Zoos may save bodies, but they destroy the spirit of a creature in its native, unfettered state. Today, WWF is fighting for the natural environments in which the animals were meant to live—in a complete relationship with land formations, plants, and other animal species.

Acts of Love, Acts of Power

Finally, the most powerful acts are those of love. Sometimes the power of love moves us to act in ways that disarm us.

While travelling in Australia, I spent two weeks on the west coast, living at a beach called Monkey Mia. Here, for the last twenty-five years, wild dolphins have chosen to swim into knee-deep water, at first to take fish from human hands, and later simply to touch and be touched by humans who came in increasing numbers to view the phenomenon.

During my stay I read the story of a woman who was the former owner of the caravan park that sits on the edge of the beach at Monkey Mia. She and her husband shared a great love for the dolphins and a growing concern for the dolphins' safety as more and more visitors flocked to the beach. She wanted to designate the beach a nature reserve and hire full-time wardens to supervise the visitors' interaction with the dolphins.

One day a crew of technicians arrived. A ship had run aground in the shallow passage at the northern end of the bay. After several rescue attempts, they decided that the only way to move the ship was to blast it off the rocks with explosives.

Knowing that the dolphins, always curious, would be attracted to the ship because of the activity around it, the caravan park owner confronted the technicians. "If you put explosives on that ship," she told them, "you'll have to blow me up, too. I'll strap myself to the hull. You know the dolphins will swim in to see what's going on, and they'll be—they'll be—you just can't do this!"

She was as surprised as the technicians by her outburst. They decided not to use the explosives and eventually succeeded in coaxing the ship off the rocks.

"You know," the woman confided to a friend, "I suddenly understood all those people who stand in front of bulldozers to save the forests. 'Til now, I always thought they were crazies. And I know, too, how much I've come to love those dolphins. I just couldn't bear the thought of them being harmed in any way."

Love catalyzes powerful action, often catapulting people into arenas they never would have dreamt of entering before being inspired by a cause. Most of the actions begin in one's own backyard. The illegal toxic waste dump called Love Canal, for example, was "discovered" by a neighborhood of mothers who noted similar unexplained illnesses among their children. When they pieced the information together and then sought the cause, the mothers became embroiled in a campaign that attracted national attention.

Look around you, in your daily life, for your next course of action. My housemate dreams of moving to Israel to plant trees while the compost heap outside needs to be turned. I want to move across the country to study naturopathic medicine in order to support people in their personal process of transformation while the local dump needs a recycling co-ordinator. A woman dreams of saving souls in war-torn Central America but is given a vision for fostering peace in her own land. Piecework, peace work—it begins here and now, with you and me and our shovels and the pile of decomposing vegetables in the back yard. It is the daily act, done within the scope of a larger vision, that brings about planetary change.

Thirteen

Re-sourcing

IN 1986 MY PARTNER ALAN AND I spent six weeks in Australia visiting rainforest activists and hiking in wilderness areas. After two years of living in the relatively desolate land of Scotland, where the forests and the native people were plundered long ago, I was relieved to feel undisturbed, healthy land beneath my feet again. The rainforests humbled and inspired me. Obviously, the land had affected others as well. The activists we met were some of the most dedicated, tireless workers I have ever encountered. Unlike many political activists I had worked with, they seemed able to sustain a grueling pace without wavering. And, unlike the spiritual seekers I had been living with, they acted decisively and accomplished much.

What was their secret? What kept them inspired? After living for a few days in Rob Blaker's house in Hobart, Tasmania, I gleaned a few clues. Rob and others living in the house are very involved in the Tasmanian Wilderness Society, the main instigator and agitator in the campaign that stopped the damming of the Franklin River. They gathered every evening for a period of meditation and chanting. They practice a particular form of yoga that honors the sacredness of all life. For them, their work in wilderness areas is intimately bound with their spiritual tradition. These daily meditation periods are a way of returning to the source of their inspiration, for themselves and for their work. Returning to source. Re-sourcing. That, I began to see, was a large part of their secret.

The activists we met at the Rainforest Information Center (R.I.C.) in Lismore, New South Wales (mentioned earlier) taught me the importance of living for something. Their work is fueled by their passion for wild places and their vision for keeping them wild, undisturbed, vital, and alive. They are working towards a vision of the kind of world they want to live in. I learned that work done out of love continuously refills, while jobs performed out of duty soon consume all internal fuel and leave a worker burned out, empty, disillusioned. Their love for the land, combined with their personal inner work, sustains them.

Combining Inner and Outer Work

John Seed, founder of R.I.C., speaks of his own personal struggle to combine his spiritual practice (Vipassana) with activist work. "There was the feeling in Buddhism that one should stay cool and not get heated up about things," he explains. "Many things happen in the world, but you just watch them come and go. I found myself doing certain things because I needed to, but a part of me felt I was going astray."

John and others working at R.I.C. inspired me precisely because they were combining their inner spiritual work with outward direct action. I had worked with hardcore activists, burned out from years of doing, and I had lived with spiritualists who were content to be without ever doing. Here, though, the inner work was expressed in outer action. The combination was powerful, effective, and extraordinarily moving. Rather than contradicting each other, the inward contemplation and outward action fed each other. The outward activity is the expression of the inner realization, and the inner work is the means of reinspiring the actions, re-sourcing, returning to the original source of love and inspiration that fueled the outward action in the first place.

Burnout

Burnout can be a reality for even the most lovingly directed activist. An inner-directed activist has chosen to dance with life rather than contemplate it. Like the Grouse, who dances in a sacred spiral, ancient symbol of birth and rebirth, we are born anew through our actions. How we move dictates how well or poorly our movement will blend with the whole of Creation.

During periods of stress and confusion, when you have "burned out" and consumed all internal fuel, you need to resource, to return to the founding spark, and rebalance. When you find yourself spinning, rather than spiraling, in a mental world of ideas and problems, take time to re-establish your connection with the Earth. Go for a walk. Dance. Lie with your belly pressed into the Earth. Pay attention to the energy in your body and note what activities open or obstruct the flow. No matter how inspiring your vision, you cannot actually live its power without maintaining connection with the Earth.

Return to your vision often. Remember why you are doing what you are doing; recall the choices you have made. Work becomes easier when you have its purpose in sight. Each task generates momentum for the next when you align with your vision. Action without any sense of purpose soon loses momentum.

"Simple Things" for the Earth?

I have leafed through at least a dozen books informing me of "simple things" that I can do for the Earth. Although the books provide valuable information, I find them lacking in vision. Let's say that I decide to recycle newspaper because it's something "simple." But when the local recycling center closes and I have to search farther afield to find a new dropoff point, will I still continue to save paper? When "simple" acts become a bit more complex, will I abide by my earlier decisions? Do I have a sense of why I am taking action in my life, or am I doing things to assuage guilt or because I want to "do the right thing"? Who says it's the right thing to do? If that direction comes from outside me, what will I do when the message grows faint, and I am left to my own devices?

A friend recently read an article in *Defenders of Wildlife* magazine about bio-diversity. When she finished reading, she looked into the trees of her own back yard. For years she had kept her cats inside to protect birds and other wildlife, but for the past year she had let them roam at night—a compromise, in recognition of their independent cat spirits. Looking in the trees, though, she discovered that last season's five birds' nests nestled among the limbs had dwindled to none. Am I supporting bio-diversity? she asked herself. What's more important, roaming cats or wildlife? She chose to keep the cats inside, hoping that the birds would return.

For both my friend and the cats, this was not an easy decision. The cats still longed to roam and were vocal about their desire. Fleas soon invaded the house. She stripped curtains and furniture covers and closets full of clothes, sending them all to the cleaners to wash out the fleas. To maintain their psychological health and provide the stimulation they lacked from being indoors all day, she committed herself to spending fifteen minutes of "quality time" with each cat every day.

My friend's decision to keep her cats inside was not a "simple thing." In fact, I suspect that the only thing that sustained her decision was the wider perspective from which she viewed her actions. She wanted to support bio-diversity, and she literally looked in her own backyard to evaluate her own contribution to the situation. Her larger vision sustained her in taking difficult steps. She was working with her vision in sight.

Enjoyment

In addition to returning often to your vision, discover activities that refill you. Cultivate methods of inspiring yourself and refreshing your commitment. Find ways of just plain enjoying yourself. A friend in India goes on meditation retreats. I thrive on dancing to almost any sort of music, from English country dance tunes to African drumming. I also spend at least a week every year in a wilderness area. If you can find a particular activity that you find inspiring that also supports your work, all the better. Be wary, though, of making every single moment "useful." Don't force every waking moment into a narrow tunnel marked "purpose." Leave spaces for surprise, for the invasion of unexpected pleasures, for contact with the numinous in the form of seaside sunsets, sand castles, and serendipitous meetings with friends. Another word for God, says Brother David Steindl-Rast, is SURPRISE. Leave some openings for God to do Her work.

Be sure to take time to smell the roses, to savor a cup of tea, to relax with a loved one for five extra minutes in bed each morning. Enjoyment happens now, in this moment. If I cannot find pleasure in my work, why bother? I stop to stretch, to listen to birds chirping in the apple trees behind the house, to smell the scent of freshly mown grass. Leisurely work is a key to success for any activist; it allows me to accomplish more with less strain.

Intensity and Tension

Leisure, however, does not excuse me from the work itself. Paradoxically, I would even suggest cultivating a sense of urgency in your work. By urgency, though, I do not mean approaching a project with clenched fists and a sweaty brow. During a violin master class, James Buzzwell once admonished a student for confusing intensity with tension. "Play with intensity. I didn't say 'Clench your violin as hard as you can.' You see, we think we are being 'emotional,' emoting, when we tense our shoulders and grit our teeth. Forget that. It's intensity that I'm after."

"Intensity," according to Buzzwell's definition, is an internal tension, the sort that gives rise to expression, that moves us toward our goals. You can lean towards, rather than away from, the tension created by your vision. If you do not experience intensity about a particular task, you are not likely to complete it. Your intentions wither like a heat-blasted plant. All green plants thrive on inner pressure—without "turgor pressure," the tension of water inside the plant cells, stems, and leaves would soon collapse. Humans, too, need an internal pressure, one that arises from a desire to move toward something, not to avoid it. You may want to finish a beading project by the end of the week to show your aunt. You may want to plant three apple trees before the ground freezes. In both cases desire moves you to the completion of a project.

Running away from things, however, trying to avoid certain situations, generates a debilitating sort of tension. I wonder if the jogging craze in the United States is symbolic of our passion for running away from our problems. Ask any runner who has recently increased her mileage why she spends more hours on the track, and she will tell you about tensions at work or domestic difficulties. No matter how enticing the prospect of leaving our problems far behind, the sad truth is that we always carry them with us. They never stay "put" because problems reside in people, not in places. Leaving a problem is as futile as trying to misplace an arm or a leg. They come attached—for good reasons. "Don't run. Really, don't," says Michael Ventura in *L.A. Weekly.* "America likes to run because running from (fill in the blank) is what we do best. Everybody who runs is running away from something terrible. Stop running and find out what's behind you."[1]

Don't get me wrong; I think exercise is very important, for both physical and mental health. Aerobic exercise can be a fantastic release for anger and other debilitating emotions that tax the body's immune system. Exercise tones the whole body system. Know why you are running. Run around the block, vent the adrenaline rush, then return to your starting point and face the source of your anger. Be prepared; you may come face-to-face with yourself. Is that who I've been running away from all along?

Look at the things in your life that you want to run *toward.* Focus on what you want to create in your life. Bravely face those areas that do not match your vision. Befriend the changes you need to make in order to cross the bridge from here to where you want to be. Don't panic if your vision changes. Change is part of the process, the only constant in the stream of experiences that fills your life. Invoking change for the planet means invoking change in your personal life as well. You can't have one without the other; it's part of the bargain. Don't kid yourself that focusing on a brave new world will take the spotlight off your own growth. You are part of that brave new world, which means that you inevitably will be touched by the floodlights.

Enduring Growth Pains

I have endured my own panic attacks. One involved Susan Griffin, author of *Woman and Nature: The Roaring Inside Her* and many other feminist-oriented books, who came to speak at the Findhorn Foundation. Her work had influenced me greatly during my college years, and I was eager to meet her in person. I was part of the organizational group for the annual conference, "One Earth: A Call to Action," intended to be a week for people to recommit themselves to take action for the planet. I eagerly awaited Susan's talk on the second night of the week-long conference.

Contrary to all my expectations, her talk jarred me. In fact, most of the audience was writhing, calling out in the middle of her talk to ask, "Why? Why are you doing this?" Susan's new research delved into the mindset that generated the Holocaust in World War II to see if she could decipher clues as to the type of personality that could perpetrate a nuclear holocaust. In agonizing detail she described Hitler and some of his chiefs of staff. She was holding up a mirror that reflected the most destructive elements of our own human personalities. Too shocked to tolerate more than a glance, most of the audience turned away in horror.

After the talk, and a very emotional "question and answer" period that nearly erupted into a fistfight, the audience dispersed in ragged bands, holding each other for support. I stayed in the hall to the very end to handle some administrative details.

A group of women were gathered in the center of the hall. "The men are meeting in Guy's caravan," I overheard one woman say. "I think that's so wonderful. Maybe we should all meet somewhere tonight. I mean, I think it's so important that the men heal the men and the women heal the women; then we can really come together."

My heart started beating harder. Two years before I had stood in the same spot, talking with the same woman, and we had been in complete agreement. Now I found her words disturbing.

"Caroline," I said, joining the circle, "I think we need to address this problem together, both men and women. We're all in pain."

"But didn't you understand what Susan was trying to say? The primary separation is between men and women. That's the root of all problems."

My heart beat faster; I was angry. Hadn't I invested my academic career in exploring the connection between the domination of women and the domination of nature? Hadn't I read and studied and debated and breathed the work of Susan Griffin and others like her? *Who are you to tell me that I don't understand?*

"We are all human beings, Caroline," I said evenly, "and we are all in pain. That's more important than whether we have breasts or penises."

I finally arrived in my room shortly after midnight, exhausted but unable to sleep. I lay on the floor, staring at the ceiling, feeling as if something was dying inside me. Had I sold out? Had I given up my feminist ideals because they were too difficult to enact in my life?

The last ember of guilt flared and then died in my heart. No, I had not sold out. I had grown to see the world in a new way. The world was no longer defined by the split between men and women. It was infinitely more complex, and ineffably simpler. I couldn't put people into predictable boxes of male and female behavior. I had met aggressive women and nurturing men. Prejudice and genius come in both packages. For so long my feminist beliefs had been a touchstone in my life, a carefully constructed collection of ideals that coalesced into a (relatively) clear lens through which I viewed the world. Who was "I" without this lens? The floor swayed beneath me. My stomach lurched. I was losing my bearings, no longer sure of up and down or in and out. My internal compass had cracked, and I had nothing to replace it. Perhaps, for a split second, I saw clearly. Then—shift. New lenses fell into place. I awoke in the morning, seasick in dry sheets, setting course for new lands.

Initiation and Aloneness

The voyage between familiar, comfortable beliefs and new lands can be rough; you may find yourself queasy in mid-passage. That is to be expected—leaving the known means facing the unknown, dying a bit, dying to the old ways that allowed you to function but no longer serve you. In fact, you may never feel dry land beneath you again. You may enter a new element and learn to swim or fly.

The caterpillar transforms into a butterfly in isolation, in darkness. No one accompanies the chrysalis on its voyage of transformation. You must be prepared to journey alone. Caroline Myss suggests that any initiation is followed by a period of aloneness. Initiations are ports that launch your ship into the sea. They are the beginnings of a journey, a "jump start" that propels you on a new course. Initiations do not guarantee a destination, only a radical departure from your former haunts. No one can physically accompany you. You must sail alone, face the fears that obstruct your path, and finally land on unfamiliar territory, accompanied only by the guides and the "unseen realms," always present to support and encourage. The journey forces you to be inner-dependent—not "independent," separate from the rest of Creation, but rather inwardly focused for your directional cues.

During bouts of queasiness, remember to scan the horizon and keep the wider picture in your awareness. The hassles of everyday living weigh less heavily when they are hung from the larger framework of your life vision. Conversely, the "mundane" tasks of life take on new meaning when they are recognized as supporting a greater purpose. While living in Scotland, for example, I knew that every job that I did, no matter how "menial," supported the work of the community. Washing dishes for 200 other people engaged in a meaningful conference or workshop supported a larger vision. The clearly defined purpose of the community provided a ready-made meaning for all of my actions.

Balancing Present and Future

Living away from the community, I have to make meaning in my own individual life. I wash the dishes for myself, my family, friends, and housemates. I wash them so that the kitchen will be clean. I wash them so that I can return to the "important" work of writing or photographing or talking on the phone. But how often do I wash the dishes simply to wash the dishes? Am I so addicted to purpose that I can accomplish nothing for its own sake?

Here, purpose and presence dance to conflicting rhythms. Re-sourcing involves balancing the need for purpose in your life with the desire to live here and now. Wash the dishes simply to wash the dishes. Wash the dishes so that you have a clean home in which to do your work. Wash the dishes to increase the sense of order and beauty in the world. Above all, wash the dishes and enjoy doing it.

Thich Nhat Hanh writes about a visiting friend who volunteered to wash the dishes after dinner. Hanh asked if his friend knew how. His friend laughed—did Hanh doubt that he knew how to wash dishes? Hanh replied that there are two ways to wash dishes—either in order to have clean dishes or simply to wash dishes. His friend chose the second way—to wash the dishes to wash the dishes. Hanh gave him the "responsibility" of washing dishes for the entire week.

> If while washing dishes, we think only of the cup of tea that awaits us, thus hurrying to get the dishes out of the way as if they were a nuisance, then we are not "washing the dishes to wash the dishes." What's more, we are not alive during the time we are washing the dishes. In fact we are completely incapable of realizing the miracle of life while standing at the sink. If we can't wash the dishes, the chances are we won't be able to drink our tea either. While drinking the cup of tea, we will only be thinking of other things, barely aware of the cup in our hands. Thus we are sucked away into the future—and we are incapable of actually living one minute of life.[2]

As a daily activist, I am challenged to sit, stand, and walk in the here and now while simultaneously holding a vision of the world I want to live in. I am rooted in the moment and yet breathe sustenance from a future world. All time is now, say the Aboriginal people. Blending past, present, and future disturbs only a linear mind. Gracefully bend the divisions of time. All spokes in the wheel of time meet at the center point—the here and now.

Rooting in Place

I also draw sustenance from place, from the roots that I have sent into a particular part of the Earth. Inhabitory people are those who have committed themselves to living in one place. For better or for worse, they have sunk their roots into the soil of a particular community, drawing strength from their chosen land.

> As Peter Nabokov says, goodhearted environmentalists can turn their back on a save-the-wilderness project when it gets too tiresome and return to a city home. But inhabitory people, he says, will "fight for their lives like they've been jumped in an alley." Like it or not, we are *all* finally "inhabitory" on this one small blue-green planet. It's the only one with comfortable temperatures, good air and water, and a wealth of living beings for millions (or quadrillions) of miles. A little waterhole in the Vast Space, a nesting place, a place of singing and practice, a place of dreaming.[3]

Uprootedness is as pernicious a disease as "ghost sickness" in these times. We are uprooted from our bodies, from place, social structure, tradition, and time. Many, however, are aware of the malady, especially the uprooting from place. Although one in six Americans moves every year, most relocate within six miles of their previous dwelling. Only 10 percent of those who move range beyond their place of origin, and most of them are in the 20-29 age bracket. Many are forced to stay in one place because of economic realities; others, weary of U-Hauls and cardboard boxes, choose to stay put.

Simply living in one place, though, is not enough. Rooting requires effort—seeking out neighbors, organizing picnics, discovering endemic birds and flowers, attending pancake breakfasts, learning where your water supply comes from. Community happens in public places: in local diners and pubs, on park benches and softball fields. These informal public places are hotbeds for nurturing friendships, discussing upcoming elections, and organizing community activities. You can hear the heartbeat of a neighborhood in its community centers, church bazaars, and independently owned grocery stores. There you will hear the dreams, concerns, and points of contention that mark a particular neighborhood. If you hear nothing, or only the faintest of murmurings, begin resuscitation immediately. Communities have strong hearts, but they need ongoing nourishment to stay healthy.

We are uprooted from our own bodies, our own bit of the Earth, as well. We speak of body, mind, and spirit—and sometimes emotions—as if we were a loosely stitched quilt of mismatched scraps. Instead of viewing ourselves as disjointed parts and feuding collections of sub-personalities, we can experience our bodies as an embodiment of spirit. We are body-spirits, not souls trapped in lumps of flesh or, as Christopher Fry puts it, "half-witted angels strapped to the back of a mule." Regarding our bodies this way is a typical expression of our uprootedness.

As mentioned above, few of us are rooted in time. We range ahead to the future and linger over the past, robbing ourselves of a true present. I daydream about the end of the afternoon, when I can turn off the computer and focus on other projects. I fantasize about visiting friends and lovers. I worry over yesterday's conversation with my mother. I tire; I have no roots in the moment, this moment, and therefore no nourishment.

What roots us in this moment, this place? One factor is keeping in touch, both literally and figuratively, with the world. Ultimately, the Earth is our source of physical nourishment, the touchstone of our existence. Take time to lie on the Earth, to listen and walk and touch and roll and swim and revel in Creation. When I am sick or physically drained, I lie with my stomach on the Earth, breathing its strength into my guts. Almost always I am refilled.

Keep a finger on the pulse of the world as well. As mentioned earlier, escaping the important news of the day, with or without a radio or television, is like trying to avoid hitting air molecules. We are surrounded by the happenings of the world in the form of conversations, printed information, and the electronic media. Often, though, the most important news is transmitted by the quietest voices—small presses, news releases from citizens action groups in remote areas, alternative news magazines. By placing your ear to the (under) ground and listening intently, you can hear rumblings that may take months or years to attract the attention of the national media.

Living in the World

Gayle Lauradunn, a long-time activist, describes her own realization of the importance of not only listening to, but also participating in the world. "When I was a junior in high school I read a lot of Emerson and William James and Oliver Wendell Holmes. I think it was Holmes, it may have been James—there's one line where he says, 'The man (sic) who does not engage in his times, can be said not to have lived.' It gave me chills at the time that I read it. And then I forgot about it for a long time.

"The very first thing that I ever did (as an activist) was my senior year in high school. The hypocrisy in my school hit me, and I wrote a scathing article for the school newspaper. I thoroughly trounced the student government, some of whom were my friends. And it was a real lesson to me because everyone just acted as if it never happened. Except people would come sidling up to me, like at my locker, and they would whisper, 'You know I really agree with what you said in that article.'" Gayle laughs. "It turns out there was a lot of support for what I said in the article, but nobody (was going to say so, out loud)."

Daily activism involves taking risks. Purely outward-looking political work shields me from inner motivations; exclusively inward-looking spirituality disengages me from the outer world. "Most of the people I've known who've been involved in the spiritual aspect have been very self-seeking, inward looking, and not politically connected at all," says Gayle. "To me, the political is where you're connecting with other people and movement is occurring. Change is occurring. It's social change. I'm not saying the spiritual is bad, that it shouldn't be there at all—I think it's important—it's just that the people I've known who've been really involved in that, none of them have been connected any more outwardly than just right here," she says, extending her arm about a foot in front of her, "and that bothers me a lot. Now I think a purely political movement without spiritual aspect is dangerous, too, but without the political the spiritual is very, very limited and very self-serving."

Combining the inner and outer view takes courage. Their union means being aware of the outer world and being vulnerable enough inside to see my own reflection in that world. Sometimes the pain is so great that I might prefer not to see or listen. Actively engaging in my neighborhood means being seen, heard, disagreed with, respected, and ridiculed. Like an old tree, I become gnarled from struggling with the winds of change. But a tree is meant for open fields, not cloistered museums. Let me contemplate within the world, actively involved with my times, alive in my knowing of this time, this place.

Creative Actions

When you take action, make your demonstrations bold, inspiring acts that express the kind of world you want to live in. I know few people who would wish to live in a world of angry words, violent acts, and broken glass. Such demonstrations may provide a needed outlet for the pent-up frustrations of an oppressed people, but they do not offer a solid foundation for a new social structure. Creative acts have boldness and genius in them that often confound the most hardened of politicians.

The Chipko Movement in the Himalayan mountains of northern India is one example of creative demonstration. *Chipko,* in both Garhwali and Hindi, means to embrace or hug. In ancient times, the Chipko people worshiped the spirit of the trees. The reigning Emperor sent soldiers with axes to cut the trees for timber. The leader of the Chipko people wrapped her arms around a tree; other women followed her example. The soldiers, vexed, asked them to move. "No," said the women, "we will not move. You must first kill us if you wish to fell the trees." Finally, exasperated, one of the soldiers chopped the Chipko leader in half, killing her. When news of the incident traveled to the Emperor, he was very angry with the soldiers. He ordered them to leave the forest and forbade them ever to cut trees there again.

Unfortunately, contemporary leaders have forgotten the Emperor's promise. Deforesting the Himalayas is a disaster for both local forest dwellers and villagers many miles downstream. Forests on steep mountain hillsides are clearcut, exposing the uprooted soil to wind and rain. The soil quickly erodes, washing into the rivers. Without soil and roots to hold it, water races down the mountains and floods the river valleys. Whole towns have been swept away in the swollen rivers. Farther downstream, towns have disappeared under the mud and silt washed from eroding hillsides.

A gentle Himalayan schoolmaster, Dhoom Singh Negi, revived the tradition of hugging trees to save them from destruction. The women quickly followed his example. As primary wood collectors for their families' cooking fires, women are acutely aware of the rapidly disappearing forests of the Himalayas. The initial Chipko movement was inspired by a woman; the revival is supported chiefly by village women. With the loving embrace of their arms, they place their bodies between foresters' axes and the trees. The women have also formed human chains across roads to prevent contractors from reaching their designated timber sites. Hugging trees—a creative, powerful act whose influence has spread throughout India and much of the rest of the world as well.

A German woman, unfamiliar with the Chipko movement, expressed her deep concern for the dying trees of her country by gathering with friends in a local park. They spent one Sunday afternoon embracing the trees while hundreds of people walked by. Many stopped to ask what they were doing. They explained that acid rain was affecting local trees and devastating the Black Forest. They talked about the number of trees felled for paper and timber production. They talked about their love for the trees. And people listened, probably more attentively than they would have if confronted with a self-righteous picket-line. Some even joined them hugging the trees.

The AIDS memorial quilt is another example of a creative act. The quilt, when fully displayed, covers nearly a mile of ground. Dying AIDS patients and those who loved them made the quilt as a reminder of the human cost of the disease, and a plea to support those who inevitably will follow them.

The Ribbon Demonstration in Washington, D.C., mentioned earlier, was an expression of what people loved, what they could not bear to lose in a nuclear war. With paint, ribbon, and thread, people made beautiful panels that, tied together, wrapped fifteen miles of the capital in a creation inspired by love.

When you are inspired to take action in your community, be bold. Think creatively. How can you act in alignment with your vision for the world? Acts of love and beauty are acts of power. They will linger in people's awareness long after the eloquent words of impassioned speakers have faded. They will inspire long after the event. One thing I know: love lasts. Anger dissipates. Actions based on anger and frustration inevitably burn out. They have no reliable source to fuel them. Love, however, refills constantly. Creation just does not have the "juice" or the interest to support violence and cowardly acts. Be bold. Take risks. Create public acts of love.

Keep Your Eyes on the Prize

Besides acknowledging the difficulties, staying in touch with the world means noticing things that work. The most effective people I know are not cynics; they are too inspired by their work to expend a lot of energy recounting the world's woes. They are not involved in "fixing" the whole of Creation; they are involved with bettering their own corner of creation, and sending ripples out into the world as a result.

While traveling in Oregon one summer, I met a woman in a roadside rest area. After we talked for a few minutes, she reached for a pad and pencil. "You've got to meet my family," she said. "My mom and dad live a few hours south, just off the highway. I think you should drop by and see them. They'll tell you they aren't anything special, but I'll tell you that what they've done is extraordinary."

Her parents, Tony and Betty Koch, moved onto a piece of clearcut land over thirty years ago. For years they labored to pull out stumps and plant an orchard. Reluctant to spray the trees with chemicals, Tony studied the land and animals and developed an alternative plan—attract swallows and other insect-eating birds and let the wildlife eat the bugs. Every spring Tony hangs 700 swallow boxes from barbed wire strung above the cherry trees. After observing a nesting barn swallow pair rebuilding an old nest, he also designed mud homes for cliff and barn swallows. He mounts them on boards that he hangs under the eaves of the machinery shed. In the autumn, he cleans out the nests and stores them in the shed.

Tony's newest project involves attracting little brown bats, nocturnal insect eaters who feed on two of the cherry trees' most destructive predators, gypsy moths and corn earworm moths. The bats usually migrate south from western Oregon, but if provided with a warm daytime winter roost, they will stay. Tony has designed a solar bat roost with hopes of enticing them to stay through the winter.

Hundreds of people visit the Kochs' farm, called "Bird Haven," each year. News of their work is spreading. Betty writes that the Oregon State Forestry Department "invited, paid, and dined us to speak and show slides to the Oregon, Washington, and Idaho Small Woodlot Owners—on 'alternative methods for controlling insects in the forests' (using birds and bats). Gypsy moths and other pests are getting a foothold out here. We were well received as the public is becoming increasingly alarmed about pesticides, etc."

What do they do during their "time off"? "The winter months are busy," writes Betty, "recuperating, redesigning, cleaning, and reorganizing. Building houses for bats as well as birds. Wished you could be here now as hundreds of swallow babies have left the nest. The year goes so swiftly. Tony is now 75 and I am 62, so the place seems to grow. We do our own work except for our son who cuts the grass once a week during the growing season."

Betty and Tony describe themselves as "ordinary folks." In one sense they are ordinary—conscientious neighbors who walk with open eyes in their own neighborhood. What makes them extraordinary, though, is their intimate involvement in the workings of their neighborhood. Their concern encompasses the entire community, including the animal and plant inhabitants.

These folks are too busy and too inspired to think about retirement. "What an interesting world," says Betty. "Each day a new adventure if one wants to be a part of it!" Being a part of the world is what makes life an adventure. Engaging in our lives, in our communities, in the life and health of the planet is what draws us out of bed in the morning and inspires us to continue. Tony and Betty teach that listening and acting in harmony with one's neighborhood produce "phenomenal" results. Small acts, applied with much love, have great effects. That is the secret of working in harmony with the land, with our communities, with our loved ones.

Gratitude and Beauty

Seeing beauty is one way of acknowledging what works in the world. Beauty, in the end, is what makes life worth living. Carol Chatfield, a passionate lover of wild places, told me recently about her experience with a patch of woods near her home.

"I walked past the forest every day on my way to work. I decided to pick up trash each time I passed. That's how I would do my bit to make the Earth beautiful," she explained. "After a while, though, I realized that I just saw the trash, not the beauty of the trees. So now I've quit picking up garbage. And I've begun to see the beauty again."

How often do I look at the world and see trash instead of beauty? Am I so focused on discarded cans and bottles that I overlook a robin's nest? Does an empty bread wrapper distract me from seeing the bloodroot blossoming near the railroad tracks? Am I focusing on the beauty or the garbage? Eventually I must learn to see both, and view them in proper perspective. Carol redefined her priorities after her experience with the woods. "I realized that's the most important thing I can do in my life—to see beauty. And to give thanks for the beauty. I want to live my life with as much gratitude as possible. That's what's important in my life right now."

Gratitude, says Brother David Steindl-Rast, re-roots us. When I am grateful, I say "yes" to the outpourings of Creation. I open myself unconditionally to the world around me. I commune with the whole of Creation. Prayer, the Native Americans have taught me, is not a series of petitions made to an indifferent God. Prayer is an expression of gratitude, a state of reverence, an act of thanksgiving. When I approach the world with gratitude, I open to the experience of wonder. The Earth becomes an annex of heaven, a world full of surprise—infused with Brother David's God.

Finally, be sure to express gratitude for yourself. Take time to nurture your own body, your own personal expression of the Creation. Fill yourself first; then you will have more than enough to share with others. You cannot pour from an empty cup. A weary body cannot serve itself, much less someone else. The Tiep Hien ("Interbeing") Order of Buddhism includes the following precept: Do not mistreat the body. Learn to handle it with respect. Do not look on your body only as an instrument. Thich Nhat Hanh explains that "the fourteenth precept (of Tiep Hien) urges us to respect our own body, to maintain our energy for the realization of the Way. Not only meditation, but any kind of efforts that are required to change the world require energy. We should take good care of ourselves."[4]

Re-sourcing: returning to source. Return often to the source of your inspiration, the fertile dreams that spawned the vision of the world you want to live in. Practice—playfully. Rehearse your dreams until they bleed into the experience of your waking world. Dance a lot. Befriend walruses. Liberate a zoo. Climb trees. Reinhabit your neighborhood. Discover what makes you jump out of bed in the morning. Refuse to do anything else with your life. Sleep under trees. Cast wildflower seeds over freshly plowed fields. Walk in the moonlight. Howl. Crack peanuts in movie theaters. Go barefoot earlier in the spring. Eat more ice cream. Live. Experience. Suck the marrow of the world. Enjoy. These are the ten commandments:

1. Thou shall love the world.
2. Thou shall love thyself. Thou shall love. Period.
3. Thou shall enjoy.
4. Thou shall follow thy bliss.

5. Thou shall refuse to do anything else.
6. Thou shall make love with thy fellow human beings.
7. Thou shall respect all of Creation.
8. Thou shall speak thy Truth.
9. Thou shall live thy Knowing.
10. Thou shall celebrate with gratitude 'til the end of thy days.

So get on with it. Get holy and roll in the grass and kiss a dog. This is serious business, and you'd better get down to it (or up to it, depending on whether you are facing up or down in your somersault.) Saving the world is heavy stuff. Chuck it. Get on with creating the world you want to live in. Who wants to repair the same old wreck? Recycle it. Build a new model. Take the best of the old design and improve it. Take the world lightly; fill it with light so that you can see what you are doing. Add shadow for depth and perspective. Add love for warmth. Make it comfortable enough to inhabit, a home for all, one that you would proudly leave your grandchildren and their children's children's children. Most of all, get on with it. Enjoy the journey; you shall certainly have many adventures before reaching your destination. The Eleventh Commandment: thou shalt have adventures, many of them. That one's guaranteed with a lifetime warranty. Adventures come with the territory—so expect the unexpected. Surprise—there's God again. I warned you this was holy business.

I'll end with the words of a wise old woman of eighty-five. I hope to apply her wisdom when I "grow up." I hope that you, too, will aspire to the same level of maturity.

If I Had My Life to Live Over

I'd like to make more mistakes next time.
I'd relax. I would limber up. I would be sillier
than I have been this trip. I would take fewer
things seriously. I would take more chances. I
would climb more mountains and swim more
rivers. I would eat more ice cream and less beans.
I would perhaps have more actual troubles, but
I'd have fewer imaginary ones.

You see, I'm one of those people who live sensibly
and sanely hour after hour, day after day. Oh,
I've had my moments, and if I had it to do over
again, I'd have more of them. In fact, I'd try to

have nothing else. Just moments, one after
another, instead of living so many years ahead
of each day. I've been one of those persons who
never goes anywhere without a thermometer, a
hot water bottle, a raincoat, and a parachute.
If I had to do it again, I would travel lighter
than I have.

If I had my life to live over, I would start
barefoot earlier in the spring and stay that way
later in the fall. I would go to more dances. I
would ride more merry-go-rounds. I would pick
more daisies.

—Nadine Stair